The In-Service Education of Teachers

The In-Service Education of Teachers

Trends, Processes, and Prescriptions

EDITED BY

Louis Rubin
University of Illinois

ALLYN AND BACON, INC.
BOSTON LONDON SYDNEY

Second printing . . . December, 1978

470 Atlantic Avenue, Boston, Massachusetts 02210.

Library of Congress Cataloging in Publication Data

Main entry under title:

The In-service education of teachers.

Includes bibliographical references and index.
1. Teachers–In-service training–United States–Addresses, essays, lectures. I. Rubin, Louis J.
LB1731.I547 371.1'46 77-20036
ISBN 0-205-06022-6

Contents

Section III Other Voices: Other Opinions 153

Preface

The professional growth of teachers and administrators is a vital element in any formula for improving public education. The conception of new theory, the initiation of experimental research, the development of new teaching materials and the improvement of instructional methodologies are useless if their benefits are not incorporated into classroom procedures. Consequently, it is appropriate to review, from time to time, ongoing events to search for clues that will enhance the professional expertise of the practitioners. This volume constitutes such an effort.

Professional development is an exceedingly complex phenomenon that can be approached from many different vantage points. Because little is known about the subtle interplay among the various factors involved, an open-minded attitude is essential if only to ensure that significant matters are not overlooked or ignored. Hence, in the following pages the treatment is somewhat eclectic, and a deliberate effort has been made to set forth disparate points of view on the major issues. For example, in the first section of the book, the present state of the art is placed in approximate perspective and some of the important, yet unresolved, difficulties are considered in the context of the changing educational scene. In addition to the more fundamental questions of form and substance, attention is given to the economic, political, and sociological aspects of professional growth that are beginning to provoke debate and disagreement.

Section II is devoted to an analysis of the dominant reform movements on the educational horizon, and to a corresponding synthesis of their implications for in-service teacher education. However good a practitioner's preservice preparation may be, continual readjustments in educational goals and procedures invariably impose new demands on craftsmanship. Each chapter in this section deals with a particular curriculum reform, and each seeks to illuminate the particular atittudes-of-mind, knowledge, and technical skills that are essential to the suggested revision. These chapters help to clarify part of the existing confusion, to specify—somewhat earlier than usual—the kinds of teachers and teaching that will best serve the schools in the time ahead, and to outline strategies for coping with inevitable transitions.

Educational change, however, is impelled not only by new curricular movements but also by policy realignments, shifting social constraints, budgetary limitations and demographic changes as well as a host of other factors. Accordingly, Section III sets forth a broad range of commentary on a variety of forces that are also likely to influence the course of professional retraining. Reflecting the special concerns of teachers, administrators, government officials, academic theorists, foundation officers, consumer protection advocates, and civil rights lawyers, the arguments serve to dramatize both the complexity of the plot and the large number of players in the cast. The affairs of the school, and the effects of teaching, are of considerable interest to many groups and thus issues regarding teacher retraining tend to command a broad spectrum of interest. In fact, recent evidence seems to suggest that the control, management, and organization of professional development programs are no less subject to power struggles than any other facet of the educational enterprise.

Although continuing professional education has recently attained unprecedented prominence, it is hardly a new concern. A respectable amount of theoretical thought, particularly during the latter part of the 1960s, was devoted to its requirements. Therefore, in a book of this sort, it seems useful to summarize an assemblage of convictions and conclusions, and to highlight a number of operational concepts derived from research and practice. Resultingly, Section IV is in the form of a primer covering a wide array of basic guidelines. While the postulations are, of course, open to dispute, and while some will engender more controversy than others, the primer is useful in identifying specific problems, and in conveying a range of possible options and processes. The concepts embodied in the primer focus on the planning, organization and implementation of professional growth experiences in the practitioner's work milieu.

In Section V, attention is given to the nature of teaching and the cumulative acquisition of adeptness. Much of the debate on in-service education centers on cost factors, time provisions, governance, evaluation, and so on. All of these, however, are in a sense secondary to the more basic questions relating to the practitioner's role, purpose, and workstyle. Whether teaching is considered an art, a craft, or an amalgam of both, it can scarcely be denied that artistry in teaching is possible, or that instruction can be carried on with either negligible or substantial skill. To provide for professional improvement with no conception of what true mastery entails, would be to train practitioners for a mystique. It is hoped that the reader will find the text reasonably useful in delineating the multiple dimensions of professional growth, in outlining the present state of affairs, and in postulating potential new requirements.

To illustrate the cumulative evolution of in-service education, the book offers us an historical perspective. However, when compared with the immediate future, the past is likely to be regarded by many as a period of comparative lethargy. We are now entering an era of unprecedented expansion in continuing professional education of teachers and administrators; not only will there be far more activity, but the activity will be definitively different. One could, in fact, postulate a series of generalizations about future trends:

1. *Greater emphasis will be placed on locally-determined programs that have maximum relevance.*
2. *Larger attention will be given to the practical applications of theoretical principles.*
3. *As school staffs are stabilized, and personnel changes sharply reduced, in-service education will become a more routine aspect of professional life.*
4. *In the sustained efforts to improve instruction, quality teaching will be viewed as more important than the development of new curricula.*
5. *Incentives will rely less on salary increases and accumulation of graduate units, than on the intrinsic rewards of superior craftsmanship.*
6. *Continuing professional education will be more collegial in nature (centering around the interchange of ideas among experienced teachers) rather than traditional (leader-participant relationship).*
7. *While many instructional problems are relatively widespread, the uniqueness of each school mandates some latitude in the adaptation and use of techniques; therefore, new procedures in in-service programs will be less prescriptive and more flexible.*
8. *Diversity in both the organization and methodology of staff development activities will be greatly enlarged, since all aspects of professional competence cannot be dealt with through any single mechanism.*
9. *The participants in continuing professional development activities will play a major role in determining content, structure and*

process, as well as in assessing programmatic strengths and weaknesses.

10. *The consultants, advisors, specialists and trainers in the in-service programs will have a high degree of practical experience. They will be especially adept at cooperative interaction with professional teachers, and will be drawn from the ranks of the profession itself.*

These trends are already manifested in a variety of state-wide plans. For example, in Michigan educators are convinced that modifications in the learning milieu have not brought about spectacular results; therefore they have begun a major expansion of their provisions for the professional renewal of instructional personnel. The United States Office of Education recently established a special Task Force, under the direction of William Smith, to organize appropriate federal leadership in improving teacher education. Colorado, along with a number of other states, has created "Talent Banks" wherein expert teachers are temporarily loaned from one district to another in order to expedite the introduction of promising innovations. In Ohio a Division of Educational Design and Renewal has been initiated. The division prepares and disseminates teacher training materials that can be used throughout the curriculum. In Massachusetts there will soon be a Commonwealth In-Service Institute, administered through regional offices, making it possible for local districts to obtain staff-development assistance more expediently and efficiently. The state of Florida has launched a study of societal changes that will affect schooling, in order to anticipate the future retraining needs of teachers. West Virginia has introduced in-service programs that focus on specific learning problems encountered by children. In sum, providing greater opportunity for professional enhancement among educators has become something of a national priority.

However, as interest in in-service education increases, there is a growing danger that the training programs, in themselves, will be regarded as a guarantee of improved practice. We would do well to remember that skills are mastered, and new knowledge is utilized, through continuous personal striving toward greater proficiency. Consequently, professional retraining should be viewed as a guide and a stimulus, rather than as a warranty of higher student achievement. Teaching is a performing art; therefore it is developed—like all other performing arts—through prolonged and intelligent practice.

Much of the recent theorizing on continuing professional education has been devoted to program organization, training methodology, resource provisions, and so forth. While these are, of course, worthy of attention, they are probably of less significance than the individual practitioner's basic sense of role and purpose. In short, if a teacher is impelled by desire, will and insight, virtually any reasonable system can be successful.

It is also important to note that the dramatic augmentation of programs could easily lead to false expectations. Professional retraining cannot cure all of education's problems. Aside from the fact that there is often a regrettable tendency to regard in-service as a fresh coat of paint, a seminar in pedagogical tricks, or common indoctrination, successful learning depends on a number of factors. Professional growth can be directed toward many ends, each of which requires a particular kind of instructional setting. For example, a lecture can serve to explain the provisions of "mainstreaming"; a teaching demonstration may illustrate heuristic instruction; and the analysis of a video-tape is useful in illuminating the fine points of classroom recitation.

Teaching is an extraordinarily complex activity that involves a great range of skills, perceptions, knowledge and sensitivity. A workshop on alternative ways of evaluating pupil progress—however useful in its own right—will not replace a badly-needed orientation in techniques for working with bilingual children. Hence, while the long overdue increase in commitment to continuous professional development is an immense step in the right direction, it will not bring about a steady production of instant miracles. The critics, already waiting in the wings to attack more investment in teacher education, must be reminded that artistry is cultivated over time; it matures and ripens from year to year. The critics must also be reminded that even great teaching cannot overcome social deprivation.

Two additional concerns also merit our attention. In a heated political atmosphere, where issues of control and governance continually arise, power rather than logic may determine the course of events. The essence of politics lies in the manner in which conflicts between the common good and special group interests are resolved. Thus, the critical question is always: "Who tells whom what to do."

It is hoped that—within the inevitable skirmishes—an aura of cooperation can prevail. Disputes are unavoidable and, consequently, take on great importance. However, for the children in the classroom, it does not really matter how and why decisions are made; what matters is whether the decisions advance or retard their education. Obviously, no one wants to sacrifice or even jeopardize the welfare of the students. We must, therefore, find equitable resolutions to the disagreements that do not violate the child's inalienable right to a good education.

We have traditionally tended to think of in-service education as "corrective"; as a means of overcoming professional weaknesses. Now, a new, more enlightened conception of professional development is beginning to take hold. The best teachers must have periodic occasions for reflection, for readjusting their tactics to shifting social situations, and for utilizing new processes and procedures. In short, in-service has finally gained its own dignity.

The recent spate of school criticism notwithstanding, one would have to search long and hard to find an individual who, in one way or another, has not been profoundly influenced by some teacher. Our preoccupation with weakness sometimes blinds our recognition of strength. The remarkable social consciousness of today's youth, for example, is attributable, in substantial measure, to teachers who helped their students to envision a better world. Similarly, few would deny that good teaching is a vital force in perpetuating desirable social values regarding energy conservation, consumerism, health, and so on. To be sure, serious educational problems do exist, but the society is beginning to appreciate the true value of a strong teaching force.

Therefore, in-service education should not be restricted to what may be regarded as the crisis of the moment; instead, it can be addressed to a broad spectrum of social and cultural concerns. Teaching techniques and subject-matter knowledge alone do not make for an inspiring classroom leader.

A new era of in-service education, based on a larger conception of what professional development entails, must have an updated rationale. What, for example, must be done to ensure that the individual practitioner's natural style is exploited to the fullest advantage? What constitutes a balance between in-service education directed at the systematic development of pedagogical artistry, and retraining aimed at specific instructional problems?

Gifted teachers rarely come ready-made. They possess a finely-honed intuition, a capacity to develop understanding out of ordinary experience, and an ability to provoke genuine thinking in their students. They are problem-solvers rather than rule-followers; creative rather than ritualistic; visionary rather than myopic; real rather than pretentious; and demanding rather than easily-satisfied. Above all, they are driven not only by ideals but by a corresponding passion for engineering their realization.

Similarly, while the movement is clearly toward teacher-determined in-service programs and the fulfillment of teacher requirements, there is an obvious relationship between a teacher's philosophy, intent and beliefs, and professional retraining interests. These, in the main, will determine what is sought in the way of growth. As a result, staff development policies must include provisions for activities that allow teachers to clarify the values underlying their in-service requests.

What we most need, in the immediate future, is a rationale that accommodates the political differences that exist; preserves the teacher's autonomy in self-directed improvement; incorporates activities directly related to major educational inadequacies; provides for progressive enhancement of technical mastery; permits sharing of local-state-federal support; generates more dollars for in-service activities; and–of greatest significance–demonstrates tangible benefits. Whether we strive for more money, or attempt to make do with less, the new programs will be closely monitored by observers who will make judgments as to their worth.

The arguments in the pages that follow represent, perhaps, the beginning elements of such a rationale.

Louis Rubin

Section I

In-Service Education in Perspective

Continuing Professional Education in Perspective

Louis Rubin

University of Illinois

Most professionals try to keep abreast of changing times and aware of new developments. However, educators' circumstances differ from those of accountants, lawyers, and physicians. Teachers and administrators are beholden, not only to the ethics of their craft and their personal convictions, but to the expectations of their clients and the general good of the social order. It is this dual allegiance, among other things, that tends to distinguish them from other professional practitioners.

The obligation to serve diverse taskmasters also spawns political and ideological conflicts. Disagreements arise, not only with respect to the ancient power question of who shall tell whom what to do, but also with respect to the proper means and ends of education. The result of these conflicts is that professional development programs are sometimes uncertain and imprecise, frequently deferential to convenient rather than optimal solutions, and often reduced in potency for lack of adequate commitment and resources. Yet, few things are as important to society as the perpetuation of good teaching and a serviceable school system.

In order to achieve a better system of ensuring the continuous extension of professional expertise among teachers and administrators we must deal with three requirements: first, the strengths and weaknesses of present programs must be assessed in order to determine what should be sustained and what should be changed; second, impending revisions in curriculum and instructional technique must be anticipated so as to clarify the professional competencies practitioners will require; and third, efficient procedures must be devised for facilitating a transition between the existing system and a better one. It is the first of these three efforts that constitutes the principal subject matter of this first section. Attention is given in subsequent chapters to pending curricular modifications and the corresponding problems of change.

Regrettably, the present state of affairs does not lend itself to an exact appraisal. The scene is characterized by a range of activity that is too broad and too indeterminate to permit an unambiguous identification of promising trends. However, it is possible to describe a variety of current events and to note emerging problems and issues. These, in turn, suggest some tentative conclusions and a partial agenda of needed development. In the interest of logical order, therefore, the following commentary begins with a short historical synthesis and then focuses on present issues. It concludes with a suggested prospectus for subsequent research.

PAST AND PRESENT IN CONTEXT

Throughout the long history of the school, provisions for the improvement of the in-service teacher have rarely been adequate. The typical program has suffered from a lack of energy, precision, direction and imagination. Two factors accounted for this state of affairs. First, in-service education was treated so casually that clumsy and inept programs survived; and second, remarkably little was known about the mechanics of teacher improvement. As long as the nature of schooling remained relatively static there was little incentive to improve matters. However, we have now reached the point where our ancient infirmities may well do us in. Not only have better schools become a matter of considerable importance to the society but it has also become increasingly obvious that any new procedure, constituting a potential improvement, can be dissipated in the hands of an incompetent practitioner. The reform of the curriculum, the invention of superior teaching technology, the investment in specially designed experiences for children with learning disabilities are all of negligible consequence if the teacher who puts them to use is ineffectual.

The tendency of careless practice to nullify the benefits of new methodologies is an accepted fact of life. Most textbooks, for example, are used somewhat ineptly for a short period of time following their introduction. Moreover, the absence of systematic school-university collaboration in teacher preparation suggests that neither institution yet understands its proper role, and that most practitioners are largely self-made; studies on resistance of schools to change show that teachers are wary of any innovation that requires a radically different instructional technique; and the effort to discover why promising new practices work in one situation and fail in another provides grim testimony to the capacity of the ill-trained teacher to imperil educational effectiveness.

As these difficulties manifested themselves, it became evident that they could not be overcome by the then prevailing system of in-service education. A majority of the programs were either so prescriptive that they insulted the teacher's intelligence, ignoring the need to fit teaching to one's own style and to the peculiarities of the particular classroom, or they were too vague to be useful. With rare exceptions, retraining activities dealt with lofty conceptions rather than with the fundamental skills of teaching. In-service programs invariably occurred in isolation from children, thus making practical application and cumulative practice impossible. But perhaps the greatest failing of the retraining activities was that they tended to focus on the temporal fads of the moment rather than on the basic problems of the classroom world.

Preparation for a teaching career includes spending four or five years at a training institution where the prospective teacher receives a sampling of man's accumulated knowledge, some ideas about the theory of education, and a few prescriptions regarding the art and science of teaching. Even if this preparation were adequate, and clearly it is not, the training becomes antiquated in the space of a very short time. For instance, it has been observed that the chemistry teacher who has not studied chemistry for the preceding five years is no longer current in the subject, and is likely to lead students to some misconceptions. Thus, obsolescence begins the day after the teacher concludes formal training. These circumstances notwithstanding, the typical teacher will labor at his or her craft for three to four decades.

The need for a sustained program of retraining that counteracts out-dated or defective teaching is hardly new. In-service education has been a standard educational trapping for most of the twentieth century. Although the need has been recognized, few workable remedies have been suggested. Humans tend to survive whatever does not cause them too much bother, and seemingly, the futility of most in-service education has not been much of a bother. Of late, however, a need to interrupt this prolonged complacency has emerged. First, bad situations, once their nature becomes known, should not go uncorrected. Second, the availability of new technology now permits an approach to retraining that promises greater efficiency and precision. Third, there is much to suggest that teachers are more responsive to professional training *after* they are in service rather than before. And fourth, the recent period of experimentation has greatly enlarged the potential for improvement.

The experiments have taken diverse paths. It has long been felt, for example, that school principals heavily influence the teaching-learning environment in their schools; accordingly, many projects were aimed at enhancing the administrator's ability to function as an instructional leader. Other endeavors, resulting from the belief that retraining should be tied to a specific teaching objective, concentrated on the introduction of innovations of one sort or another. Still others sought to reduce instructional error through diagnosis and correction. From all of these disparate efforts, a basic conclusion has emerged: any attempt to improve children's learning depends on some form of teacher growth. As this conclusion was substantiated in one situation after another, it also became obvious that many training instructors were laboring under a misconceived rationale: they assumed that initial preparation was far more important than in-career development. Although it was obvious that schools differ from instance to instance, there was a peculiar assumption that an able practitioner in one situation would be equally competent in all situations. Far too little allowance was made for teaching individuality. And, contrary to the time-honored principles of incentive, almost nothing was done in the way of motivating teachers to perform somewhere near their highest level of efficiency. As a consequence, many of the old problems of staff development are still with us. Thus, an awareness of the problems has not been enough. It is not the crisis, the philosophers say, but the way in which people respond to the crisis, that determines survival. Until very recently, the profession had not responded to the professional development crisis with anything that even approached appropriateness.

It is widely known, for example, that the introduction of a new practice must be accompanied by a corollary program of teacher reeducation. Similarly, the ease with which carefully tested improvements can be distorted and misused makes it clear that virtually nothing in schooling is teacher-proof. Not only is instant success in educational reform rare, but a kind of reverse Hawthorne effect often occurs. That is, the introduction of a new practice produces, at the outset, less learner gain than was obtained before the change was initiated. This is frequently the case even when the alteration is as relatively undramatic as a shift to a new workbook. Upon reflection, however, these consequences are not unreasonable: the cook must grow accustomed to a new kitchen gadget, the golfer to a new set of clubs, the teacher to a new method or new materials.

Finally, in a curious incongruity, the training of teachers often violates many of the canons that are held sacred in the training of students. Put bluntly, the methods used in in-service education have been for the most part, bad educational practice. With a few notable exceptions, most of the programs are sporadic and disorganized. A lecture here, a meeting there, are used with little success as substitutes for systematic strategies aimed at well-defined objectives. There does not, moreover, appear to be any workable process (or any strong desire to find a process) with which to accommodate teacher individuality. The typical program presumes that all teachers are precisely the same in background, belief, knowledge, technical finesse, and teaching style. Teacher complaints of meaninglessness and irrelevance in in-service education programs have been acknowledged in spirit and ignored in practice. Even when they have gained a bit of attention, makeshift and inconsequential adjustments are dismissed as a necessary evil of bureaucracy.

Teachers not only teach different grade levels and subjects, but their working environments vary considerably from school to school. The nature of the student population, the expectations of their parents, the aspirations of the school system, the customs of the particular faculty, and the school's physical resources all influence the ways in which the teacher must function. It follows, therefore, that these same environmental factors also affect both the competencies teachers need, and the procedures for their development. Such differentiation, however, is not often reflected in the standard professional improvement program.

What is of greatest significance, however, is the changing job market. In the period ahead there will be a progressively declining need for preservice training. As the supply of teachers approaches overabundance, colleges and universities are likely to produce fewer and fewer practitioners. The opportunity for greater emphasis on continuing professional development will therefore increase proportionately. Put another way, our greatest hope of improving the quality of instruction may rest—not in the training of new personnel—but in the continuous upgrading of the teachers already at work. It is worth noting, in this connection, that although substantial research funds have been appropriated for the purpose of refining preservice training, far less has been earmarked for the betterment of in-service education. This imbalance may have been somewhat defensible in the past, but we have now reached the point where a reversal of priorities is in order.

It is probable that the new research presently being supported by the National Institute of Education will lead to a further expansion of teaching technology. This, in turn, will necessitate a corresponding reeducation of teachers. Wisdom dictates that we anticipate this impending need and try to reduce the historic time lag between the development of a new pedagogical technique and the reorientation of its users.

All in all, the existing state of affairs strongly underscores the need for usable research on staff development. The list of problems requiring solutions is impressive: (1) there has been a profound lack of continuity between preservice and in-service learning; (2) present programs generally lack vitality and rigor; (3) many current practices suffer from a conspicuous lack of precision, at least in the sense that teacher-growth objectives are not coupled with an efficient means for their attainment; (4) we have failed to exploit the rich potential inherent in the processes through which teachers can educate one another; (5) our preoccupation with teaching technique related to subject matter has caused us to overlook the importance of what might be called the "personological" skills of teaching; (6) little systematic attention has been given to the educational and social values teachers embrace; and (7) not much has been done in the way of anticipating the kinds of teachers that will be required as school and societal change follow their inexorable course.

To sum up matters, then, the historical legacy of in-service education has been characterized by randomness and fragmentation, by programs that deferred more to expediency than to need, and by methodologies that have been largely atheoretical. These infirmities have persisted, mainly, because of three conditions. First, whether or not systematic professional development provisions exist, teachers do learn, intuitively, through their day-to-day experience. While, in the case of some, true artistry and master craftsmanship have not been reached, sufficient competence to ensure survival is not too difficult to achieve. Second, the reforms of the past twenty-five years have not, in general, demanded major readjustments in teaching technique. Most have unfolded with such tentativeness that average teachers have been able to keep pace, at least on the surface, by making minor adaptations in their customary habits. Third, since capable and highly motivated students seem to learn no matter how they are taught, many pupils learn to compensate for poor instruction.

It is unfair to imply that all in-service education is defective, or that excellent teaching does not, in many instances, go on. It is legitimate to note, however, that the machinery for sustaining the professional development of educators is in need of an overhaul.

THE CURRENT SCENE

A number of events serve to dramatize the need for a better system of in-service education. An analysis of education's resistance to change during the past decade demonstrates that much of the trouble is inherent in the counterfeit assumption that teachers adapt quickly and easily to change without any special preparation. The intrinsic relationship between curriculum improvement and teacher development has, as a result, become more widely appreciated. In addition, it has become abundantly clear that any teaching objective can be accomplished in alternative ways and that master teachers rely on a repertory rather than on a single method.

The accountability movement has also had an effect. Although the precise meaning of the term remains vague, and there is considerable disagreement as to the proper criteria for assessing pedagogical effectiveness, the importance of enhancing teacher proficiency is now taken a good deal more seriously than in the past.

Sovereignty has also become a major point of contention. The rise of teacher autonomy, and its attendant political struggle, has raised serious questions as to the following: (a) who determines the substance of in-service activities, (b) who serves as the training expert, and (c) who evaluates the outcomes. The answers are being hotly debated since control converts into power. The stewardship of in-service training is a significant political issue and substantial controversy has developed over who governs it. To date, the only predictable outcome is that the traditional monopoly of the academic professor will almost certainly deteriorate.

Teachers contend, with reasonable cause, that the skilled practitioner is an infinitely better trainer of teachers than the professor who is knee-deep in theory and removed from the real world. The academics, on the other hand, are quick to point out that without the infusion of insights derived from scholarly analysis the state of the art would remain static. To complicate matters further, school administrators suggest that professors and teachers are not in a good position to sense the public pulse. They argue that if the schools' image and credibility have become tarnished, the only viable corrective is to make education more responsive to community concerns. Accordingly, many administrators maintain that public expectation—not teacher or professorial opinion—should serve as the primary basis for revitalizing teaching, and improving professional retraining programs.

The result of all this, not surprisingly, is that with a great many actors contesting for parts in this drama, competitiveness may overshadow reason. Most of the efforts leave something to be desired. Any activity that gives promise of improving teacher performance can be labelled in-service education. Therefore, building principals, district supervisors, college and university professors, teachers, and a host of specialists from other fields (social workers, psychiatrists, systems planning experts, librarians, urban planners, legitimate and illegitimate group psychologists, and behavior modification technicians) are devising and delivering "professional growth experiences" that will supposedly improve teaching. Their promises span a broad gamut: the extension of individual creativity, the humanization of learning, the diagnosis of students' affective needs, the improvement of peer group relations, the elimination of sexist bias in teachers' attitudes, the development of role-playing skills, and so on.

At the same time, a somewhat smaller number of endeavors, rooted in the systematic application of pedagogical principles, is also under way. Situated in teacher centers, research programs, curriculum implementation projects, and frequently, in the school districts themselves, these ventures show more real promise of elevating the state of the art.

Much of the chaos surrounding the extension of in-service education is attributable to three sources of confusion: (1) differing ideological conceptions regarding teaching and the teacher's role; (2) conflicting notions regarding what in-service education should accomplish; and (3) the absence of a tested system for implementing professional growth activities within the work day environment.

From the moment when the first school opened its doors, ideas regarding the purpose of teaching have been the subject of endless debate. If, for example, teaching is viewed as the didactic transmittal of factual knowledge, certain implications for in-service education will logically follow. If, instead, teaching is viewed as the guidance of learning, wherein the student functions heuristically, the implications take another direction. If we conceive of the curriculum in terms of cognitive learning alone, specific pedagogical capabilities are suggested. But when we think of instruction as having both cognitive and affective dimensions, a rather different set of teacher skills becomes germane. As long as there are contradictory conceptions regarding the purpose of education, corresponding differences will exist with respect to the nature of teaching. And, as long as we disagree about the nature of teaching, we will also disagree on the optimum methodologies of instruction, and on the technical requirements for expert teaching performance. Thus the ideological contradictions come full circle: when beliefs regarding the technical requirements of teachers are inconsistent, the same inconsistency must exist with respect to appropriate training and retraining programs.

A second source of confusion is therefore inevitable. Many educators still regard in-service education as a mechanism for the remediation of technical defects. Others, more skeptical about our ability to precisely identify defects, view in-service training as a vehicle for open-ended professional development, especially in areas that seem important to the individual practitioner.

Moreover, the question of retraining objectives is itself subject to disparate sentiments. The liberal and humanistically oriented are committed to the belief that teachers can determine and organize their own self-development. In contrast, conservatives remain convinced that at least minimal external direction is mandatory. While a dichotomy is perhaps unnecessary, professional education that is seen as a device for familiarizing teachers with desirable change and promoting reform must be demonstrably different from that which is conceived of as personal maturation.

In most districts, administrators are still legally charged with establishing tenure criteria and determining which teachers do or do not qualify for permanent appointment. In many cases, appropriate in-service activity could make a difference in whether the teacher improves sufficiently (in the eyes of the evaluator) to warrant tenure status. Many observers insist that administratively-determined professional development experiences are not only advantageous but indispensable to a teacher's welfare.

Other theorists are persuaded that the curriculum should be planned and organized by teachers, and that this responsibility should serve as the basis for planning in-service education. Those in disagreement adhere to the traditional presumption that teachers should follow the instructional policy set by designated authorities. In the latter scheme of things, teachers are seen as agents who carry out the plans of superordinates. In point of fact, many teachers might be content to abide by such a division of responsibility, but teacher organizations in particular, and autonomy conscious teachers in general, are unwilling to settle for such pawn-like subservience.

Differences persist even within the ranks of the theorists. There are those who regard teaching as an organized system of tactics and strategies that are acquired through guided practice. They contend that in-service development should be restricted to those instructional skills that can be demonstrated and modeled. But there are also theorists who believe that finely honed technical skills are not, as a general rule, trainable, and that the individual teacher's attitudes, beliefs, and values are the crucial wellspring out of which creative technique, appropriate to the particular circumstance, is fashioned. Consequently, it comes as no shock that since knowledgeable people disagree about the legitimate function of in-service professional development, current activities are a discrepant collection of miscellanea.

Besides conflicting ideologies and contradictory conceptions of purpose, difficulties also stem from the conspicuous absence of systemization. There is, for example, no standardization with respect to the kind of professional development activities that should be offered, when, where, how, and by whom. Nor is there any uniformity in legal mandate. Participation is sometimes voluntary and sometimes compulsory. Many districts lure teachers with extrinsic rewards while others rely on more intrinsic motivation. In some places, sanctions for nonparticipation are imposed; elsewhere teachers can virtually survive the length of their professional careers without any formal efforts at professional enhancement.

Similar inconsistencies prevail with respect to financial support. A few districts reimburse teachers for tuition costs associated with university-based postgraduate study; most support programs of one kind or another through local district funds; and state and federal monies are often available for special programs, particularly those related to specific innovations. Still, there is virtually no consensus as to the proper roles of the federal, state, and local authorities. Neither is there an established, widely-endosed process for assuring continuity between one activity and another, nor a generally agreed upon pattern for cohesive collaboration among colleges, universities, teacher organizations, and school supervisors. And, in what is perhaps the greatest omission, there is nothing approaching an effective procedure for evaluating the outcomes of most programs.

The trends and events characterizing the current state of in-service education in the United States must therefore be seen against the historical background. Some difficulties owe their origin to unresolved dilemmas of the past. Other, somewhat newer problems, are the result of the troubles and tribulations that now afflict education in general. It must also be acknowledged that, whatever the past and present impediments, the efficacy of planned professional improvement is viewed with skepticism by many observers. The net gains, from the dollars invested in the programs of the last decade, are less than impressive. Thus, along with the other requirements is the pressing need to rekindle credibility.

What is most heartening in the overall evolution is the fact that in-service education will probably be taken far more seriously than it has been in the past. More and more, the making of a teacher is conceived of as a continuum that begins early in the baccalaureate experience and extends into the first few years of professional service. For those, in fact, who subscribe to the belief that even the oldest of dogs can learn new tricks, it is conceptualized as a career-long development. A period of unusual ferment is under way, important issues are being contested; thus, there is reason for modest optimism about the future.

The Teacher Center Movement

In summarizing present teacher in-service education in the United States, it is probably most useful to begin with the Teacher Center movement, whose rationale reflects the centripetal concerns of our time. This movement, which derives its impetus chiefly from earlier English models, constitutes a shift away from in-service as a "course," and toward a more heuristic and autonomous endeavor. Since there is little standardization in format, a Center can be organized in almost any way. The purposes and objectives, moreover, are equally variable.

Some Centers are sponsored by teacher collectives, some by school districts, and some by colleges and universities. A few function in specially designed facilities, but most tend to be more of a process than a physical entity. As Devaney and Thorn have noted, the essential common denominator among Centers is a basic philosophy regarding the role of teachers.

> Teachers must be more than technicians, must continue to be learners. Long-lasting improvements in education will come through in-service programs that identify individual starting points for learning in each teacher; build on teachers' motivation to take more, not less, responsibility for curriculum and instruction decisions in the school and the classroom; and welcome teachers to participate in the design of professional development programs.[1]

1. Kathleen Devaney and Lorraine Thorn, *Exploring Teachers' Centers* (San Francisco: Far West Laboratory for Educational Research, 1975).

The guiding spirit of the Center movement is captured in the following description of a typical program. The Campbell County Teachers Center is more than a building where teachers participate in in-service activities; it is a concept based on the following beliefs:

1. Teachers are key agents in affecting fundamental changes.
2. Teachers are unlikely to change simply because administrators or outside experts tell them to.
3. Teachers will take reform most seriously when they are, at least partially, responsible for defining their own educational problems, delineating their own needs, and receiving help on their own terms.[2]

The major function of the Center is to generate greater teacher involvement and self-direction. Motivationally, the energizing mechanism is creative participation. When teachers are given control over the substance of their instruction, when they are allowed to invent appropriate methodology and provide for learner relevance in whatever way seems most desirable, professional dedication, enthusiasm, and effort are likely to increase sharply. As a result, teachers invest greater excitement and energy in their tasks, take greater intrinsic satisfaction in accomplishing their objectives, and become considerably more knowledgeable about effective teaching.

The attraction of the Center concept is attested to by recent federal legislation providing for the establishment of a national network of such programs. Interest is also mounting in "training centers," agencies specifically designed to facilitate the preservice and in-service development of teachers. The underlying assumption here is that a rich supply of teacher-made and industry-made instructional materials might greatly enlarge the practitioner's professional repertory.

Politically, however, two problems exist. Many administrators contend that if school district funds are used to support Centers, designated district officials should play a role in their governance. Furthermore, some administrators doubt the virtues of total teacher self-direction, preferring instead to interject at least some external guidance.

Other critics suggest that the Centers will be unproductive as long as they depend on voluntary participation, and deal primarily with parochial concerns. They feel that the teachers most in need of what the Centers can offer are the ones who are least likely to become

2. Edward Yeats, "Staff Development: A Teacher-Centered In-Service Design," *Educational Leadership* (March 1976): Vol. 33 No. 6, 417.

involved. They also argue that little good can emanate from even well-intentioned and persevering efforts if the wrong problems are attacked.

The Ford Foundation, long associated with innovation and experimental reform, has recently been interested in teacher centers. Its interest lies in in-service education evolving out of teacher-determined needs. According to Marjorie Martus, a program officer with the Foundation, the projects that were funded in the early 1970s were principally intended to encourage experimentation. Out of the belief that different forms of teacher participation and different kinds of teacher centers are possible, and the conviction that curriculum-specific skills (teaching techniques related to one specific program) lack general application, the Ford-funded projects were generally organized around alternative procedures for perpetuating teacher self-development.

In assessing the pros and cons of the Teacher Center potential, it is instructive to cite the comments of David Burrell, a British scholar, who has followed the movement in England for a sustained period of time. Burrell has this to say:

> There is certainly nothing incidental about the philosophy of the centres. Indeed in some ways this philosophy is the most characteristic and significant aspect of them. Several basic assumptions are worth noting. First, there is the notion that basic and effective innovation and reappraisal of work in the classroom will come about mainly through the efforts and activities of practising teachers, assisted by whoever can contribute in some way.
>
> The second assumption is that there exists among teachers a vast reservoir of untapped expertise and experience. If they are given the opportunity, good teachers are capable of drawing on these and using them as a starting point for professional renewal and growth. The good practitioner is seen to have great potential as the trainer of other teachers. Third, it is assumed that centres can be effective instruments for reconsideration or development of current practice in the schools. The fourth assumption is that centres can provide a neutral arena in which teachers can work relatively free of constraints and pressures and the hierarchical assumptions often present in other training institutions. Many would argue that the rejection of the latter is the initial decisive factor in the development of true professionalism among teachers. It is certainly associated with the idea of teacher control of in-service planning, for the fifth assumption is that centres should be organized and controlled as far as possible by the teachers themselves through the centres' programme and other decision-making committees.[3]

3. David Burrell, "The Teachers Center: A Critical Analysis," *Educational Leadership* (March 1976), Vol. 33 No. 6.

In subsequent commentary, Burrell also observes that "despite the rhetoric, a major activity is the traditional course, and that it tends, in the centre context, to be short in duration and very practically based." Dissatisfaction with contemporary in-service programs in the United Kingdom seems to parallel that in the United States—teachers feel that topics related to practical problems are considerably more valuable than incidental lectures, and they prefer to deal with professional rather than personal solutions. "There is an obvious tendency," Burrell says, "for activities run by teachers for teachers, particularly if they are rather short in duration, to be merely a recounting of successes or the subjective pooling of experience. These can provide a valuable starting point for significant activities, but it is extremely difficult to move many teachers beyond this starting point." Burrell also fears, as do some American observers, that the resources essential to the Center movement may be forestalled by dollar constraints; that adequate time, during salaried hours, for teacher participation in the Center's endeavors will be difficult to achieve; and that many self-directed practitioners, seeking to overcome technical problems, may confuse symptoms with cause.

All of this should not suggest that the Center concept is a predestined failure. It seems more reasonable, instead, to assume that the movement is still in its infancy. While the potential remains promising, the evidence is not yet all in and judgment must be delayed.

Other Innovative Programs

The customary in-service program is most likely to follow a traditional formula. Teacher institutes are commonplace, practitioners are often given incentive credit for participation in college and university courses, and periodic workshops are offered, particularly in connection with current educational development. Individual teacher interests are accommodated through provisions for choice among the available options; the evaluation of programs is predominantly based on participant opinion; and, generally, there is a limited amount of sustained and well-planned connection between professional growth opportunities and teachers' daily classroom concerns. Depending on the size of the district and the available funds, in-service activities are organized according to grade levels (elementary, junior and senior high school) or according to subjects (mathematics, English, social studies) or according to special themes (accountability, peer tutoring, grading procedures). Apart from these conventional trappings, however, a number of other experimental innovations are also underway.

In an effort to join research on teaching with improvement of in-service education, several ideas are being pursued at the Far West Laboratory for Educational Research. Labeled an "interactive approach to research and development on teaching," the distinctive feature of the plan involves the use of teachers as researchers. Teams consisting of a researcher, a trainer, and a teacher, collaboratively gather and interpret case studies of ongoing classroom practice.

In another exploration by the same group, the potential of using teachers as self-trainers is being tested. Employing a three-step format, teachers first choose a new program or procedure that has interest and appeal. Next, through self-directed study and occasional use of an external consultant, the teachers attempt to master the innovation. Finally, the process is evaluated in order to determine the particular mechanisms and strategies of greatest efficacy. Prototype experiments have been conducted in Vancouver, Washington; Traverse City, Michigan; and Weymouth, Massachusetts.

An additional pursuit of the same Laboratory is also worth mentioning. Using criteria based on "21 dimensions of effective teaching," teacher behavior is studied in regard to fostering independent learning, mathematics tutoring, and questioning techniques. The objective is to learn more about the allocation and utilization of teacher time. Through an ethnocentric approach to data gathering, teachers serve as participant-observers. Descriptions of classroom activity, gathered through recorded observations, are subjected to analysis. The data is categorized into three separate teaching stages: preactive (teacher intent), active (actual teacher behavior) and reactive (teacher reactions to the outcomes of the instruction).

All three projects are built upon several fundamental presumptions. First, generic (widely applicable) teaching techniques not only exist, but are identifiable and teachable; second, the appraisal of teaching performance, based on children's daily learning, is more valuable than evaluation based on end-of-year tests; and, third, despite great variations in teaching style, there is a common nucleus of effective pedagogical technique.

A number of current trends are also illustrated by the in-service procedures of the Lincoln, Nebraska schools. This school system boasts of one of the highest budgets in the nation—roughly 2 percent of Lincoln's funds are devoted to teacher professional growth. The primary strategy of the program rests in the use of school principals as staff development specialists. Since the district favors decentralized administrative control, principals have the freedom to plan, organize, and implement whatever staff development programs they deem desirable. Although policy leadership emanates from the office of the district in-service supervisor, and although program outcomes are assessed on a district-wide basis, great latitude is given to the specialized concerns of the individual schools. Nebraska has also organized an informal consortium of school districts that works cooperatively to design programmatic improvements. Once a year "caravans" composed of specialist teams visit school districts, observe staff development practices, and offer criticism, encouragement and advice.

Significantly, in the Lincoln, Nebraska in-service program, 75 percent of the training is provided by the district teachers themselves. Benefiting from a superintendent strongly committed to the importance of teacher professional growth, the district's emphasis is broadly eclectic. Training activities deal with human relations, organizational consistency, skills and understanding associated with a contemplated instructional change, and positive teacher attitudes.

In another program, the schools of a suburban Chicago high school district (Arlington Heights) in cooperation with the University of Illinois, provide teachers with mini-sabbaticals. Teaching interns replace career teachers for short periods of time, enabling the career teachers to engage in professional development activities. The regular teachers do not go on formal leave, but time made available through the use of the intern substitutes is used for participation in courses taught by University faculty. A variation of this procedure is used in a similar relationship between the University of Massachusetts and the schools of Worcester.

In Madison, Wisconsin, a type of "management by objective" system is in operation. District supervisors hold individual conferences with teachers and cooperatively plan in-service experiences that promise to enhance the teacher's capacities. Similarly, in Des Moines, Iowa, a procedure known as a *charrette* is utilized. Small groups of teachers convene, determine their professional needs, debate alternative plans for accommodating these needs, and ultimately develop professional improvement activities. The tactics used in Des Moines, Madison, Worcester, Arlington Heights, and Lincoln are noteworthy in that they all respect the belief that teachers are the best judges of their own professional strengths and weaknesses.

This similarity in trends is perhaps in large measure attributable to the National Staff Development Council. A relatively small organization, the Council's membership is composed of district in-service education specialists, who convene annually to consider mutual interests and problems. A consistency in view seems to be the natural outgrowth of this cooperative approach to problem analysis.

One of the most comprehensive enterprises is situated in Jefferson County, Colorado. The operation is both a physical entity and a planned sequence of activities. Housed in its own facility, the "Academy" offers teachers an extraordinary range of professional experiences. Courses are organized in conjunction with colleges and universities as well as with educational development laboratories. There are also cooperative arrangements with publishers engaged in producing innovative curricula. A liberal sprinkling of most contemporary teacher training activities are, in one way or another, represented in the programs. Despite the great scope of activity, observers seem generally impressed with the quality of the Jefferson County organization.

Elsewhere, a number of other nontraditional programs are in evidence. However, most are either so new, or so small-scale, that generalizations are difficult. For example, Minneapolis has experimented with "retreats"–group meetings carried on away from the work site so as to reduce distractions–aimed at administrator in-service education. It might be observed, in this regard, that strong connective tissue between the continuing professional education of teachers and that of administrators is important. Even with the growing degree of teacher autonomy, the principal's conception of good education has an appreciable impact on the instructional organization of a school. As a consequence, there is an inevitable link, either implicit or explicit, between the kind of instruction that goes on, school policy, and the pedagogical beliefs of teachers. For example, Intermediate Service Unit XIII, an organization similar to a conventional county office, located in the environs of Austin, Texas, has tried in various ways to increase the correspondence between the educational commitments of teachers and administrators. Noted for its willingness to depart from convention, its efforts to attack problems in depth, and its extensive outreach, the Service Unit typifies recent efforts to interrupt antiquated organizational arrangements.

As yet there is still a peculiar lack of centralized programming in most State Departments of Education. All state agencies, of course, acknowledge the great importance of continuing professional education for teachers, and all support programs of one sort or another. For example, the state of Florida has mandated a regular provision of training that increases teacher proficiency in Early Childhood Education and other priority areas. Five dollars per student, per year is allotted for staff development, with the proviso that diagnostic-prescriptive techniques and the teaching of basics be emphasized. Nonetheless, in most states, administrative responsibility for teacher in-service activity is divided among different offices and bureaus. There seems to be a striking absence of departments in state agencies that are specifically and exclusively concerned with teacher development and able to exert state-wide influence.

As a result, in most states, the ongoing trends and events create a somewhat fragmented picture. The Intermediate Unit near Austin, Texas, for instance, gives special attention to a fifty hour modularized training program emphasizing individualization techniques. In contrast, the Jefferson County Academy offers district-wide courses based chiefly on teachers' interests. The breadth of the program, in fact, is so great that more than 1700 different meetings have been conducted in a single calendar year. Much of the activity stems from arrangements with seven area universities offering graduate credit courses, applicable to advanced degrees, in the Academy facility. Sometimes teachers pay their own tuition charges; in other cases the costs are defrayed by a grant from the Teachers Corps; and on occasion training expenses are shared jointly by the teacher and the Academy.

Similarly, the Des Moines schools have a working relationship with Drake University that makes it possible for in-service courses to be used in qualifying for graduate degrees. In the Des Moines situation, however, the teacher programs are intended primarily to bridge the gap between new research findings and the practical exigencies of the classroom. Although both Des Moines and Jefferson County have provisions for individual, teacher-determined, professional growth projects, the points of thematic emphasis are somewhat different. An issue, yet to be resolved, thus becomes central: Is policy standardization desirable or undesirable?

The most dramatic and bold departure from convention is perhaps reflected in Georgia's recent revisions. Teachers seeking certification renewal will soon be required, by law, to undergo evaluation and demonstrate adequacy. In the pilot program, now underway in Griffin, Georgia, the local CESA unit, headed by R. E. Flanders, is testing sweeping new arrangements. Teachers interested in certification renewal are evaluated on the job by a team of three trained evaluators. Using rating scales, the evaluators, who are professional teachers, determine whether the individual has achieved a minimal level of competency in various areas. In each of the technical skills where the performance is judged inadequate, the teacher must take a prescribed sequence of ten hours instruction in order to upgrade capability. Parallel training is also being provided for leadership personnel as a part of the comprehensive effort to improve student achievement. If the Georgia pattern is a forerunner of things to come, competency-based in-service–and minimal standards–have clearly taken hold.

Theoretical Exploration

A number of trends are also observable in the theoretical arena. At the Stanford Center for Research and Development in Teaching, in a study sponsored by the National Teacher Corps and the National Center for Educational Statistics, an attempt has been made to extract operational concepts, basic teacher needs, and practical implications from the great mass of professional literature. The study sought to improve the knowledge base for in-service education by clarifying fundamental conceptions, defining significant issues and problems, contrasting conflicting ideologies, and describing prospective new directions. The study, carried on by Bruce Joyce and his colleagues, included a compilation of "expert opinion" in the form of commissioned position papers, as well as an attitudinal survey of teachers and administrators.

The investigation reaffirmed the inadequacy of present theory, the lack of definitive models, and the exaggerated reliance on college and university courses. Teachers object to the lack of relevance between professional development programs and their daily responsibilities; they resent the fact that improved performance tends to be unrecognized and unrewarded; and they believe the existing system makes it difficult for teachers to pursue their own job-related interests.

The investigators were also critical of the typical criteria used to assess teacher effectiveness: "Unfortunately, pupil learning (often measured in achievement gain scores) is seen as a direct reflection of the teacher's ability to 'teach'–and more frequently than not, the classroom teacher is unable to remove his/her own personal feelings of self-worth and self-concept from these standardized test scores."[4] What this suggests, self-evidently, is that responsible teachers embrace pedagogical aims that go beyond the subject-matter measured on standardized tests.

In another theoretical exploration, also being conducted at Stanford University, an effort is being made to apply concepts derived

4. "A Study in In-Service Teacher Education: Concepts, User Needs and Literature," (Stanford, CA.: Stanford Center for Research and Development in Teaching, 1975), unpublished document.

from Aptitude Treatment Interaction (ATI) to the problems of teacher professional growth. The dominant constructs are: (1) teacher education should function as a self-corrective system; (2) teachers must adapt to changing situations; (3) teacher-training programs should accommodate individual differences; (4) training systems should therefore be adaptive because teacher needs vary according to time and circumstance; and (5) adaptation must be viewed as a transactive process–that is, teachers both teach and learn in their daily classroom encounter.

Of greatest significance, perhaps, is the fact that the research is based on the premise that a quest for guaranteed teaching methodologies and universal strategies in training teachers, is largely fruitless.

> Over the past decade, educational psychologists have learned to ask some new kinds of questions about teaching and learning in schools. A cognitive psychology has emerged that emphasizes the structure and process of mental events, and the complexity, individuality, and situationality of human interaction with environment.[5]

The approach constitutes a sharp departure from traditional experimental designs and correlational procedures. The effect, if not the intention of the rationale, is to acknowledge that teaching-learning is so sensitive to variation that idiosyncracies of the particular environment overshadow operational principles. As a result, little can be gained from asking questions such as "What teaching methods work best?" or "How much time should be devoted to a particular instructional objective?" or "What provisions should be made for level of student intelligence?" The answers to these questions depend on a large number of external factors ingrained in the specific situation, and on the interplay and cross-effects among the factors themselves. In short, everything rests on the characteristics of the setting, the natures of the people involved, the goals at hand, and the ways in which all of these intrude upon and affect one another. Consequently, the search for tactics that are free from failure–irrespective of the contextual scene and the human elements–is not likely to be of any real avail.

In a study sponsored by the Florida Department of Education entitled "Patterns of Effective In-service Education," and carried out under the direction of Gordon Lawrence, ninety-seven studies of continuing-teacher education were analyzed. Notable among the findings were the following:

5. Richard Snow, "Toward the Effective, Evolutionary Teaching of Teachers," (Stanford, CA.: Stanford Center for Research and Development in Teaching, 1975), unpublished document.

1. In-service programs in schools and on college campuses are equally capable of affecting teacher behavior, but the school settings tend to be capable of influencing more complex behavior changes in teachers.
2. Minicourses sponsored either by colleges or schools tend to emphasize the development and application of specific teaching skills, with a corresponding lower emphasis on beliefs, values, concepts, and information objectives. Minicourses have a high rate of success in achieving the specific skill objectives.
3. No medium of the instruction is broadly inappropriate or distinctly inferior in the accomplishment of the objectives of in-service education.
4. Training in the use of an observation system, such as Interaction Analysis, is effective in changing a teacher's capacity to perform certain verbal operations; but it is relatively ineffective in influencing teacher attitude and in influencing pupil behavior.
5. School-based programs in which teachers participate as helpers to each other and planners of in-service activities tend to have greater success in accomplishing their objectives than do programs that are conducted by college or other outside personnel without the assistance of teachers.
6. The success rate of in-service education programs is substantially higher when change in teaching behavior is the criterion rather than when subsequent change in pupil behavior is the criterion.
7. In-service education programs that have differentiated training experiences for different teachers (that is, "individualized") are more likely to accomplish their objectives than are programs that have common activities for all participants.
8. In-service education programs that emphasize demonstrations, supervised trials and feedback are more likely to accomplish their goals than are programs in which the teacher is expected to store up ideas and behavior prescriptions for a future time.[6]

Recently, much has been done to clarify the distinctions between preservice and in-service training. In a report prepared by the American Association of Colleges for Teacher Education, *Educating a Profession,* in-service education is defined as training that relates to specific instructional programs.[7] In contrast, continuing education is used to denote more general professional development. The Association's Commission,

6. Gordon Lawrence, "Patterns of Effective In-Service Education," Principal Investigators: Department of Education, Tallahassee, Florida, December, 1974.
7. Robert B. Howsam, et al., *Educating a Profession* (American Association of Colleges of Teacher Education, Washington, D.C., 1976), p. 65.

chaired by Robert B. Howsam, recommended that primary responsibility for the preservice preparation of teachers should be vested in colleges and universities. The planning and governance of in-service education, in turn, should be assigned to the school system. Finally, continuing education–aimed at personal growth and enhancement–is viewed as the responsibility of the teachers themselves and their professional associations.

The Commission also emphasized the need for better professional curricula. Arguing that the training of teachers should serve as a model of pedagogical excellence, the report advocates a longer, more comprehensive period of training, coupled with transitional internships. Multi-level certification also is suggested: basic credentialing, at the conclusion of preservice training; secondary certification, once acceptable competence has been demonstrated; and professional status, identifying those who have attained the highest levels of proficiency. More generally, the report concludes that too little time is spent on the science of pedagogy during preservice training; more attention should be given to the creation of a "professional culture" symbolizing master craftsmanship in teaching; and the provisions for developing true expertness must be enlarged.

The critical connection between attitudes formed during preservice preparation and in-service aspirations was similarly underscored in a commentary by the Study Commission on Undergraduate Education and the Education of Teachers. In view of the mounting demand for increased professional autonomy among teachers, the educational beliefs and convictions of the individual practitioner have become crucial. Citing survey data collected in 1970, the Study Commission report notes that not only do teachers gain limited social sophistication before beginning their teaching careers, but attention to sociological awareness is likely to be equally scant in their subsequent professional development.[8] Theorists have long puzzled over suitable ways of overcoming the generality of preservice training and the specificity of teaching assignments. Since teachers receiving the same preparation often take jobs in very different communities, it is only through continuing professional education that the indispensable familiarity with the students' culture can be provided. When this socialization fails to occur, a considerable period of time may elapse before teachers eventually

8. Pal Olson (Director), Study Commission on Undergraduate Education and the Education of Teachers, *Teacher Education in the United States: The Responsibility Gap* (Lincoln, Nebraska: University of Nebraska Press, 1976).

develop a "sense" of their clients. One of the impressive contributions of the Teachers Corps, in this regard, has been the development of training protocols that sensitize teachers to the lifestyles of their students.

Haberman and Stinnett have pointed out that the tasks of in-service training can be greatly complicated by poor initial selection.[9] Entry to teacher-training programs is based largely on the individual's ability to study education, rather than on teaching ability. As in most other professions, correspondence between college grades and professional success is anything but strong. In other words, it is virtually impossible to determine, at the conclusion of a training program, whether a graduate will become a successful or an unsuccessful teacher. The National Institute of Education has sought, through a variety of projects, to enlarge our present range of selection and training procedures. To date, however, the problem remains as intractable as ever, and no easy solutions are in sight.

Nonetheless, one can detect a degree of consensus in the conglomeration of theory, conjecture, speculation, and wishful thinking now being brought to bear on the continuing professional education of teachers. Writings by Roy A. Edelfelt of the National Education Association[10] and publications of the American Federation of Teachers[11] espousing the convictions of Robert D. Bhaerman, emphasize collaborative planning, parity in decision-making, and teacher autonomy. Both organizations, along with the Association of Teacher Educators–a group of school supervisors, state department officials, college instructors, and others involved in professional training–are convinced that, even if for political reasons alone, cooperative governance is vital. Similarly, all agree that the finance factors are crucial. In a time of dwindling resources and rising costs, it is a foregone conclusion that the organized profession will resist virtually everything that stands in the way of salaries. It would be irrational, hence, to design professional development programs without due concern for budgetary constraints. The question, therefore, is not merely what is good but also what is economically feasible. It may be necessary to first conceptualize an

9. Martin Haberman and T. M. Stinnett, *Teacher Education and the New Profession of Teaching* (Berkeley, CA.: McCutchan Publishing Corporation).

10. Roy A. Edelfelt and Margo Johnson, eds., *Rethinking In-Service Education* (Washington, D.C.: National Education Association, 1975).

11. Robert D. Bhaerman, AFT QUEST Paper No. 7, "Several Educators' Cure for the Common Cold, Among Other Things," (Washington, D.C.: Department of Research, American Federation of Teachers).

ideal arrangement, however elegant and costly, but sooner or later, we will have to generate mechanisms that are serviceable as well as inexpensive.

Although the preceding overview does not cover all ongoing theoretical endeavor, it does provide a cross-section of current directions. For example, there is relatively widespread agreement on the need for restructuring the logistics of professional development, as well as considerable unanimity regarding the desirability of clarifying means and ends. Goals and strategies, however, must of necessity spring from a basic credo regarding the nature and purpose of schooling. Competency-based training, to wit, makes abundant logic from one ideological perspective but is completely senseless from another. As long as philosophical differences divide the profession, theories of in-service education will provide cause for dispute and contention.

Yet, for all these differences, there is a growing acceptance of certain realities among the various camps. Few would quarrel with the argument that teaching artistry must be cumulatively extended. Most observers acknowledge that alternatives exist both in teaching goals and teaching methods. Since the evidence that learner achievement, and thus teacher effectiveness, is heavily affected by unpredictable events, situational circumstances and flexible in-service arrangements, *in situ,* are now generally viewed as mandatory. Similarly, there are movements toward the cooperative planning and control of activities, toward greater allowance for teacher-determined professional objectives, and toward diversity rather than uniformity in program design. All of these trends emanate from deficiencies in the present system and are therefore presumed to be steps in the direction of a better system. Issues, nevertheless, remain. In the following section, some of the more significant dilemmas are considered.

CRITICAL ISSUES

Basically, issues are questions that involve substantial disagreement. In-service education in the United States is currently beset by a full slate of these issues. Opinions differ with respect to who should determine appropriate training content, who should provide the training, who should pay for the training, and, ultimately, who should judge the usefulness of the training. Further arguments exist with regard to optimum delivery systems, procedures for individualizing training, the extent to which "natural style" in teaching should be respected, and the comparative advantages of emphasizing generic or subject-specific skills. These disputes, of course, have always been with us; their current vogue stems from emerging interest in continuing professional education.

Matters are further complicated because attention often diverts from "what is right" to "who is right." The teachers' unions believe that practitioners should determine their own needs, receive expert counsel from other practitioners, benefit from at least some on-the-job release time for professional growth, and be protected from the dangers associated with a merit-pay system. Administrators, school boards, and some theorists tend to see the circumstances differently.

Although the political maneuvering is inevitable, and perhaps necessary, much could be gained if less attention were focused on the disputes and more on the discovery of rational solutions. For instance, in the case of program determination, it seems reasonable that the individual practitioner have an opportunity to satisfy personal interests and ambitions. At the same time, the failure to achieve basic educational objectives, however such failure is determined, must also be considered in determining in-service goals. Similarly, as new programs are invented and new procedures introduced, the changeover from old to new is almost certain to pose special retraining needs that must be met. Thus, rational action is less a matter of quibbling about different points of view than of establishing a reasonable balance in priorities.

The question of who should serve as training specialists is a bit more complicated. Experiences suggest that teachers are most responsive to guidance from other teachers, and master craftsmanship is more likely to be found among teachers than anywhere else. At the same time, there are supervisors, school principals, and college professors who, out of special talent and commitment, have been extraordinarily successful in facilitating teacher growth. The problem, therefore, may be more with individual adeptness than with occupational category. Be this as it may, in a massive system involving millions of students and teachers, expertise and competence could easily be subordinated to organizational convenience, or to political negotiations. Some degree of irrationality is hence inevitable. Ultimately, teachers exercise their own prerogatives; since it is not hard for practitioners to distinguish between good and bad tutors, the choosing of trainees will undoubtedly be done—once the extraneous factors have been eliminated—on the basis of ability. In any event, perhaps the happiest consequence of the issue is that the performance of future in-service teacher-trainers will most likely constitute an improvement over what we have now.

A major dilemma does exist with respect to the problem of individualization. Since teachers vary in individual development, in their work situations and in their personal styles, group training sessions will, at times, but not always, be appropriate. Therefore we have a complex spate of difficulties: How is individual need best determined? Once determined, how is it best accommodated? And once accommodated, how are the results best assessed?

The difficulties emanate from a multiplicity of factors: substantive needs and interests of teachers differ; preferences with regard to time and organization vary; and two teachers, interested in the same goal, could easily choose to attack the problem in alternate ways. Finally, since individualization is usually more expensive than nonindividualization, what economic constraints must be considered?

The delivery of in-service education is fraught with debate. Training can be provided in the teacher's own classroom, in group seminars held on college campuses, in demonstration centers, and so on. It can be of a general nature or directly related to the teacher's immediate classroom concerns. For example, various techniques in teaching, say, fractions can be dealt with while the teacher is actually teaching, before the teaching ensues, or after it has been concluded.

Training can make use of children, video presentations, or didactic tutoring. It can be pursued through modeling or discussion, before or after school, during evenings or summer vacations, for short or long periods of time. In one way or another, all of these pieces must fit into the puzzle. It might be possible, if finances were unlimited, through trial and error, to discover and implement an ideal program of professional development for every teacher. But the era of plenty is a thing of the past; resources are likely to be increasingly scarce, and compromises must be made. The task, therefore, is to find a sensible basis for working with less than the optimum.

The points surrounding curricular focus are also debateable. From a budgetary point of view, efficiency requires that primary emphasis be given to general teaching skills with universal application across various subject-matter. Studies of innovative failure, made during the 1960s, however, plainly show that many promising programs accomplished far less than they might have because teachers were not given sufficient opportunity to master the specific techniques involved. Obviously, provisions should be made for both approaches but this is easier said than done.

Some theorists argue that teachers can transfer general principles from one teaching situation to another with little difficulty. Others dispute this contention and suggest that unless teachers perceive opportunities for transposition, extrapolation does not occur. Moreover, certain skills (those associated with the teaching of reading) are unique, and do not lend themselves to cross-application. Since no instructional method is infallable, a repertory of devices is undoubtedly more desirable than reliance on a single solution. Finally, there are those who question the virtues of skill-based teacher training *in toto*. Their conviction is that it is the teacher's personal interpretation and application of general principles, not the mimicking of a prefabricated method, that will produce the greatest advantage. They believe, in short, that insight and conceptual grasp are the only legitimate foundations for professional improvement.

The issues surrounding training mechanisms, therefore, are somewhat clouded and solutions are anything but close at hand. Above all we are confronted with the inescapable fact that some teachers are able to obtain good results with virtually any method while others depend on what, for them, is the most workable strategy. It is thus difficult, in a manner of speaking, to generalize about generalizability.

There are a number of other questions regarding the management of teacher in-service education that may be more or less critical than methodology. For example, some reviewers hypothesize that since teacher intentions are the best predictor of ultimate teacher behavior, and since teacher intentions basically stem from teacher attitudes, the attitudes, values and beliefs of practitioners are of primal significance. Other specialists believe that the greatest good will come from sustained efforts to define the particular competencies teachers need. Once these are established, program development becomes a process of systematic skill development. Because of recent preoccupation with parity (equal participation in policy determination), decisions regarding the organization and structure of activities are reached a good deal more slowly than in the past. A sizeable group of critics remain convinced that the surest path to expertise in teaching lies in encouraging teachers to function as researchers in their own classrooms, to test alternate solutions to their problems, and to develop what Dreeben calls a "technology of teaching."[12] Thus the role of academics, traditionally the dominant stewards of teacher training, has—in what may be an unfortunate case of over-reaction—been diminished.

It is in this connection that still more disagreement arises. Lortie, in *Schoolteacher,* has observed that a technology of teaching really does

12. R. Dreeben, *The Nature of Teaching: Schools and the Work of Teachers* (Glenview, Illinois: Scott, Foresman and Co., 1970).

not exist, and further, that the privacy of professional life militates against its development.[13] He maintains that teachers must, of neces sity, invent their own wheels, as the need arises, because: (1) their craft lacks a systematic body of operational principles that have practical utility; (2) their teaching aspirations derive from personal convictions about how schooling can best serve the young, and must therefore be achieved through personally-constructed endeavors; and (3) their conceptions of good technique, appropriate standards, and classroom control, are all intensely idiosyncratic. Teacher anxieties, frustrations, satisfactions, and self-esteem, consequently, are tied more to their own psyches than to the norms of the craft. The logical extension of this thesis, presumably, leads to the following conclusions: professional socialization is largely impossible; planned in-service activities, in the absence of an accepted taxonomy of method, can only yield marginal benefits; and the effects of training must always be subordinate to individual personality. The thesis has won neither wholesale endorsement nor been free of criticism, but if it is even partially valid, there are strong implications for a modified approach to continuing professional development.

PERSPECTIVE

The major elements of a summation should be apparent: a considerable amount of activity is taking place; the volume of effort—coupled with the haste in which much of it was mustered—has generated a good deal of uncertainty; and a sure sense of direction is missing. Nonetheless, it is to be hoped that as this sorting-out process continues, the form and substance of effective teacher in-service education will materialize.

Irrespective of the particular framework that emerges, new perspectives on the making of a teacher are sure to develop. A continuum of sequential growth, spanning preservice and in-service experiences, is likely to materialize; discriminations will be made as to what kinds of training are best provided before and after entry into service; and, as a consequence, the badly-needed training typology will begin to take at least rudimentary shape.

It also seems likely that the present shortcomings of in-service education will become more widely apparent—especially to those with the political power to fund improvements—and interest in enhancing the

13. D. C. Lortie, *Schoolteacher: A Sociological Study* (Chicago: University of Chicago Press, 1975).

practice of teaching should increase. Teacher collectives will accumulate greater autonomy and control, the traditional role of academic trainers may alter, and new kinds of organizational collaboration will materialize. The establishment and legitimization of professional standards may (or may not) happen. Much depends on our ability to reach a consensus on educational purpose, define teacher responsibilities with greater specificity, and reach agreement on a basis and a method for evaluating performance. All of these changes, however, must be paralleled by a philosophical realignment that places continuing professional education in a framework of open-ended, self-directed maturation.

If there is to be significant improvement in education, the nation's teachers must manage their own professional development. In short, they must have periodic opportunity to enlarge their own artistry.

Such a program must first acknowledge that the expertise and zeal of the teacher are by far the most important factors in quality instruction. Teachers vary greatly in their strengths and weaknesses, intellectual backgrounds and educational allegiances, as well as in their adaptation to teaching situations. Yet, in teacher education arrangements, we tend to treat them as a homologous species. We often forget that the difference between teaching that which is routine and teaching that which is inspired depends to a great extent on the teacher's passion and commitment. The desire to change, if it is to be consequential, must come from within. Mediocre teaching can distill and even pollute the value of everything that goes on in the classroom. Nothing we can invent in the way of content or method will be worth very much unless it is used ingeniously. In-service education should not be, as it has sometimes been, merely another theatre for puppets. It should set a stage for growth in the tradition of the Comedia del Arte, where actors do not memorize, but improvise their lines.

The teacher functions in a school environment that is often antithetical to the elevation of competence. The educational fraternity, on occasion, has behaved as if teachers were meant to be pawns acting out the genius of others. Practitioners have been trained according to nondescript and weak prescriptions. The profession, it must be said, has not been entirely oblivious to these problems: teachers, administrators, and professors have often warned that to prize change for its own sake, and to underestimate the importance of individual role and style, would be to border on folly.

Inept programs have remained–perhaps because it is virtually impossible to teach so badly that no learning takes place–and the price has been an inhibition of experimentation and a lack of progress.

Indeed, the pressures for preserving the status quo have easily overpowered those that favor the search for something better. Moreover, since we have never been too clear about the delicate balance that must exist between the artistic and scientific dimensions of teaching, nor about the essential equilibrium between stylistic variation and the need for consistency and unity within the school, our tendency has been either to leave well enough alone, or to impose meaningless innovations that serve to create an impression of newness.

In sum, the present scene is characterized by: (1) a tendency to devaluate the professional integrity and sophistication of practitioners who must initiate educational improvements; and (2) an inclination to disregard the teacher's right and obligation to have a voice in his or her own professional development. We have become too preoccupied with the quick fit–the introduction of visible innovation without sufficient concern for the internal restructuring within the system–and with the reorientation of the teacher. We need, therefore, an effective machinery that will generate professional growth among teachers as a necessary precondition to rational change and better schools.

What, then, can be said about the needed restructuring of teacher in-service education?

The basic problem, distilled to its essence, is that the traditional devices of continuing professional education–the workshops, the one-session inspirational meetings, the district committees–have, in the main, had negligible effect on the teaching body politic. We lack a usable strategy to overcome the chronic obstacles and, concomitantly, advance the cause of professionalism. The chief hurdles are familiar: in-service education is no different from other types of education wherein achievement is influenced by the learner's attitude, incentive and purpose; the curriculum fluctuates in piecemeal fashion, making it difficult to avoid a fragmentary approach to retraining; we cannot conceive of teaching in any one image or mold, but must cope with an almost infinite variety of professional behavior differing in both degree and kind; and the logistics of time, cost and evaluation must be satisfied in realistic ways. It follows, therefore, that any workable strategy must concern itself with the matter of incentive, with provisions for overcoming disjointedness, with procedures that ensure personal relevance, and with the requirements of practicality.

In-service education is not merely something that is done to teachers; it can be something that teachers do to and for themselves. If we can infuse the activities with an aura of pertinence, and provide the substantive wherewithal for self-directed development, we can perhaps achieve the larger objectives of professional growth and at the same time, aid and abet the improvement of schooling. We can also exploit the teacher's capacity for uniqueness, for initiative, and for the simple joys that derive from exercising one's own creative powers. This is not to say that all traditional in-service techniques ought to be abandoned, or that continuing education cannot be nurtured through a group process. It is, rather, to suggest that such efforts should be facilitated through stratagems that make allowances for the private strengths and weaknesses of teachers, for their special imperatives, and for the pleasures of constructive self-improvement.

When all is said and done, the curriculum is what occurs after the classroom door is closed and teacher and child begin to interact. We often overlook the fact that technique and content should direct each other, and reduce in-service training to putting mimeographed directions in the teacher's briefcase. At the heart of any acceptable strategy there must be a profound concern for things that cause a high sense of involvement, a personalized preoccupation with the yet unattained, a continuing quarrel with the senseless and ineffectual, and an unfettered inventiveness in style and approach.

From a technical standpoint several cautions are worth noting. We will not progress unless someone in each school is given responsibility for facilitating an effective program of professional development, and unless such responsibility is given to a person who is both an imaginative and skilled entrepreneur. Moreover, we cannot indefinitely continue to beg the question with regard to incentive. After all, we are asking for a rejection of the easy in favor of the better, for a yielding of the familiar and an exploration into the unknown, and for the plain investment of energy and devotion beyond what is necessary for tolerable performance. We must in turn give something—whether monetary compensation, or prestige, or even perhaps the simple freedom to pursue one's own inclination. Beyond this, we must also give time. As long as professional enhancement is subsidized by time stolen from the teacher's golf game, stamp collection, or literary browsing—or by dollars drained from salary checks—progress will be slow. Teaching, admittedly, is not without its dedicated souls, but even dedication is an exhaustible commodity.

In its simplest context, teacher in-service education should work toward three ends: the extension of knowledge in general and pertinent subject-matter information in particular; the acquisition of new techniques for teaching; and a shaping of attitude and purpose. These ends are neither mutually exclusive nor alien to the crux of any educational ideology. A continuing education experience for a chemistry teacher, for example, should add to the teacher's knowledge of the world as well as of science. It should make unfamiliar methods and materials familiar, and, ultimately, it should help to define what is important and what is trivial, as well as nurture a sense of mission. The realization of these objectives lies in the things teachers read, in the meetings they attend, in the conversations they have with colleagues, in their testing of new methods, and in the careful analysis of the differences between their intentions and their results. In the pursuit of craftsmanship, as in love and war, virtually all is fair. In sum, teaching is a learnable art.

The five postulations that follow are applicable to a district of one school or fifty. Size creates problems of organization and procedure rather than of fundamental philosophy. The postulations are intended as a guide rather than as a fixed prescription–their structure can be tailored to fit the particular setting. The principal components are as follows:

1. Each teacher must believe that he or she can contribute to educational improvement by assessing the shortcomings of instruction, by seeking to better it through one's own experimentation, and by testing the value of methods suggested by the experiments of others.
2. Each teacher must guard against complacency, work to enhance personal artistry, be governed by self-insights, and draw systematically, from the aggregate resources, whatever contributes to better teaching performance.
3. Each teacher must have an opportunity to be consistently informed about new developments, to judiciously select alternatives, and to make periodic judgments regarding the adequacy of instructional outcomes.
4. Each teacher must have recourse to the special kinds of technical assistance that he or she requires, whether in the form of special consultation or faculty cooperation, and each must have an opportunity for cumulative skill mastery, theoretical study, and the planning of instructional improvements.
5. The task of leadership is to promote professional development, provide the means for its achievement, unshackle the individual teacher from those aspects of organizational life that are constricting, and cooperate in instituting desirable change.

The essence of the strategy idea is its emphasis on the individual, matching idiosyncratic training with what is a highly idiosyncratic endeavor; in its provisions for reducing the pitfalls of fragmentation; and in its proviso that the nature of in-service activity be governed by the teacher's particular objective at the particular time. While the stress on personal rather than group orientation will increase program complexity, the complications are not insurmountable, and the end gives promise of justifying the means.

There is much to be said, as well, for giving attention to impending educational problems rather than restricting professional development to current concerns. For example, the mounting interest in early childhood education, ethical-civic education, multi-cultural education, and community-based learning establishes an impetus for corollary teacher retraining. By anticipating the teaching requirements of such movements, the relevance of in-service programs can be enlarged, a logical basis for soliciting budgetary resources becomes available, the inherent relationship between curriculum development and teacher improvement is strengthened, and the pragmatic advantages of continual professional growth can be made more obvious. It might even be conjectured, in fact, that it would be sensible to link *most* in-service activity with the probable needs of the immediate future.

A RESEARCH AND DEVELOPMENT PERSPECTIVE

A research and development agenda for the future must, of necessity, take partial direction from the unfinished business of the present. It is evident, for example, that many of our existing problems do not lend themselves to instant relief. The difficulties are so intricate that a decisive "break-through"—one that might suddenly make everything right—is not likely. Research and development can serve many purposes, and the present scene suggests that there is a place for most of these in the quest to upgrade in-service. Specific weaknesses must be analyzed, potentially promising solutions must (under controlled circumstances) be tested, hypotheses must be explored, and the results of all of these must be put to the test in a variety of real-world situations.

It does not seem important to worry excessively about a particular order of priorities. The problem-spectrum is sufficiently broad, and the impediments in school environments so varied, that it is doubtful whether any one ordering could be defended as superior to another. The separate components must be worked on whenever and wherever conditions permit, and then combined in alternative "mixes" so as to determine what works best in what context. Thus progress will be cumulative and gradual.

These considerations notwithstanding, a list of unresolved dilemmas is not difficult to devise. More must be learned about effective organizational support, alternative training methodologies, incentive structures, integration procedures, and so on. The necessary research agenda, perhaps, can best be illustrated by synthesizing a set of arguments that the writer prepared for a publication of Stanford University.[14]

One, successful teaching depends on a repertory of distinct skills. Teachers differ markedly in the extent to which these have been mastered; hence, their retraining needs are far from uniform. Yet, we lack ways to individualize retraining with reasonable economic efficiency.

Two, all parents do not have the same expectations of their children's schools; all students do not learn in the same way or have the same characteristics. The teaching of eighth-grade history, for example, will vary according to the situation—often, it must be of a different form within two classrooms of the same school. We therefore require methodologies through which the teacher can be assisted in accomplishing a specific task, in a specific situation, with a specific kind of learner. We must have programs that make it possible for teachers to adapt to the environment and to the subculture of the particular work situation.

Three, present in-service training programs are usually based on one of the following formuli: (1) expository exhortation, either spoken or written, through which teachers are implored to utilize a particular method, emphasize a particular set of ideas, or accept a particular set of assumptions; (2) demonstration teaching, wherein an expert demonstrates a teaching method with students; (3) supervised trials in which teachers use a specific teaching method, or teach a prescribed lesson, and are then subjected to critical appraisal; (4) performance analysis through which the classroom behavior of teacher and students is recorded and interpreted for the teacher so that an analysis of strength and weakness can be made. But, since teachers are subject to as much individuality as other humans, and respond differently to training stimuli, and since the appropriateness of a training procedure varies with the task at hand, teacher retraining must be approached multilaterally rather than unilaterally. We need systems that will permit us to integrate a variety of training devices within the same program.

Four, we have tacitly assumed that a supervisor, a principal, or a college professor—as a privilege of ordainment—can train teachers in whatever pedagogical tactics are needed. This assumption is unreason-

14. Louis Rubin, "The Societal Future and Teaching," ISTE Report #5 (Stanford, Cal.: Stanford Center for Research and Development on Teaching, June, 1976).

able. If we are to exploit the potential of continuing professional education promoting useful educational change, three conditions are indispensable: we must develop effective training methodologies; we must train trainers to use these methodologies; and we must persuade those who judge teachers, and who measure their worth, to understand and value the training objectives.

Five, our attempts to improve teacher in-service education are hampered by a lack of systematic theory. In the absence of such theory, it is difficult to build effective procedures, particularly with respect to the necessary balance between self-directed and other-directed growth. In order to accomplish significant teacher improvement we must help teachers develop their own techniques, acquire techniques that have been developed by others, blend both in appropriate ways, and gain insights that ultimately make them self-sufficient in solving their own instructional programs. The teacher, in short, must know what to do, as well as why and when to do it.

Six, when the issues of teacher retraining are debated, there is often a presumption that better training will, in and of itself, produce better teaching. The fact is that few teachers function anywhere near their optimal capacity (neither, for that matter, do most administrators and researchers). Thus, if many teachers can already teach better than they do, how can matters be improved if we increase capability but not incentive? Respectable experiments have demonstrated, again and again, that teaching performance is substantially improved when the grounds for reward are made explicit and when tangible payoff actually occurs. Two reforms are therefore desirable. First, schools must reorganize their system of staff development so that perhaps 10 percent of the teachers are able to engage in professional growth activities at any given time, and, second, the profession itself must begin to invoke sanctions against poor performance, and rewards for good performance.

Seven, because of the great difficulty in measuring the results of teaching, we tend to avoid precise efforts to distinguish the pedagogical assets and liabilities of each teacher. Moreover, in the present way of things, improved performance does not always produce any direct benefits for the teacher. While most practitioners, of course, have a genuine desire to teach as well as they can, their impulses are frequently distilled by an assortment of personal and organizational inhibitors. As a result the typical teacher rarely finds it imperative to increase competency through continued professional development. Teachers adjust their labors to the standards of their faculty group, and tend to perform at the particular level required for survival in the system. Therefore, even when a training program is of exceptional quality its efficacy may be diminished by low incentive. As a consequence, retraining programs should, among their other obligations, raise professional expectations.

Above and beyond these general tasks, an additional reform agenda will stem from the inevitable need to adapt public education to the requirements of the future. Despite occasional protests that accurate social prediction is impossible, futurism has become something of a current vogue. Still, all institutions plan, at least for the short-run, and education would do well to consider its own immediate posterity and, if possible, relate teacher in-service education to prospective developments.

Any generalizations we make regarding predictable changes, however, should be qualified by the conditions that prevail generally. Teachers function at a particular level of expertise with respect to technical knowledge and skills, they reflect private values regarding what, educationally, is good and bad, and they manifest particular pedagogical preferences. Efforts to design professional growth experiences that prepare teachers for the educational future—in both method and content of instruction—must therefore begin with our present dilemmas. Some school children still find their classrooms boring; some continue to be alienated by what they feel is meaningless curricula; and some remain convinced that school life is singularly unresponsive to their developmental interests and emotional well-being.

One of the peculiarities of human nature is that our self-images are so deeply entrenched that we are often oblivious to reality. Similarly, our conceptions of the way things should be are so firmly ingrained that social changes evoke stubborn resistance rather than docile readjustment. Teachers do not take to disturbances in their belief system any more than the rest of us. Educational modifications, in anticipation of what lies ahead, are rarely viewed with either enthusiasm or conviction. Societies and schooling, nevertheless, do change.

The major solutions for teacher in-service education in the time ahead would seem to embody the following: (1) the need to emphasize, throughout the curriculum, a high degree of social awareness; (2) the need to develop among youth the skills associated with problem-analysis and problem-solution; (3) the need to inculcate students with a better understanding of participatory democracy, a stronger commitment to its ideals, and a clearer sense of moral and civic responsibility; (4) the need to strengthen students' values and priorities with respect to personal and public good; (5) the need to instill greater optimism regarding the human capacity to overcome social crisis and enhance the quality of life; and (6) the need to nurture–in every student–a sharper perception of how one's personal future can be shaped.

These objectives may seem amorphous, so vague in meaning as to be practically useless. Or, for the more cynically-minded, they may smack of the platitudes that are sometimes used as substitutes for well-defined goals. Many ideals, however, can only be expressed in imprecise terms. And despite their imprecision, they may be of considerable help in pointing the way.

A skillful and imaginative teacher, for example, can do a great deal to expand social consciousness. The lyrics of popular songs, newspapers, contemporary social-commentary television programs, and a vast abundance of similar material can be used in literature, social studies, science, mathematics and even career education classes to increase student sophistication regarding family disintegration, drug abuse, the havoc wrought by human greed, and so on.

Moreover, virtually everything we wish to teach can be taught in a social context. During the last decade much of the curriculum has become inquiry-oriented. Children have grown accustomed to searching out cause and effect, testing hypotheses, predicting the consequences of events, comparing alternatives, and so on. A good foundation already exists, consequently, for the extension of these procedures into a generally more comprehensive emphasis on various kinds of problem-analysis techniques. What must be underscored, in this regard, is that the point in encouraging children to think about prospective solutions to social dilemmas–and personal ones–is not the quest for workable solutions (although the notions emanating from the minds of children might not be much worse than many that have stemmed from adults) but rather the building of a constructive mental set toward problem-solving.

For the same reasons, life in the classroom must offer a better example of democracy in action. Wherever the subject matter permits, learning should sharpen insights regarding negotiation and compromise, as well as provide direct experience in conflict resolution. Through such activities students can learn, not only a tolerance for divergent points of view, but a respect for the mechanisms of the democratic process, and even more fundamentally, a familiarity with what recently has come to be called "people power."

The matter of ethical behavior, too, transcends particular areas of the curriculum. Whereas in the past the chief problem was to choose between right and wrong, in the future we will face infinitely more difficult choices between two conflicting "rights." The curriculum, therefore, should provide routine exercise in choice-making—a special form of problem-solving. And, since the exercise of choice is in itself often anxiety-provoking, emotional as well as intellectual dimensions are involved. Seemingly, then, the call will be for instructional activity that helps students formulate healthy values, translate these values into moral judgments regarding personal and public priorities, and minimize the inherent emotional tensions. The seven instructional movements, described in the section that follows, document these requirements in considerably greater detail.

The futurists who serve us best are those who preach an optimistic rather than a pessimistic outlook. Pessimism debilitates psyche and spirit alike. What, after all, will be lost if our faith in the perfectability of humankind eventually proves false? A belief in the capacity of teachers to grow, to reach increasingly higher levels of maturity, and to serve youth with greater compassion, skill, and understanding, is, perhaps, what will make the greatest difference.

Section II

Dominant Reform Movements

The Individualization of Learning: Teacher-Related Problems

Robert H. Anderson

Texas Tech University

In the culminating section of a series related to the American Revolution Bicentennial, Tyler recently examined some of the challenges and opportunities that will characterize tomorrow's education. In his introduction, Tyler praised America's schools for their "amazing success" in responding to the needs and expectations of a continuously changing society, and noted that in over the 200 years of their existence these schools "have also sought to serve Americans as individuals, offering them opportunities to develop their own special talents, pursue their own particular interests, and achieve their own personal goals."[1] Lamenting that by no means are all the nation's children served by the schools, and that many are inadequately served, he noted that the role of the school has evolved from that of a sorting agency to one that is "expected to help every child to achieve the full limit of his or her potential."[2]

Although individualization of learning is identified as one of the dominant educational reform movements, Tyler suggests that individualization is not so much a new idea as it is a currently focal one. In this regard, it may be recalled that the National Society for the Study of Education issued a yearbook in 1925 entitled *Adapting the Schools to Individual Differences*; in 1962, the yearbook was entitled *Individualizing Instruction.* Taken together, the titles of these yearbooks and of this reading reflect the subtle but significant shift that has

1. Ralph W. Tyler, "Tomorrow's Education," *American Education* 11 (August–September, 1975): 16.
2 Ibid., p 17.

occurred in the concept of individualization over the years. Currently, emphasis is upon the individualization of learning.

In a recent overview of innovations in organization for learning, Heathers asserted that individualization is the "most pervasive theme in current efforts to improve the arrangement for instruction and learning."[3] Noting that there is no generally accepted definition and that many persons erroneously restrict individualization to conditions in which the student works independently or receives private tutoring, Heathers proposes the following definition:

> Individualization of instruction-learning refers to any arrangements whereby the student engages in learning activities that are specifically selected and designed to accommodate his learning needs and his characteristics as a learner.[4]

Discussions of individualization usually indicate, as does Heathers, that individual differences in learners are (or can be) reflected in:

1. the choice of objectives and learning tasks
2. the learning materials and equipment employed
3. the choice of learning arrangements or settings
4. the choice of instructional methods
5. the choice of teacher-student matchups
6. the provisions for varying the rate or pace at which advancement takes place.

To the extent that a school program is based on a very narrow range of choices in each of these six categories, individualized learning is likely to be accidental and fortuitous whenever it occurs. On the other hand, the effort to maximize the available options in each instance is at least theoretically likely to result in more universal benefits to the learners.

Among the more formal efforts at developing systematic approaches to individualized learning are several about which a great deal has been written. First to be noted is Planning for Learning in Accordance with Needs (PLAN) developed by the Westinghouse Learning Corporation. Second, is Adaptive Environments for Learning, an extension of the system widely known as Individually Prescribed Instruction (IPI), developed by the Learning Research and Development Center based at the University of Pittsburgh. Third, is Individually Guided

3. Glen Heathers, "Overview of Innovations in Organization for Learning," *Interchange* ? (1972).
4. Ibid., p. 50.

Education (IGE), a term that is associated both with the Wisconsin Research and Development Center headed by Professor Herbert J. Klausmeier of the University of Wisconsin and with the Institute for Development of Educational Activities (/I/D/E/A/) of the Kettering Foundation in Dayton, Ohio. Detailed descriptions of PLAN, of Adaptive Environments for Learning, and of the Wisconsin IGE program are included in a paperback volume recently published by the National Society for the Study of Education.[5]

Equally familiar is the approach known generally by the term "open education." Although use of the term "open education" appears to have crested, the idea is thriving. The extensive literature of open education is a vigorous and well-informed plea for truly individualized schooling. In some ways, this approach is an outgrowth and extension of the literatures, first, of progressive education and, more recently, of nongradedness and related organization arrangements. In fact, in a recent volume I traced the historical antecedents of open education and attempted to demonstrate its compatibility with team teaching and other frameworks that provide more flexibility for the teaching-learning environment.[6]

Other efforts in recent years to enhance learning by making school experiences more directly suited to the needs and history of each child include:

1. team teaching and differentiated staffing
2. alternative pupil grouping (interschool, interclass, intraclass) and subgrouping
3. provision of structured instructional materials (as in PLAN and IPI) that permit pupils to progress with minimum external direction
4. opportunities for learning with guidance from one's peers as in the Durrell approach to Pupil Team Learning
5. open-space architectural arrangements
6. arrangements that are described by the term "independent study."

Since the focus of this paper is primarily on the problems that major reforms such as individualization create for teachers, and vice versa, the examples cited are selective rather than comprehensive. It is anticipated that any generalizations discussed will prove applicable to other examples.

5. Harriet Talmage, ed., *Systems of Individualized Education* (Berkeley, CA: McCutchan Publishing Corporation, 1975). This is from the National Society for the Study of Education Series on Contemporary Educational Issues.

6. Robert H. Anderson, *Opting for Openness* (Arlington, VA: National Association of Elementary School Principals, 1973).

By way of introduction, then, I have reviewed some definitions and examples of individualization and recalled the rather long history of American efforts to individualize. Given the current emphasis on individualized learning, the critical question is: "What are some of the problems that teachers and other school workers confront when they *do* become involved in Individually Guided Education (IGE), in one of the other systematic approaches that are available, or in more informal efforts at individualization within their own school?"

CAUSES OF DIFFICULTY

Recently, sociologists from the University of Denver pointed out that the occasional failures of open classrooms have been due almost always to the attitudes of teachers.[7] They isolated six reasons:

1. The teacher was an insecure person (unable to take risks).
2. The teacher did not accept the basic values of open education (e.g., the value of freedom and openness; the value of autonomous activity).
3. The teacher failed to set clear limits for students (e.g., via student-teacher contacts).
4. The teacher refused to yield her position-based teacher power (in favor of competency-based power).
5. The "provisioning" for learning was inadequate.
6. The classroom was "opened" too suddenly, without preparing students for the freedom they would have. In this latter connection, they suggested that a "warming-up" period be used to help students to put their (unfamiliar) autonomy to productive use.

In a somewhat similar analysis, following the introduction of an independent study program in a New York secondary school, Plunke.t reported that students in the early stages require a good deal of structure, direction, and guidance in making the transition to the new arrangement, being required to submit much more detailed plans at the outset than will later be necessary.[8] Incidentally, Plunkett noted that one of the most serious problems was the passivity and noncooperation of many faculty members.

7. Stephen V. Dillon and David D. Franks, "Why Open Classrooms Close Down," *Nation's Schools* 93 (February, 1974): 43–45.
8. William T. Plunkett, "Independent Study at Syosset High School," *Phi Delta Kappa* 50 (February, 1969): 350–352.

These two reports are representative of the numerous commentaries that have been made by observers of innovative efforts that are now underway. I recently reviewed a number of research reports about open education and was impressed with: the many references to the almost-universal failure of school administrators and would-be "change agents" to provide teachers with sufficient advance preparation; guidelines for phasing into the new arrangement; adequate resources and materials; time for doing all the extra work that accompanies a major change-over; advice and counsel during the adjustment period; and evaluation technology to help them assess how the new program is succeeding. For the most part, it is evident from the record that the new programs are not adequately defined, teachers have too little opportunity to participate in the decisions that lead to program adoption, and they are left "to sink or swim." Even when teachers hold values that especially predispose them to be sympathetic with proposed changes, such little help is provided that energy and enthusiasm may soon wane. Hence, teachers may retreat to the procedures with which they are more familiar and that are more comfortably accomplished within the time and resources available.

As the Denver report indicates, however, many projects suffer not only from inadequate resources and support but also from the psychological and/or philosophic inability and/or unwillingness of teachers to embrace the proposed arrangement. Not all teachers have the sturdy self-assurance, the healthy emotional stability, the attitudes of respect for children as human beings, the essentially kind and tolerant personalities, and the general personal maturity that seem increasingly essential to the maintenance of a healthy classroom atmosphere and productive interpersonal relationships. A surprising number of teachers, even those without symptoms of psychological maladjustment, find security in following established rules and routines, avoiding confrontation with colleagues and parents, maintaining a low profile and demonstrating loyalty to the conservative mores of both the school system and the community. Such persons can be greatly disturbed by the introduction of arrangements that they do not understand, that appear to violate or disregard the familiar rules and routines, and that make them both more visible and more vulnerable to making recognizable mistakes.

When the teacher *does* suffer a more serious personality maladjustment, the aforementioned problems become much more dangerous. Brodbelt, in a strong protest against practices that allow psychologically maladjusted teachers to remain in service, reviews several studies that imply fairly high percentages of teachers with mild-to-moderate impairment.[9] He proposes means for coping with the problem—screening out teacher trainees with identified problems, and much more on-the-job attention and correction.

One of the most dramatic side-effects of introducing various approaches to individualized instruction, especially team teaching with its built-in requirement that adults work intimately together, is that such arrangements tend (fortunately for the children) to bring the maladjusted teacher out into the open. Within the privacy of the self-contained classroom, following familiar routines and otherwise remaining inconspicuous, many a neurotic or even psychotic teacher has managed to survive for years without detection. Given the sorry state of supervision in American schools, plus the ignorance and cowardice of some principals who choose to ignore the symptoms of such maladjustment, some of these persons are inflicted on class after class of unlucky children.

Little wonder, then, that team-teaching and other projects have proved a painful experience not only for the maladjusted teachers whose careers may be upset by the new arrangement, but also for the otherwise well-adjusted teachers who have had to suffer through the embarrassment, the soul-searching, and the painful decisions that involve their troubled colleagues.

Even where school systems have been diligent and effective in detecting and correcting actual personality problems within the staff, the essential authoritarianism and methodological conservatism of American schools has created an atmosphere that is often less than congenial to innovation. Furthermore, resistance is probably in direct proportion to the amount of trust that the innovation accords to the learner. Many teachers and administrators, especially in secondary schools, rely blatantly on the carrot-and-stick approach inherent in A-B-C-D-E report cards (or their equivalent); for some, the concept of intrinsic motivation in adolescent pupils is foreign. High schools have sometimes been depicted by their critics as regrettably similar to prisons, especially with reference to controls that govern pupil movement within the building, pupil accountability for their whereabouts, and general discipline. A high school without *some* system of rules and discipline is of course almost unimaginable even to the most liberal reformers. But the point here is that many schools are so undemocratic that the shift to a more open and trusting arrangement

9. Samuel Brodbelt, "Teachers' Mental Health: Whose Responsibility?" *Phi Delta Kappa* 55 (December, 1973): 268–269.

will require a tremendous change in both the philosophy and the operational habits of the teachers and administrators involved. Such change does not come about except through concerted effort.

Among the conservative operational habits of teachers are those associated with two discredited but persistent patterns of school organization–the self-contained classroom and graded instructional groupings. The latter, in particular, is almost totally incompatible with philosophies of individualized learning and of "humane" schooling. Hardly anyone today actually argues that the lockstep graded organization is good for modern children or more likely than an open, nongraded approach to produce high academic achievement. Yet the vast majority of American schools continues to classify and assign pupils by grades (first grade, fourth grade, etc.) and to employ the related mechanisms of promotion-and-failure and competitive marking systems. The irony of this is apparently lost on the conscience of the profession.

Given that many superior alternatives exist, the continuing predominance of self-contained classrooms is an impediment to all kinds of educational progress including individualization. On the other hand, many of the systems designed to promote individualization have rejected self-containment and embraced one or another of the multiple-adult staffing patterns for which the term "team teaching" is still a useful label. In the late 1950s and early 1960s team teaching was the subject of much virulent debate. For a time, it was the topic of a great many articles, books, and discussions in state and national meetings. Eventually the *idea* of teaming gained fairly general acceptance. Although the research never did achieve a very high quality, it soon came to be recognized that the self-contained classroom was not as sacred a cow as it was once thought. In fact, the intellectual and social well-being of children, and also of their teachers, seems clearly to be less well served in self-contained classes than in team situations. General agreement with this view is reflected in the fact that thousands of new (or newly-renovated) school buildings have flexible and open interiors that facilitate team teaching. Many of the major plans for improving school programs, such as IGE in particular, are based on the premise that teachers and other adults will work with pupils (and, significantly, with each other) in teams.

Among the most powerful characteristics of team teaching is that it mandates a very great deal of professional interaction, much of which resembles the interaction that takes place within graduate courses in Education (and for that matter in the academic disciplines). Whereas the self-contained teacher could spend a lifetime in intellectual isolation from his or her peers, the team member has almost constant opportunity for informative discussions about pupils, curriculum topics, teaching strategies and materials, and professional values. Further, team members have available to them many more options for individualizing learning than exist in the self-contained arrangement. Therefore, it would seem that more widespread adoption of IGE and other team-based arrangements could be not only a great boon to the pupils served by them but also a powerful stimulant to the professional, and even personal, in-service growth of the adult staff.

In a later section, training programs available for assisting staffs to understand, to embrace, and to implement some pattern of teaming will be discussed. However, at this point it is relevant to note the crucial role that is played by principals and other leaders in these processes. It appears to be fairly well established that where principals "buy" the idea of teaming it tends to work well; conversely, where they are cool to the idea, it never heats up in the school.

This leads to examining the overall influence that principals exert in their schools, and especially to consideration of how they utilize their available time and energy. The need for more enlightened and energetic *supervision* in the schools seems to be critical. According to Cogan, the failure of many useful instructional innovations to secure a foothold in schools and universities can be related to inadequate supervision.[10] Cogan asserts that the neglect of in-class or clinical supervision deprives the teacher of necessary support while he or she is trying to develop new classroom competencies. Without continuing specialized help, the teacher is likely to fall back to familiar and "safer" modes of teaching. In Cogan's view, teachers under *all* circumstances, not only where major changes in procedure are being introduced, have need for a focused, continuing, clinically oriented, and highly individualized program of in-class support. No doubt this is especially true where the goal is to accomplish significant improvements in the ways that teachers individualize their instruction. It would seem from available accounts that the great majority of American teachers receive only token supervision (by Cogan's standards); and even among those principals and supervisors who make the necessary effort to provide adequate supervision all too few seem well-qualified to do so.

Probably the greatest single cause of the teacher-related problems to which this paper addresses itself, then, is chronic neglect of leader-

10. Morris L. Cogan, *Clinical Supervision* (Boston, MA: Houghton Mifflin Co., 1973), p. xi.

ship services. Conversely, research and experience seem to clearly confirm that when the principal and other leadership personnel have a manifest commitment to the program or practice in question, e.g., IGE, along with a thorough understanding of what it is and how it works, continuous involvement in the efforts of teachers to bring it about, and ready access to the resources and materials that it requires, the chances for success of that program or practice are remarkably high.

SUGGESTIONS AND REMEDIES

Improving Preservice Education

Individualization is facilitated by the adoption and energetic support of administrative policies and arrangements such as those that characterize the IGE program, and further by providing an appropriate and flexible environment that is well-supplied with a great variety of high-quality instructional materials. However, even the most perfect combination of resources and structures will not nurture individualized learning unless the teachers who function in that situation have (1) relevant attitudes of mind and heart, i.e., values; (2) necessary knowledge and understanding of individual differences in children; (3) thorough mastery of the content (broadly defined) of the school program; (4) depth and breadth in the technologies and arts that comprise "teaching"; and (5) plenty of practice in dealing with learner differences under a great variety of circumstances.

It is unrealistic to expect that teachers, whose preservice training has not emphasized and illustrated such attitudes and skills, can be converted in sizable numbers during their years of salaried service, even if school systems were to make a gargantuan effort to do so. So long as colleges and universities, and especially the departments and schools of Education within them, remain aloof and distinct from those reforms associated with individualized learning, their example and influence will be largely negative: their alumni will be poorly prepared for serving children as unique individuals. On the other hand, where the university environment *does* exemplify and demonstrate effective approaches to personal learning, its graduates carry all sorts of helpful attitudes and insights into the classrooms where they will work. If the current literature of teacher education offers reliable clues, it does seem that in the mid-1970s there is a substantial effort underway in the U.S.A. to break away from old patterns and to make the management of undergraduate

Education courses more consistent with the individual-oriented values those courses espouse. Examples include: extensive utilization of electronic and other technology, development of competency-based units and modules, reorganization of staffs into teaching teams, increased use of clinical approaches and field-based experiences, greater reliance on independent study and tutorials as modes for specialized instruction, student participation in program decision-making and management, modifications of the competitive grading system, and major overhaul of teacher-education curriculum sequences.

One of the major spin-offs of the reforms has been the ever-increasing involvement of active public-school personnel in the enterprise of preservice teacher education. The increasing desire of university professors for partnership with public school practitioners, along with the growing demands of teacher organizations for more involvement (and, in fact, control) with respect to teacher education, portends, among other things, that teachers, principals, and others in ever larger numbers will be engaged in the training of new teachers. Given more intimate association with university personnel and the need to be well-read and more thoughtful about philosophical and methodological issues, teachers so involved seem likely to grow both conceptually and operationally. Also, in a very real sense, the future teacher with his recent training and his idealistic view of the teacher's role can have an educative impact on the more veteran teachers with whom he associates during the field-based phase of his preparation.

Strengthening Teacher Skills

Individualization of learning inevitably calls for a great amount of diagnostic-prescriptive activity on the part of teachers, compelling them to pay more attention to the thoughts, feelings, and actions that the instructional prescription is intended to produce or to enhance. Although these days we in education seem to be more comfortable with behaviorally-defined objectives than we were ten or fifteen years ago, it is disheartening to note how confused many teachers become when they are required by the system, e.g., IPI, PLAN or IGE, to specify learning objectives in terms of performance skills. When the teacher perceives his or her goal in terms of "covering" a certain body of material (such as the next chapter in the textbook, or the Civil War unit) with the whole class, the teacher's role is relatively simple. It becomes the child's problem to digest what is offered and cope with the eventual paper-and-pencil test. On the other hand, when the teacher's goal calls for enabling every child to end up with a set of predefined behaviors some of which are different, at least at this moment in time, from those expected of other children, the textbook or unit is no longer an all-purpose vehicle and the teacher's role is considerably more complex. The intellectual and other skills that go into the functions of needs assessment, of selecting appropriate activities, of preparing and selecting materials, of managing the multifaceted learning situation and of evaluating the obtained outcomes are of a very high order. Even those teachers with excellent preservice preparation for such work require much more supervisory assistance and in-service training than is usually provided. They also require constant interaction with colleagues who are facing the same problems and whose insights and solutions become available through sharing.

An oddity, if not an anachronism, is that many teachers seem to be ill at ease in the one-to-one relationship that is so much a part of individualization. Several explanations are possible.

1. Prior experience, and even teaching training, has over-emphasized whole-class teaching and work with presumably-homogeneous groups of six to fifteen.
2. Time has never seemed available for one-to-one relationships.
3. The teacher has guilt feelings that the one-to-one relationship leads to neglect of the rest of the class.
4. One-to-one interaction makes certain psychological and emotional demands upon the teacher.

In a project with which I once worked in Concord, Massachusetts, seeking to develop a superior method of evaluating and reporting pupil progress, it was observed that the teacher-pupil reporting conference seemed more difficult for a majority of the teachers than did the teacher-parent conference. These and other clues suggest that both preservice and in-service programs should attempt to equip teachers with the psychological, intellectual, and procedural insights they will need to function more effectively in the one-to-one situation.

It follows that assistance must also be given with respect to the several types of small group activities that are a necessary part of any individualized program. Furthermore, most teachers need both intellectual and psychological assistance in adapting to various other types of learning settings, such as pupil tutoring arrangements, at one extreme, and computer-assisted instruction at the other. In these settings, the teacher functions at the periphery of the learning that is going on, and interpersonal contacts of the teacher and child are only occasional and incidental.

Shifting Focus to the Learner

That teachers need not be at the literal center of ongoing learning activities is, in fact, one of the hardest ideas for many teachers to accept; often their maladaptive behavior in efforts at individualization grows out of unwillingness to relieve learners of dependency upon them. Often this grows out of the sincere conviction that children and youth are not capable of self-direction, that teaching is necessarily a didactic process, or that society would disapprove a more passive and subtle approach on the teacher's part. Almost always, such convictions persist because teachers have little experience with such approaches and thus no first-hand evidence of their efficacy.

Individualized-learning programs emphasize pupil self-direction, and presume that direct and immediate intervention and/or assistance from teachers is generally not necessary or even desirable. Under normal circumstances, when a teacher is not conducting a lesson either (1) learning materials being used provide all the necessary cues; (2) pupils seek help when needed from other pupils; or (3) pupils make use of problem-solving skills in order to determine the best course of action. Under such circumstances, turning to the teacher ought to be regarded as a last-resort solution. The teacher who has carefully nurtured these circumstances and helped prepare children with coping and problem-solving skills gets great satisfaction out of *not* being needed (in an overt sense) most of the time

Providing Resources, Techniques, and Training

To create a learning environment that nurtures pupil self-direction requires ample and varied resources in whose use the teacher has been well trained. It requires specific structural arrangements such as IGE provides, and it calls for teachers to learn techniques for dealing with a variety of dissimilar ongoing activities and fairly rapid shifts from task to task. Especially, it calls for a high level of intellectual activity on the part of teachers dealing (as does the general medical practitioner) with numerous patients each with a different need and each requiring unique treatment.

Although this may sound like a tall order it is not unreasonable to subscribe to a high performance standard for presumably professional educators.

Robert H. Anderson

From my experiences as a school administrator, as an IGE trainer, as a director of pilot team-teaching programs, and as a consultant to hundreds of other projects stressing individualization, it is evident that most teachers and administrators are well-motivated persons who are capable of adapting to far more complex and demanding roles than they usually give themselves credit for in advance. Furthermore, twenty years of experience with introducing individual-oriented innovations has taught a great deal about the change process in schools. Although only rarely are they coordinated within the same macrosystem, as in IGE, useful materials and mechanisms for the reorientation and training of teachers are now available. Fewer failures and misfires need occur in the future, if we have but the wit and the will to use them.

Probably the major lesson from the recent past is that leadership people must themselves be extremely knowledgeable about practices such as those associated with individualized learning and its underlying philosophy. A visible commitment to the successful implementation of such practices is not sufficient. Lacking detailed information, principals and others can scarcely be effective trainers and supporters for the teachers who carry the major implementation responsibility. In study after study, it has been found that teachers, parents, and children respond positively when leadership is both expert and enthusiastic.

It is also essential that a solid foundation be established over enough time so that all concerned are comfortable with the definitions, the basic values, the operational characteristics, and the emotional overtones of the new or different approaches through which individualization is intended to occur. For the teaching staff this obviously must occur primarily within the framework of the in-service program, both the formal variety and the more incidental and continuous training that is possible under conditions of expert clinical supervision.

In the IGE training program, one of the first items on the agenda is a series of "human development" games and activities designed to help the workshoppers become personally acquainted and at ease with each other. Another series of activities, described by the term "We Agree," is intended to help the participants reach a mutual commitment to the basic values and philosophy that underlie all decisions about curriculum and methods. Within a self-study format, individuals and groups have access to a collection of films, filmstrip-cassettes, and published materials that describe individualized learning and the mechanisms that are recommended for bringing it about. All of this connects with the real-life experiences that the trainees have in teaching teams working with groups of children. Planning together, becoming familiar with the IGE system together, and doing group observations and critiques of each other's professional activities, these persons have an intensive and profound in-service training experience that, for most, is reportedly of unprecedented significance.

Some of the specific components of the IGE training program are included in other programs that are offered throughout the country: sometimes in the form of sensitivity training, values clarification activities, human relations training, self awareness programs, and human potential seminars, and sometimes in workshops or conferences that deal with interest centers, uses of new materials, pupil "contracts," learning packets, development of mini-courses, mastery learning, independent study, multi-media centers, and programmed learning. The regional, state and national conventions of professional organizations often offer assemblies, action groups, simulations, and other opportunities for learning more about these and related aspects of becoming a more skilled and qualified professional. Larger school districts sometimes have in-service programs that also employ some of these approaches.

Exploiting Available Help

There are some other things that can be done to help the typical classroom teacher acquire the insights, skills, and attitudes associated with more child-centered teaching. For one thing, most school systems employ personnel with special training to serve as remedial teachers, tutors, special-education teachers, helping teachers, and consultants or counselors of various types. A lively effort could be made to draw upon such persons as models and as teachers for the rest of the staff. Usually such persons have both the necessary skills and the attitudes of mind that are associated with effective one-to-one instruction. If it proves uneconomical to divert these people from their special assignments, then *at least* every principal should be required to spend a significant fraction of his or her time observing them at work, soaking up ideas and attitudes that can later be shared with the other teachers.

Another necessary step is to take greater advantage of the great quantity of materials now coming out of the large federally-funded laboratories and research-and-development centers around the country (such as RBS, CEMREL, LRDC, EDC, and the Far West Lab). Many of these materials are expressly designed to promote individualization, as indeed are many materials now coming out of *university centers* and from some of the *major publishing houses.* Granted that quality varies and the quantity of available materials almost numbs the would-be buyer, it is hard to imagine a time when teachers had a more exciting opportunity for selecting materials to be used by children.

The same is true of the available resources for helping teachers learn about learning goals, about different instructional approaches, about various ways to set up classrooms, about teaming, about the tutorial process, about the teacher-pupil relationship, about evaluating learning outcomes, and many other topics that are presented in films, filmstrip-cassettes and, of course, books.

WRAP-UP

When one attempts to review so complex and so crucial a topic as individualized learning, there is a tendency to exaggerate the profession's failure to accomplish it and to oversimplify and oversell perceived solutions. The role of the reader is to filter out the excesses and to seek a perspective from which he or she can operate. I would be disappointed, however, if the filtering is so thorough and so anesthetic that it leaves us content with where we are. Especially those of us who prepare teachers, who supervise the work of teachers, and who as teachers have high ideals of authentic professionalism, must permit ourselves to be tormented by the gap between those ideals and the prevailing standards of practice. The several systems and procedures selected for discussion here are only examples, and we are free to choose or to invent others. But I doubt that we are free of the obligation to make choices and commitments, if the individualization of learning is to be achieved.

In-Service Teacher Education—Paradoxes and Potentials

H. S. Broudy

University of Illinois at Urbana-Champaign

ROLE REVERSAL–WHICH SIDE IS UP?

In-service training for school teachers has a long history in American education. Teacher institutes go back to the last century, and the taking of courses for degrees and/or professional improvement is a way of life for many classroom teachers. In-service programs have been a reliable source of income for colleges of education, and they have enabled school administrators to substitute the counting of credits for the distasteful task of judging merit.

The strong and continuous demand for in-service programs, in large part, is a result of the peculiar character of the preservice preparation of teachers. This preservice training resembles the production of automobiles that are designed to go into the repair shop immediately after delivery to the customer. Or, to invoke another analogy, the preparation of teachers operates with the strategy of people who cannot afford to have a house built all at once. So they pour the foundation, fix up the basement, and move into it. As funds become available, they construct the house itself.

On either analogy, preservice training–to use still another figure of speech–is a survival kit fashioned to keep the teacher alive until the in-service rescue squad can supply first aid and resuscitation. Needless to say, such a view of teacher preparation would be no more reassuring to parents (if they were aware of it) than the putative manufacture of cars that just about make it to the repair shop would be to prospective owners.

Relying on in-service study to supply the basic training for an occupation allegedly so important as teaching, reverses the relation of preservice to in-service study that obtains in such occupations as engineering, medicine, law, and accounting. In these professions the basic concepts, theories, technologies, and problems of practice are part of the preservice curriculum. Experience on the job provides familiarity with particular working situations and develops adeptness in dealing with them. In-service study is used to update personnel in theoretical and practical developments. It is not, as far as I know, used as a substitute for the preservice curriculum. This, then, is the first of the paradoxes or anomalies that bedevil in-service teacher education, namely, that instead of supplementing a high-quality preservice program, it is expected to take the place of a makeshift preservice curriculum.

The paradox is sharpened by the systematic illusion that the preservice preparation of teachers is comparable to that demanded of engineers, lawyers, doctors, accountants, and other occupations of "professional" grade. This illusion is shared by parents, taxpayers, and, for all I know, by the teachers themselves. It is a mischievous illusion because it arouses expectations that are bound to be frustrated. The rhetoric of educators, the existence of colleges of education and departments of education, and the circumstance that most school teachers nowadays hold a bachelor's degree, all nourish the illusion.

Now to a person standing on his head, upside down becomes right side up. Thus if one stands on one's head long enough, reversing the order of preservice, in-service preparation becomes habitual and the paradox disappears. A highly developed aptitude for standing on one's head may account for the reluctance to increase the professional components of teacher-education curricula as well as the zealous search for ways of reducing it. This zeal is shared by (1) many liberal arts professors, who have been known to assert in the same breath that education courses are vacuous and that they undo in one semester the benefits of the other seven semesters of college, and (2) prestigious philanthropic foundations bewailing the certification requirement in "education" that keeps brilliant liberal arts graduates from teaching (the Einstein-couldn't-teach-physics-in-the-local-high-school argument). Furthermore, the low rating given by teachers to many of their education courses fuels the perennial criticism of education courses and educators in general.

There is a socioeconomic factor that may be of even more importance in explaining why preservice preparation of teachers—especially its specifically professional components—remains minimal and marginal. Lortie has pointed out that the pool from which teachers are drawn is a by-product of the widespread desire to secure an A.B. or B.S. degree. In many states one or two semesters in what is regarded as relatively undemanding exposure to courses in education and student teaching yields a teaching certificate.[1]

This modest investment in professional courses does not add much to the cost of getting the general A.B. or B.S. degree either for the student or the institution; it certainly does not match the institutional costs of highly specialized study in some of the other professional curricula. Furthermore, the certificate program does not disqualify the student for the kind of jobs that are usually filled by graduates of the A.B. or B.S. curriculum. Indeed, it has been argued that taking the certificate program for teaching is like taking a minor in any disciplinary field and that to prevent or discourage students from taking the teacher-training option because there is a surplus of teachers would be no more justified than inhibiting them from taking a minor in English history because there is no obvious occupational pay-off for such study. Yet this modest professional preparation—which would not satisfy, as far as time and effort were concerned, the licensing requirements for plumbers, electricians, or nurses—does provide the student with an entry into teaching jobs. The certificate serves as a hedge against unemployment in ordinary times and as a transition to more favored employment at all times.

By design or circumstance, therefore, our society has acquired an inexpensive way of recruiting personnel for its classrooms. The beneficiaries of these economies—prospective teachers, taxpayers, schoolboards—are not likely to be enthusiastic about proposals for preservice teacher education that would increase the cognitive investment on the part of the student and decrease the ease of entry to the job. Teacher organizations may be interested in such proposals and parents ought to be, albeit for somewhat different reasons.

SUPERMARKET OR STRUCTURE

The expectation that in-service study will repair or even rebuild the ill-prepared teacher provides in-service agencies with a great opportunity but also entrains some of the embarrassments that have plagued preservice programs. One of these is the extraordinary variety of needs

1. Dan C. Lortie, *School-Teacher: A Sociological Study* (Chicago, Illinois: University of Chicago Press, 1975).

that teachers in service seem to acquire. As Lortie notes, the cellular structure of the ordinary school shuts the teacher up with the class and away from outside interference. Each teacher daily enacts the drama of overcoming threats to the control of the classroom. From day to day the teacher relies on subtle, vague clues as to how well things are going. As B. F. Skinner once put it, the teacher relies on such pupil reactions as excitement, willingness to volunteer answers, and interest in the task for the reinforcement of her efforts. Often these behaviors are misconstrued as signs that learning has taken place. In such cellular circumstances, all sorts of idiosyncratic difficulties surface. Some teachers suffer from deficiencies in didactics, heuristics, or philetics, and some in all three.[2] Some need help in what to teach, some in how to teach, and some in what to teach with.[3] And some have difficulties they do not recognize. How then can in-service agencies do other than organize supermarkets that will minister to as many of these needs as possible?

The supermarket model has much to commend it for the consumer who has a firm understanding of nutritional principles, but it is no substitute for it. The layman foraging for specific remedies for ailments in the pharmaceutical area of the supermarket is not to be compared with the physician prescribing specific drugs. The layman does not possess the cognitive resources to understand, explain, or rationalize the drugs he chooses. Lacking a strong preservice training the teacher resembles the layman more than the physician.

The alternative to the supermarket model of delivering educational services is the structured curriculum. Structure in a professional field is provided by the distinctive problems that confront the practitioner. They are the girders upon which are assembled the disciplinary facts, theories, and all sorts of information relevant to the problems of practice. By contrast, the structure of an intellectual discipline is constituted by the entities, relations, theories, and modes of inquiry peculiar to it. In time, as Thomas Kuhn puts it, a set of paradigm problems emerge upon which most of the practitioners gnaw for their daily sustenance and on which the prospective practitioner sharpens his

2. Inasmuch as only a small proportion of classroom teachers are proficient in all three modes, a teaching clinic could easily be organized on such an etiology although whether becoming a triple threat is a realistic goal for teachers is open to question. For a discussion of these modes of teaching, see *Educational Theory*, 22:3 (Summer 1972) 251–261.

3. "Teaching *with*" goes along as a component in teaching with "teaching a content *to*" and "teaching a content how." Of the three, the first is not least but it is least understood. One teaches *with* the concepts, precepts, images, and values that constitute the person as a whole; and a pupil "learns with" an analogous apparatus. What one teaches or learns *with* is not always explicit or even conscious. Herbart's "apperceptive mass" comes close to it.

teeth. In time, also, a guild is developed, the members of which share a consensus on the basic principles, bodies of fact, and modes of inquiry. These rationalize the practice; they serve as principles of practice. Into this consensus the newcomers to the profession are initiated. Only a few of the guildsmen (in a discipline or a profession) will ever go beyond the paradigm problems to create new paradigms, and even these geniuses usually go *through* the paradigms before they venture *beyond* them.[4]

Little, if any, such consensus obtains to the study of education or to the preparation of teachers for the public schools. There are as many conceptual schemes and structures as there are people writing books on the subject. No two taxonomies of school outcomes or curricula or of anything else are designed to mesh. No two analyses of teaching or learning need to be commensurable, and usually they are not. There are no standard topics or literatures with which all entrants into the occupation are expected to be conversant. Little wonder, therefore, that teacher training is either grossly empiristic or wildly speculative, that there is no common body of technical or theoretical tradition on which the teacher can lean for rationalization of practice or the solu tion of problems, and that she or he feels all alone in each classroom confrontation with pupils.

In such a state of the art each new set of predicaments–such as those created by the increase in crime and violence in the schools, cultural diversity within the urban community, and irate taxpayers refusing to pass bond levies for schools that do not support the values of the dominant group in the community–elicits responses that seem plausible to somebody in the establishment or to its critics. If a response attracts the attention and the purse of a government agency or a foundation, it may well become a bandwagon that lurches down the corridors of schools with vigor and the *eclat* of publicity until it joins other such bandwagons in the oblivion reserved for "hunch-inspired" educational reforms. It is difficult to recall even the names of all the bandwagons of the last decade. At the moment accountability, value education, alternative schools, career education, and back-to-the-basics are still around.

4. Whether these paradigms are "true" or held with the same degree of assurance by all members of the guild is not the point at issue here. This is the proper concern of philosophers of science, many of whom are busily attacking the "tough" empiricism of the logical positivists. Whatever validity may attach to paradigms philosophically, there is little doubt about their being a social reality and their role in the credentialling guilds.

In the absence of a consensus on content and structure of the teacher-education program, there cannot emerge a strong guild that will legitimate it. Lacking a legitimating guild, there is no authoritative criterion of procedural correctness, without which there can be no adjudication of charges of malpractice. Without such a guild, moreover, the criteria for training, certification, and entry into practice must remain mired in controversy. Hence the perceptual restating of objectives in ever increasing specificity and prolixity: in the absence of consensus everything must be made explicit to the professional as well as to the layman.

It is doubtful that teacher-training faculties or teachers' unions can constitute such a guild; the former lack credibility because professors of education very often are not and may never have been public classroom teachers, the latter because too few of the membership have undergone the kind of preparation that characterizes a profession or even a respectable craft. The general expectation that teachers will be rebuilt by in-service courses is itself strong evidence for this conclusion.

Teachers who go on for the master's degree in education might be the nucleus for the sort of guild I have in mind. But while master's degree programs give added exposure to formal schooling, it is doubtful that they can generate the paradigms of theory and practice to command the consensus so essential to a guild. For in these programs, as in undergraduate ones, variety is king, and while I join in reverent genuflexion to the blessings of diversity, it does not provide what guilds must have—a legitimating consensus.

FORMAL INFORMALITY

In-service agencies pride themselves on their flexibility, functionality, and fine-tuned relevance. They are not tied to standardized courses and modes of instruction, not bound by degree requirements and the restrictions of the academic bureaucracy. This freedom enables in-service offerings to utilize a variety of informal arrangements for delivery of educational services—workshops, encounter groups, field experiences, travel, and mini-courses, which, like miniskirts, are thought to be instructive in proportion to their brevity.

Although teachers dislike the restrictions imposed by formal study, they are addicted to credits and degrees. But credits and degrees raise the troublesome problem of standards, because traditionally they (credits and degrees) certify scholastic achievement. A great deal of in-service training, on the contrary, promises to improve the coping adequacy of the teacher, of which scholastic measures may not be significant indicators. Indeed, the criteria for scholastic quality and practical adequacy are so different from each other as to be virtually incommensurable. It is like trying to measure milk in feet and inches.

Academic quality is judged by conceptual clarity and logical cogency. The disciplines making up the curriculum of the university are systems of distinctive entities, relations, and modes of inquiry developed over long periods of scholarship. Professional courses in established fields, such as engineering, agriculture, law, and medicine, also take on the character of a discipline, albeit the content is organized around problems of practice, e.g., courses in jurisprudence, pathology, design, etc. Academic quality is no mystery. The respective guilds of scholars know what it is and guard it jealously. Quality in professional practice is judged by success in serving the client. When the client is dissatisfied with the service, the practitioner can plead that he had used correct procedure but that variables over which he had no control vitiated the results. But acquittal on charges of malpractice only exonerates from blame; it does not constitute success. Into success flow many, many variables over which control may be imperfect indeed.

For these reasons, while credit based on grades is a feasible way of registering or certifying academic accomplishment, it is not very useful for certifying quality of practice. In-service work that may help the teacher in the fight for survival, motivational devices, variations in approach, or even a change in dress may not signify growth in knowledge. The use of grades, exams, credits, and degrees to measure improvements in practice does not really measure improvement, and in fact, can impair the usefulness of the apparatus as a measure of academic quality.

I realize, of course, that the salary schedule is often tied to credits and degrees and that in-service agencies in offering them are responding to a social reality. Yet they need not be quite so zealous in pressing collegiate institutions to give academic credit where credit (although due) is not appropriate. In-service agencies might even refuse to collaborate with collegiate administrations that make a virtue out of their need for tuition fees. By a strange sort of logical cynicism, the propositions "Degrees and credits signify nothing important" and "It is important for people to get degrees" are made compatible in the minds of seekers and purveyors of academic degrees. When a college awards *its* academic credit for previous experience, practice of techniques, or personality development, it is debasing the academic currency. It can award honorary degrees and other marks of distinction to recognize practical accomplishment, but to confuse accomplishment in practice, however socially useful, with academic achievement confounds everything and solves nothing.

The handicaps of teachers taking late-afternoon and evening classes are familiar, and some accommodation to them is reasonable. After a day in school, teachers are tired; there is little time for reading, study, discussion, and contemplation; and not too much can be demanded in the way of papers and examinations. When these limitations determine the quality and the grading of academic work nobody really benefits, because the grade loses whatever validity it ever had. This is not a defense of the academic grading apparatus; it is vulnerable to criticism even as a measure of scholastic achievement, but this is no reason to misuse it as a measure of existential success or of the sincerity and efforts of the student, for which it is totally unsuitable.

There is no inherent impossibility in teachers studying a high-grade professional teacher-education program through in-service courses, just as there is no inherent impossibility in taking a good engineering degree through in-service programs. But in teacher education, the difficulty is two-fold: one is the lack of the guild consensus that makes the theoretical components acceptable–if not always palatable–requirements; the other is the ubiquitous demand that all in-service work contribute as directly and quickly as possible to mitigating the predicaments of the teacher. Under such pressure, teacher-preparation curricula preservice and in-service gravitate toward the technician (paraprofessional) level.

QUESTIONS AND CONJECTURES

These three paradoxes or problems or anomalies engender certain questions. First, is in-service work to be remedial or reconstructive? If it is to be the latter and remedy the lack of a good preservice program, it probably cannot do so by stitching together an assortment of remedial patches into a costume. It has to find or create a theory-*cum*-practice structure that makes sense functionally and justifies professional status and responsibility for the teacher.

Second, the chances of creating a credible credentialling guild are slim at best but perhaps better for in-service agencies than for either collegiate institutions or teachers' unions acting on their own. The in-service agencies have greater freedom and flexibility for bringing the resources of unions, colleges, and school administrators together than any one of the three can command. In concert they might devise a program that could nurture a guild of really professional teachers from among those already certified to teach.

The current surplus of teachers, real or alleged, may be an opportunity for testing the possibility of such a development. The increased investment of time and cognitive effort that a truly professional program necessitates would sift out the people committed to teaching as a career from those to whom it is a hedge against unemployment or as a transition to more preferable employment. Inasmuch as pay differentials are already tied to post-baccalaureate study, there should be no problem in enlisting the support of administrators and teacher unions for what might be called "Rebuilding Programs of Teacher Education" (RPTE).

Third, the in-service agency can deal with formal informality honestly. It does not have to translate every component of the program into grades and credits—some components may not be academic. And it need not accept for academic credit much that is academically respectable but has no relation to teacher education, or at least not to that portion of it designated as professional. It could use credits and grades to evaluate those portions of the program that are scholastic and maintain standards sufficiently high to give the credit or the degree solid academic stature. It might, for example, not allow teachers in service to undertake courses requiring lots of reading, analytic study, and time-consuming research after a full day's work in the schools.

Nevertheless, the basic paradox remains: no consensus, no guild; no guild, no standards; no standards, no profession; no profession, no professional program. An illusion of consensus or the glorification of diversity in the absence of it won't do. The breaking of the circle may not be possible or not yet possible. Nevertheless, it seems incredible that the mountains of educational research cannot yield more than the skittering mice of *ad hoc* courses, workshops, and workouts of one kind or another. I believe that there is enough reliable knowledge and theory for a professional degree. The faculties of teacher-training institutions, for the socioeconomic reasons cited earlier in this paper, may not be able to mount such structured programs as preservice requirements. So it may be the fate or the destiny or the opportunity for in-service teacher education to take the first steps in this direction.

As one example of such leadership, one might note that teachers enrolled in in-service programs are in a strategic position to help crystallize a standard set of paradigmatic situations that constitute the problems of the teaching profession at various levels of schooling. Such a set of paradigms could serve not only as organizing foci for courses, but also for clinical work and advanced internship. Translated into video tapes and other simulation media, they could do more to professionalize the field than educational theorists or practitioners have been able to do. The detection, selection, criticism, and general study of these paradigm situations could by themselves constitute a valuable target for research.

So, paradoxical as it may sound, the reform of the preservice program may in the end rest with the in-service training of teachers.

The Confluence of Affective and Cognitive Learning: Requirements for Teaching

George Isaac Brown

Graduate School of Education, University of California

Arthur Combs of the University of Florida has developed a childhood education program (whose theoretical base is derived from perceptual humanistic psychology) that holds that the causes of behavior may be found in the belief system of the behaver. "It follows that teacher education is not a question of learning 'how to teach,' but a matter of personal discovery, of learning how to use one's self and one's surroundings to assist other persons to learn." This is seen as an alternative to the more behavioristically oriented thinking that may now prevail.

Combs and Richard Usher of the University of Northern Colorado differentiate between good and bad teachers: (1) "good teachers always seem concerned with how things look to the person they are working with, while poor ones believe the important data is how things look to themselves." Good teaching might be equated with sensitivity or empathy; (2) good teachers perceive themselves in positive ways while poor ones have negative self-concepts; (3) good teachers view others in positive ways while poor teachers "suffer grave doubts about the nature and capacity of the persons they are working with"; (4) good teachers tend to be purposefully freeing, opening, and expanding while poor teachers move in opposite directions, tending to be constricting, narrowing, directing, and controlling; and (5) good teachers use methods that fit the teacher who is using them and the context in which the teacher is working.

On the basis of findings, Combs developed the following basic principles for a teacher education program:

1. There is an emphasis on process wherein teachers are engaged in a journey of personal discovery, so that they can learn how to use themselves effectively in carrying out their work.
2. This process starts from a feeling of security and acceptance; a strong support system is essential, with a heavy emphasis on success and a minimization of the experience of failure.
3. The focus of teacher training is on personal meanings rather than on behavior. This is based on the thesis that behavior comes from the originating meaning system. Originally the meaning determines how one perceives, and how one perceives determines how one behaves.
4. Accordingly, in order to focus on meaning in a productive way, professional training must emphasize subjective aspects of human experience instead of objectivity, scientific methodology, etc.
5. It follows that such a program must operate within the context of an open system of thinking.
6. It is basic to learning that people learn best when they have a need to learn. The implications here are that orderly sequence may have to be sacrificed so that learning may come first, with "order" to come later when attempts are made to organize what is learned.
7. Such a program must actively seek student involvement so that students become more and more responsible for their own learning.
8. Self-concept research must be directly applied to the training program so that constructive feedback is continually available.
9. Because these teaching methods use the self as an instrument they must be discovered by the individual. This requires a cafeteria approach to methods where many alternatives are available to the students.
10. Because of the diversity of backgrounds of teachers in training, professional training must have the widest possible flexibility to meet diverse needs. This means that students will not be required to move through sequences of experience within certain time periods.
11. The training programs must be congruent; they must demonstrate in their own practices the philosophy and methodology that they are attempting to teach their teachers-in-training. There is to be a strong emphasis on human relationships, which of course requires a unique kind of faculty, a faculty who serve both as facilitators and consultants.[1]

1. H. Ivars, R. A. Blume, A. W. Combs, W. D. Hedges, *Humanistic Teacher Education: An Experiment in Systematic Curriculum Innovation* (Fort Collins, Colo.: Shields Publishing Company, 1974).

It is obvious that Combs, in this program, is attempting not only to help the individual grow but also to provide an environment that supports this growth; the focus is both on individual and environment.

Under the leadership of Gerald Weinstein and later with the addition of Professor Al Alschuler to the faculty, the School of Education at the University of Massachusetts developed a Center for Humanistic Education. The Center has trained about 500 professionals with a focus on self-science and self-knowledge education. Self-knowledge is conceptualized as having three analytically distinct components: (a) experience, which includes feelings, actions, sensations, and thoughts; (b) processes, which include operations and structures; and (c) theory, which is made up of hypotheses. Experience is private and existential, occurring in the present time and changing momentarily. An individual makes sense of the experience through the mental procedures of processes. Processes are relatively stable across time, are hierarchical and develop in sequence.

Weinstein and Alschuler are attempting to create a developmental theory for the affective domain. One developmental aspect states that "at each stage of development the level of processes available to a person determines the nature of the hypotheses they can generate about their experience, its antecedents and consequences. As individuals develop new processes, the corresponding self-hypotheses or self-theories are progressively more adequate, accurate, economical and useful. . . . The adequacy of any theory depends in large part on the adequacy of the data available to be conceptualized."[2]

Over a period of time there are developmental changes that influence how much of a person's original experience is recalled and the way that it is to be reported. This is also true of the nature of the individual's hypotheses. Another dimension of their theory is the nature of *value*. How experience is valued seems to be developmental in terms of a regular sequence of stages. While admitting the possibility and likelihood of a number of other stages, they describe four stages of self-knowledge growth:

Elemental Self-knowledge Theory. Here each single event is described as discrete and "visible." Elements are not explicitly summarized as a single complex situation; instead they are juxtaposed or serially ordered. Separate adjective and adverb modifiers are used for value descriptions.

2. A. Alschuler, *Self-knowledge Education Project* (Amherst, MA.: University of Massachusetts, unpublished paper).

Situational Self-knowledge Theory. Although here each instance is not presented as an example of a more general pattern, feelings are included with values assigned to these feelings, and a gestalt is formed through integration of all the elements in a situation.

Patterned Self-knowledge Theory. Here, single situations are generalized over time into patterns that are "named in terms of traits, roles, obligations, similarities, and lasting interpersonal reciprocal relationships," and "value is assigned to these patterns."[3]

Transformational Self-knowledge Theory. Where, in the previous stage an event would define a stable pattern, here the experience of change becomes stable and continuous. Categories for the emotions involved are labeled as "abilities," "capacities," "personality," "interests," "mind," "soul," and "feeling." The future possibility is introduced as a consequence of recognizing internal conflicts. Here we have experiences that are described as unforgettable by the individual. "At this stage, value is assigned in terms of the meanings and inner significance of these processes of change."[4]

Weinstein's approach to psychological education as practiced at the School of Education is called Self-Science—the self becomes the content, just as in geology we are concerned with the earth or in chemistry with elements and compounds. A systematic approach for examining the self as content is provided through a mechanism called the Trumpet (also known as Individual Concerns, which are identity, connectedness and power). There are eight steps in the Trumpet. Step One, Experience Confrontations: Here, I interact with a situation that generates data. Step Two, Inventory Responses: How did I respond? What was unique? What was common? Step Three, Recognize Patterns: What is typical of me? Step Four, Own Patterns: What function does this pattern serve for me? Step Five, Consider Consequences: What does happen or could happen in my life because of this pattern? Step Six, Allow Alternatives: Will I allow myself any additional patterns of response? Step Seven, Make Evaluations: I appraise the alternatives including my original behavior and decide how to make choices, on what grounds. Step Eight, Choose: I take responsibility for choosing among the alternatives and act according to that choice. (A variety of more specific questions are provided under each stage step.)

3. Alschuler, *Self-Knowledge Education Project.*
Ibid.

The work at the University of Massachusetts continues to change as witnessed by the efforts toward a developmental theory for the affective domain that has emerged only in the last two or three years. Change also includes a shift from a strong focus on a self-centered concern to a more socially centered concern. For example, among the professional competencies to be required of those working for a master's or doctoral degree is "demonstrated commitment to combating the causes and effects of racism, sexism, and other forms of systematic dehumanization."

For me, the most *heroic* ongoing project (which, while maintaining continued effectiveness, has moved into newer and more exciting dimensions) is the Affective Education Development Program in the Philadelphia Public School System, under the direction of Norman Newberg. This project has not only survived for more than seven years (in the midst of the stresses and strains of a large urban school district going through rapid and dramatic change, and subject to political, economic, and other community forces) but has continued to grow and flourish. The project staff has been creative in designing teacher training models, and from the project's inception has carried out a careful evaluation of its procedures.

The Affective Education Development Program bases its work on two major assumptions: first, that the content presented to students must be organized around *processes* and second, that affective learning takes place for students only when there is a direct connection between what is being structured in the classroom and the concerns of the student. These concerns are described in terms of the same three basic needs used by Weinstein in the Trumpet: the need to develop a positive concept of self, also called the need for identity; the need to develop meaningful, satisfying relationships with others, sometimes called the need for connectedness; and the need of each student to feel a sense of power or control over what is happening to him, here called the need for potency.

Before providing teachers with a variety of strategies to deal with these concerns, and producing models of the curriculum that make the connections between concerns and academic subject matter, the trainers in this program help teachers become more aware of the students' concerns and how these concerns are manifested within the classroom.

The staff of the project believes that it is more effective and efficient for teachers to focus on both logical and psychological processes, such as decision-making, questioning, and value clarification, rather than, (because of the information explosion) trying to explain large quantities of subject matter, meanwhile sacrificing the students' opportunity to learn these overall processes. There is much emphasis on group dynamics, based on the assumption that students will continue to function as members of groups throughout their lives.

Some of their research findings indicate that in a four month period students in an affective group, when compared with a similar nonproject group, were absent from school half as often and tardy less than one third as often. Parents were enthusiastic about the effects of the program on their children and in fact provided a political base that helped in the maintenance and continuation of the project. Students with an affectively trained teaching team improved significantly in reading over a comparison group as measured by a silent reading comprehension test. In another school, in which teachers were trained in the project, the students' claims that they had learned more basic skills this year than the previous year under a conventional classroom structure were supported by analysis and grades. English grades of 62 percent of the new students increased an average of ten points, and social studies grades increased for 51 percent of the students according to Dr. Wendy Golub, director of evaluation at that time. In this latter school, an alternative school focusing on human services and located in a large comprehensive high school, average monthly attendance over a three-month period exceeded the average for the students on the rest of the campus.

One interesting finding, supported by my own experience in California, is reported by Mark Levin, teacher training coordinator: experienced classroom teachers master affective skills during training much more successfully than do student teachers or new teachers. This may be because experienced teachers have already solved control and organizational problems, and, feeling relatively secure in the classroom, can experience their own dissatisfaction with what is being learned in the classroom and are able to move into new areas of professional experience in order to do something about this.

Work in Philadelphia is based somewhat on the theoretical work of Terry Borton and Norm Newberg that posits that an awareness on the part of the students of the differences between what they intended to have happen and what actually happened can provide data that they can then use to modify their own behavior. This awareness, when applied to the concerns of identity, connectedness and potency, as described above, can lead to intentional processes of sensing, transforming and acting. These processes are formulated by Borton and Newberg as "What?" (for sensing the difference); "So What?" (for immediately transforming this into relevant patterns of meaning); and "Now What?" (in order to choose the best alternative for action and generalizing this, where appropriate, to other situations). Training in Philadelphia is divided into three phases covering a period of a year. During the first phase, called Awareness-Responsibility, teachers receive experiential training along with classroom assignments that are focused on deepening awareness of feelings of self and others in their professional lives. In the second phase the teachers choose a curriculum model, such as the Trumpet or the Confluent Model developed by a group (myself included) in California or the Borton-Newberg method described above, and develop lessons that are field tested in the classroom through the use of experiential and simulation techniques. The third stage is committed to developing an equality among the personal, interpersonal and public types of knowledge taught, and among the dependent, interdependent and independent kinds of experiences all students need.

Perhaps the most exciting development that Newberg and his colleagues have recently initiated is the transgenerational school where people of all ages are involved together in learning. This is helping to break the set of conventional school organization and is helping to lead us back to more community involvement in the schools, which, I believe, makes ecological and holistic sense.

There are a number of other programs concerned with the confluence between the affective and cognitive domains that have made important contributions. These include the following: the recently developed Program in Humanistic Education at Boston University, under the direction of Professor Paul Nash, which has a strong base in philosophical considerations; the work of Barbara Biber and the group at Bank Street College in New York; the original work of Ralph Ojenann in the Educational Research Council in Cleveland; William Glaser's emphasis on success rather than on failure; Thomas Gordon's Teacher Effectiveness Training; Ralph Mosher's work in psychological education at Boston College; Albert Ellis' use of Rational-Emotive Therapy Training for the classroom; Synanon; Bessell and Palomaries' Human Development Training Institute in San Diego that introduces the magic circle, incorporating "group dynamic techniques in a structured learning environment"; Self-Enhancing Education, developed by Norma Randolph, which draws heavily on Transactional Analysis; the Program for Human Development at Fairleigh Dickinson University; Diagnostic-Prescriptive Teaching developed by Robert Proudy at George Washington University; the Nicolet High School Project in Confluent Education in Milwaukee, Wisconsin; and a number of inter national projects and centers such as the Province of Manitoba Confluent Education Project that has involved over 800 teachers; the Kristiansand Project in Norway; the work at the University of Utrecht in the Netherlands; studies at the Center for Confluent Education at Yamaguchi University in Japan; projects in Confluent Education at the Fritz Perls Gestalt Institut at Neuss, Germany; the international course in pathology developed for medical students under the sponsorship of the World Health Organization, which has a strong Confluent Education component; and many others.

My own work in the field of Confluent Education came out of early theoretical and empirical work in the field of creativity. During this period of my professional life I was fascinated by the interplay of feelings and thinking in the creative process. Later, I started to do more sophisticated work in the so-called nonverbal humanities at Esalen Institute, which is concerned with the development of the human potential. At the same time I continued as a professor at the University of California, Santa Barbara. I began to make attempts to integrate these two worlds. Consequently, with a small grant from the Fund for the Advancement of Education, and assisted by teachers from elementary and secondary schools, I was able to attend more explicitly to the union of the affective and cognitive domains. Our early formulations simply insisted that it is impossible to have a cognitive experience without an accompanying affective component; and vice versa—with almost all affective experience there has to be some intellectual activity. An example of this symbiotic relationship in the first case may be found in the passion of the scholar, for even in that most abstract of disciplines, mathematics, it is the scholar's pursuit of truth, knowledge, wisdom, fame, or perhaps the personal satisfaction of the process of his work that sustains him in his endeavors. In the second symbiotic case, whatever our emotional response we usually attach words, concepts or generalizations, trying to make some intellectual sense or meaning out of that emotional experience. We may not do this intentionally, but it still goes on. The separation of the affective and cognitive domains is, of course, an artificial one, but useful for theoretical purposes.

The original attempts to develop a theory and practices are described in detail in my first book, *Human Teaching for Human Learning: An Introduction to Confluent Education.*[5] During and immediately after this original attempt the group realized that our theoretical formulations were indeed simplistic and we began to pay

5. G. I. Brown, *Human Teaching for Human Learning: An Introduction to Confluent Education* (New York, N.Y.: Viking Press, 1971).

more attention to both theory and practice. At the same time we were formalizing an academic program in the Graduate School of Education at the University of California, Santa Barbara. With a larger four year grant from the Ford Foundation we were able to strengthen this academic program and at the same time carry out a number of projects in Confluent Education in the field at various educational levels.

Describing the role of affective loadings in the curriculum, John Shiflett, now at the University of Maryland, states "there is no topic or goal within conventional curricula that does not have an integral affective component. Loadings are those affective aspects of all learning tasks stemming from basic concerns or not, which, if taken into account, may enrich personal meaning, increase relevance, and broaden understanding in a manner not possible, or only haphazardly done, by focus on the cognitive dimensions alone." He describes three categories of affective loadings: orientation loadings, which are those affective elements that are concerned with wanting or not wanting to learn. They could be thought of as affective readiness on the part of the learner along with his affective response to his cognitive readiness for a particular learning task. The second, engagement loadings, are those perhaps more obvious affective elements that can be associated with what is learned and the learning process itself. The third, accomplishment loadings, are associated with those affective elements connected with the completion of a learning task. These, when positive, could be feelings of satisfaction, self-esteem, and may also be feelings that influence the internalization of what is learned so that what is learned becomes personally meaningful to the student and a part of his personal organization. Accomplishment loadings in turn, during a sequence of learning activities, may become part of the orientation loadings of the next learning task in line in that sequence.[6]

Gloria Castillo has built her model for teaching in Confluent Education upon Shiflett's work as presented in her book, *Left-Handed Teaching.*[7] Here, circle number two represents the affective domain and circle number three represents the cognitive domain. These two overlap in a common territory where there is confluent learning taking place. These two circles represent then our original model dealing with the integration of the affective and cognitive domains within the teaching-learning process. Circle number one is described as readiness-awareness

6. J. M. Shiflett, "Beyond Vibration Teaching" in *The Live Classroom: Innovation through Confluent Education and Gestalt* (New York, N.Y.: Viking Press, 1975).
7. G. A. Castillo, *Left-handed Teaching* (New York, N.Y.: Praeger Publishing Co., 1974). Reprinted by permission.

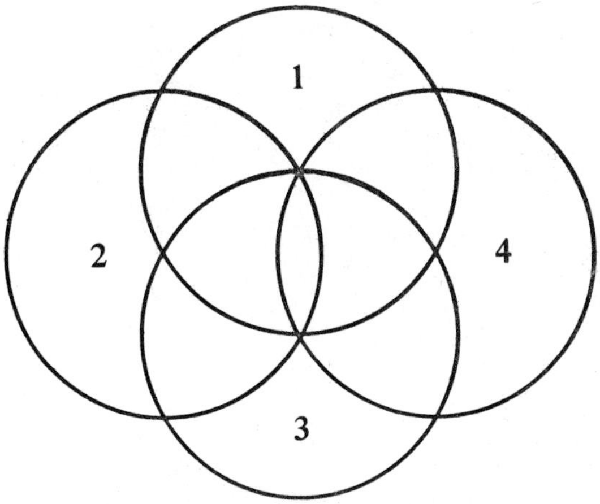

Castillo Model for Confluent Education

by Castillo. This incorporate's Shiflett's orientation loadings, although the circle also includes cognitive readiness. The fourth circle is again an elaboration of Shiflett's concept, in this case, that of the accomplishment loadings. Castillo describes this as the circle of responsibility, wherein the individual learner, if he has learned effectively, takes responsibility for his learning; that is, he incorporates or integrates his learning into his view of the world and his ways of, or approaches toward, coping with the world and finding satisfaction in his personal existence. Castillo points out that if the learning has not been effective, this circle will not be in evidence and thus the teacher will be alerted to return to his lesson to examine where, within the other three circles, adequate content or experience may not have been provided.

The Shiflett and Castillo models are useful when examining individual teaching-learning acts. They are, however, simplistic in the sense that they do not incorporate a number of other factors and consequent relationships that have to do with the process of learning development and personal growth.

One of the more useful models for me has been that of Dr. Thomas Yeomans.[8] Here Yeomans has taken the original concept of confluence (that focused on the integration or flowing together of the affective and cognitive domains) and extended it. He examines confluence as an

8. T. Yeomans, *Toward a Confluent Theory of the Teaching of English* (Santa Barbara, CA.: University of California, unpublished Ph.D. dissertation, 1973). Reprinted by permission.

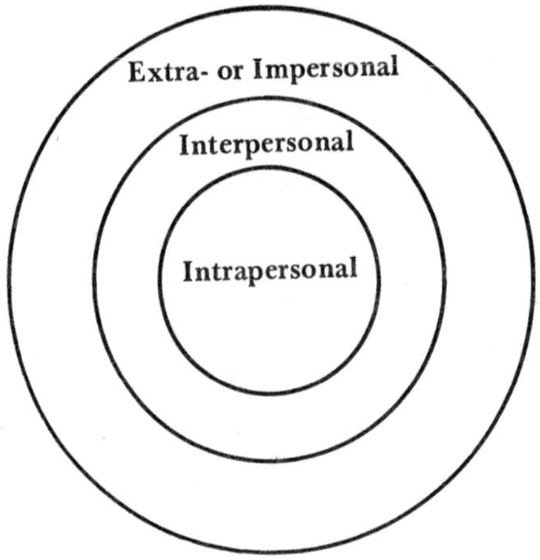

Yeomans Model of Confluent Education

internal process of integration so that there is not only confluence among all aspects of personality, but also within the triadic relationship among the self, others, and the context or environment. The latter might include the curriculum as presented in the abstract, the institution such as the classroom or the school itself, or the community or the society as a whole, including the physical environment. He conceptualizes self as lying within the inner circle that could be called the intrapersonal. Immediately surrounding this is another circle representing the interpersonal. This, in turn, lies within the context of a third circle that contains the impersonal or extrapersonal. Academically, this third circle is manifested as subject matter or disciplines. In the ideal confluent situation all three become one, so that the flow of experience moves among the realms in an integrated harmonious way; this process is called confluence.

What is happening here is that there are a number of subordinate but important confluences occurring within a total gestalt confluence. In effect, we have an ecological system where what happens within one of the circles affects each of the others. To begin, there is a confluence within the intrapersonal realm between affective and cognitive. Another confluence could be that of the number of subpersonalities that exist within one individual; the more the integration among these, the more integrated the individual's personality. The next confluence to be considered is that between the individual and others—how the individual relates to his peers, to his teachers, to his parents, to other adults, and how they relate to him all fall within the province of the second circle. Obviously the existential state of each individual involved in this interaction will affect the interaction itself, so this is an example of confluence between circles.

If, as commonly occurs, there is a major emphasis on subject matter or curriculum (that which lies within the extrapersonal circle) to the exclusion of the first two circles, one can see that the quality of experience in the inner two circles can be significantly affected. The more confluence or connectedness between what occurs in the third circle and the other two circles, the more effective the learning will be within the third circle. In other words, the more meaning for the individual from his experiences as he interacts with others, and his attitudes and feelings towards others, including his teachers, the greater the qualitative and quantitative learning of content will be within the third circle.[9]

Although not included in Yeomans' model, a fourth circle could be added, that of the transpersonal. The transpersonal realm would include religious, spiritual, mystical, metaphysical and other experience that is somehow transcendental in nature and that transcends our everyday experience. Each of us has had experiences of this sort. This might have been as simple an incident as viewing a sunset and being in awe of its magnificence, or some special, profound moment when we unintentionally make the vital connection between our secular existence and the cosmos. I believe that ordinarily we are truly "overawed" by these experiences and tend to leave them quickly, perhaps from not knowing how to fit them into our everyday world. From time to time we may look back wistfully perhaps, but then withdraw into the daily programs that we and others have diligently designed for ourselves. Recently I heard a report of interviews of a cross-section of the population in which over half the participants volunteered that they were concerned with questions of the meaning of their existence. In addition, they admitted to a reluctance to discuss this concern with others, whether out of awkwardness, shyness, or fear that they might be unlike other people. In my work as a therapist, I am continually encountering this issue, which seems to be pervasive regardless of the degree of success in one's life.

In Confluent Education we have begun to attend to the whole question of the relevance of personal meaning through the brilliant work of Dr. Stewart Shapiro, one of my colleagues, who has developed a special interview called the "Life-Meanings Survey."

9. Yeomans, *Toward a Confluent Theory.*

If we add this fourth circle, the transpersonal, we then have, I believe, a comprehensive model from which to begin to develop an even more complete new paradigm for education. Once this model begins to be utilized it can be swiftly seen that education no longer becomes the sole concern of the classroom or the school, but becomes part of a total ecological learning system that would include the community and society and, in fact, the universe. Some of our later thinking and work may be found in *The Live Classroom: Innovation through Confluent Education and Gestalt,* by Shiflett.

This work has manifested itself through a number of projects in the field and a graduate academic program offering an M.A. for experienced teachers and a Ph.D. for potential leaders in the field. Required courses include: The Creative Process, Encounter Group Leadership, Group Dynamics, Human Relations in Education, The Dynamics of Planned Change, Instructional Strategies in Confluent Education, Self-Science Education, Philosophical Dimensions, Curriculum Design in Confluent Education, etc. Emphasis is placed on empirical, theoretical, or clinical approaches or some combination thereof, depending upon individual needs.

In our endeavors in the past seven or eight years, we have discovered some principles in working with teachers integrating the affective and cognitive domains. First, we have learned that this integration is a natural process and would go on as normal development if not interrupted by conflicting external social values and consequent interferences. Such is to be expected, for here we are faced with a persistent dilemma (whether our field is politics, economics, sociology, psychology or education); that is, the conflict that continues between the needs of the individual on the one hand and the needs of the society in which he finds himself on the other.

This dilemma is another clear example that demonstrates the practicality of the Yeomans model. What we apparently need then is a set of social values and practices that maximize the full holistic development of the individual, allowing for a healthy interplay of affect and cognition. At the same time, and I stress, at the same time, we need individuals who will collectively make up the kind of society that will permit and nurture the development of the potential of each individual making up that society.

It is tempting here to fall into the chicken or egg argument. I believe that while the question of what comes first cannot be completely ignored, we do not have to be restricted by its parameters. There is a growing sympathy and demand for a more pluralistic approach in our educational structures. Furthermore, there is at the same time increasing sophistication in the development of approaches to family therapy and education. If there can be a number of innovative approaches to education that are more holistic in nature, and if each school district makes use of at least one of these, and if at the same time there is increased attention paid to the family as a social system, then, I believe we may be able to move forward in terms of creating individuals who in turn will have the strength and ability to modify the larger social context in which they find themselves. I neglected to say that, of course, the immediate social context, whether an educational system or the family itself, has to be a supportive social system while the process of developing these individuals goes on.

We have also learned that groups of teachers, when going through training sequences in Confluent Education, can be expected to go through an initial phase of being turned on with the excitement of the new experiences as they discover more about themselves and meet each other in open and nourishing relationships. At the same time, teachers begin to use techniques they have experienced in the training with their students in the classroom. As teachers increasingly internalize their experiences, their teaching approaches change, and they seem to move from simply replicating the experiences they have had to owning the values and philosophy that begin to permeate their teaching. This is a second phase. In a sense they move from using the techniques of Confluent Education to becoming a confluent teacher. The total teaching personality can be changed so that, to use the Coombs model, the consequent perception and resultant behavior also change. We then begin to find a third phase emerging that could be called the creative or innovative phase, in which the teacher begins to design new approaches, consciously anticipating the needs of the students and the teacher's own needs and juxtaposing these two in a healthy, creative, productive way.

There is another sequence that might also be expected in the training process. After the initial high, teachers sometimes fall into a low energy or depressed period. This is especially true when they no longer have the immediate support and reinforcement of the group in which they are training. If, instead of trying to combat or avoid this, the trainer can capitalize upon this, seeing it as a natural process, he or she can help the teacher to move to a more centered position and relying more and more on his/her own strength and ability (but knowing when he or she needs support from a group and knowing how to get it). It is in this centered position that he moves into the second phase described above.

A third bit of knowledge we learned was that teachers can be self-directive in terms of designing their own training programs, that they can be trusted to seek help when they need it, and if not, will learn from the mistake of not doing so. We have learned from the number of projects in which we have been involved that innovation and reeducation imposed from above is nowhere near as effective as when teachers can truly participate, not only in the choice of what to do, but also how to do it. This is sometimes difficult for an administrator or an outside consultant or expert to accept. The self-directive process does take time, and does require some skillful structuring in terms of making such opportunities available. Perhaps the biggest initial problem is in helping teachers to become aware that *there are* alternatives available to them. In providing this awareness, the administrator or outside consultant is truly challenged in his own role as a teacher, for he must here *teach* this awareness without *imposing* it.

If work in the field of Confluent Education or humanistic education is based on one or two workshops, calling in an expert for two or three visits, or the distribution of how-to-do-it manuals, then we will have (as we have had so often) another Mickey Mouse use of techniques, gimmicks, etc. The consequent professional indigestion leads to pedagogical flatulence, another odor up the corridors of education. What is needed instead is continuous, ongoing professional and personal growth opportunities, from training in individual and group growth processes through a combination of experiential and theoretical in-service training. This training should be held during released time. When combined with an emphasis on the desperate need we face in this country for the improvement of the quality of education, the decrease in pupil load allows for this. We need to *teach* the community this need, not through public relations but through actual teaching. And for the first time we begin to have concrete, legitimate, and respectable evidence of this need. This is a consequence of the careful, rigorous, empirical, split-brain research.

J. E. Bogen, who with Roger Sperry did much of the original split-brain research, in the Spring 1975 issue of the *U.C.L.A. Educator* states:

> What may well be the most important distinction between the left and right hemisphere modes is the extent to which a linear concept of time participates

in the ordering of thought. . . . (H. W.) Gordon and I have recently urged a scheme in which the right hemisphere is specialized for processing time-independent stimulus configurations and the left for time-ordered stimulus sequences . . . since education is effective only in so far as it affects the workings of the brain, we can see that an elementary school program narrowly restricted to reading, writing, and arithmetic will educate mainly one hemisphere, leaving half of an individual's high level potential unschooled. . . . For example, the usual justification of "I.Q. tests" is that they predict further scholastic achievement and that the latter is in turn predictive of "life success." This is ultimately based upon a criterion of "success" which is not only most often measured monetarily but seems to depend in part upon an analytic attitude hypertrophied by centuries of contention against nature. It is a view which culminates, when extreme, in measuring national "success" by the gross national product and in measuring progress of the human species in terms of total population. The latter criterion was explicitly adopted by Childe; such a criterion is clear, quantitative, and graphable; and it avoids altogether any concern for the quality of human existence.[10]

Robert D. Nebes, in the same issue of the *Educator,* points out,

Given the results to date on hemispheric specialization, it seems natural to many researchers in related fields that the scientific and technological aspects of our civilization are products of the left hemisphere, while the mystical and humanistic aspects are products of the right. The right hemisphere has thus been enthusiastically embraced by counter-culture groups as their side of the brain. They see in it the antithesis to an upright technological western society, identifying its synthetic abilities with eastern mystics' view of the interrelationship of all things. . . . How well such a grafting of philosophy onto anatomy will stand up is unclear, but certainly right hemisphere attributes will continue to be explored in the coming years, and their role in the various phases of human life examined.[11]

However, Nebes goes on to say,

if there is any truth in the assertion that our culture stresses left hemispheric skills, this is especially true of the school system. Selection for higher education is based predominantly on the ability to comprehend and manipulate language—a fact which may help explain why it took so long for science to come to grips with right hemisphere abilities. If the right hemisphere does indeed process data in a manner different from the left, perhaps we are short-changing ourselves when we educate only left-sided talents in basic schooling. Perhaps, when people talk about the inverse relationship between scholastic achievement and creativity, they are really talking about the effect of over-

10. J. E. Bogen and Roger Sperry, *U.C.L.A. Educator* Spring, 1975.
11. Robert D. Nebes, *U.C.L.A. Educator* Spring, 1975.

> training for verbal skills at the expense of nonverbal abilities. Many problems can be solved either by analysis or synthesis; but if people are taught habitually to examine only one approach, their ability to choose the most effective and efficient answer is diminished.[12]

No longer does right-brained creativity, intuition, metaphorical or holistic thinking have to fall within the province of soft-thinkers, do-gooders, idealists, or those who emphasize "frills" in education. The right hemisphere or brain obviously involves one half the functioning of each of our brains. We have emphasized left brain functioning for the most part to the exclusion of the right brain. At the least we have ignored right brain functioning; at our worst we have repressed it.

Fortunately there are some who have survived the constrictions of their educational bonds and prisons. Their right brains still function in a mature way in spite of the neglect or repression of their formal educational experience. Thus, we still have with us some creative and innovative workers in the vineyards, although I worry lest their numbers diminish each year. The paucity of innovative thinkers and leadership in some areas of our lives "causes me to tremble."

One example is in our own house, professional education. I believe education is currently going through one of the most severe crises of its history. There is an increasing lack of confidence in the educational enterprise. The clichés, verbalisms, slogans and assumptions we have gotten away with for years are now being called to question. There is a growing lack of confidence in our research and in our research methodology (witness the problems of the N.I.E.). Communities are looking at their educational systems in a very hard way and taxes are becoming more and more difficult to obtain. There are increasing regressions to "the traditional ways," a consequence of fear, or confusion, or anger, or frustration with the schools, some implicit and some explicit.

For years achievement test constructors have been getting away with murder–and I choose that word deliberately. I am not a psychometrician but according to my colleague, Chester Harris (and I trust this distinguished scholar in the field), construction of achievement tests typically assumes latent traits that are general over all students under all instructional conditions. This view does not allow for teachers or teaching as an independent variable that could affect test results. How absurd this is. We could consequently ask "Why *have* teachers?," and yet achievement tests have been the tail wagging the dog of educational

12. R. E. Ornstein, *The Psychology of Consciousness* (New York, N.Y.: Viking Press, 1972).

practice for as long as I can remember. Fortunately, Chester and others, whose right brains apparently still function well, are trying to develop a new, more realistic, functional and utilitarian achievement test theory.

Kuhn, in *The Structure of Scientific Revolution,* states that when a paradigm no longer fits reality, when there are an increasing number of anomalies that are not satisfied by the rules and values of a paradigm, we then have a crisis. For example, we had a minor crisis after World War II, when the Russians produced Sputnik and we didn't. We then rushed to math and science as the panacea that further reinforced our emphasis on left brain functioning. We seem to have a new crisis upon us now. Many students, their parents, other people in the community, politicians and even some professors of education are voicing their awareness that something is radically wrong, something is missing in education today.

When a paradigm enters a crisis state, then new paradigms, or suggestions of new paradigms, begin to emerge. We see this in the work of Paulo Freire, Ivan Illich, Mario Fantini, Al Alschuler, Arthur Combs, and others. I have been standing before you also, advocating the beginnings of a new paradigm. In keeping with my suggestions, let me return to the material on the split brain for a moment. I am not, I repeat, am not advocating the abandonment of teaching for the left brain. We need empirical, analytical, linear and rational kinds of thinking and brain functioning, but this must, I again repeat, must be integrated with the special, invaluable contributions (holistic, function-related, spatial, and perhaps intuitive) that our right brains can make.

Just as what has always seemed so obvious to me (that as emotions and intellectual functioning both occur within each individual, they should both be utilized in learning) so should right and left brain functioning be explored so as to develop ways for the harmonious and appropriate functioning of the whole brain.

This immediately raises a question: Is there overlap between these two concerns, right and left brain, and emotions and thinking? Bogen claims that "the affective states of the two hemispheres are usually quite similar." However, this is based on observation of gross affective response like being repulsed by odors. Just as cognitive functioning differs for each hemisphere, so might affective response. For example, a subtle affective response like the "hedonic impulse" that is experienced pleasurably and vaguely by creative people as "something about to come together" before they achieve new insights or eurekas, may well come from right brain affective apparatus that can lead to new holistic breakthroughs.

I find myself in deep sympathy with the need for rigor, clear analysis, and critique of work in humanistic education and in Confluent Education and in affective education. We need to be cautious here. Wherever there is a call for a return to an equalizing emphasis on feelings, emotions, and the need for a consideration of the human condition in educational practice, we must not be overwhelmed by our passions. At the same time I would like to critique the critique method. As I have stated earlier, research on the brain indicates the differences between left and right brain functioning. Analysis, appraisals, and critiques as conventionally conceptualized are left brain functioning. My reservation is simply that, as valuable as they may be, they are insufficient in and of themselves when accepted as an exclusive way toward the betterment of teaching. We need two additional components in our efforts toward the improvement of teacher education. First we need emphasis on some kinds of right brain functioning. This means some way or ways to examine what is occurring in a more holistic, ecological, and perhaps even aesthetic way. Such a proposal is unsettling, at least to me, and perhaps to you, for we move here into a realm that lacks precision, accuracy of measurement, and the comfort of the quantitative dimensions. You may perhaps find some reassurance in my second component wherein I propose that we somehow integrate this nebulous, illusive metaknowledge with the more rigorous, empirical and analytical methods with which we are so familiar. But how do we put these two together? How can we find standards or agreed upon measures that provide the objectivity of reality that we treasure so dearly in our empirical and scientific methodology? Of course, such objectivity is a myth unto itself. Michael Polanyi in his work on personal knowledge, Roger Williams in his descriptions of the distortions and abuse of data in biochemical individuality and the history of science itself, in which personal biases and prejudices govern the behavior of the practitioners of science, provide strong support that science is, in itself, a belief system like many other mythologies.

I do not believe that we have to be appalled by this fact. Instead, let us be aware of its existence along with the possibility of our own subjective input in viewing and reporting of the world. In fact, this, in a strange, convoluted way, may be a cue toward ways to begin to integrate the two brain functionings. What seems obvious is that for a person to function with his whole brain he must himself be a whole person, someone who is personally sound, who has integrated his feelings and intellect within himself with the world around him, who can accept new data without threat or overeagerness, who is concerned with *his* process as well as the process of institutions and communities, and who sees process as a goal. I believe there are many cues here and I hope that we will not only get assistance in our quest from the formal philosophers, but also from the philosopher within each of us.

As might be expected with the emergence of any "new" educational approach, in the area of the confluence of affective and cognitive learning the entrepreneurs and predators are swift to seize the nearest teat from the munificent bosom of Mother Education, proceeding to milk every drop they can. As a consequence, we find how-to-do-it manuals, turn-on weekend workshops, ready-made packaged materials and a plethora of "experts" willing to come in for a day or two, tell you how to do it, and then vanish when the real work begins to emerge.

Among the special dangers intrinsic in this "movement" is that the affective domain can be very attractive, even seductive. The unfulfilled personal needs within each of us sometimes seem to be more safely dealt with within a professional context. This need not be detrimental or deleterious, however; in fact, if carefully utilized, our personal needs can contribute importantly to our professional growth process. On the other hand, when these personal needs are not confronted and made explicit, much confusion and counterproductive behavior can be manifested.

Other issues in this field include the need for a more rigorous attempt to define operationally and clearly the purpose and goals of putting the affective and cognitive together. Most of the objectives commonly used tend to be loosely defined, with much room for interpretation and confusion. Attempts are being made to be more precise, this to some degree receiving support from an increasing interest in evaluation.

If there is one obvious need in this field, this is for instruments to measure affectivity along with ways to measure the interrelationships between the affective and cognitive domains and the consequences of these interrelationships. I mentioned earlier the work of Chester Harris in developing new achievement test theory. I imagine the time will come when most of our postulates and premises for evaluation may have to be reexamined.

I would like to conclude with the last paragraph in my latest book, *The Live Classroom:*

"We have much, very much, yet to learn. Basic questions still remain—with whom, when, under what conditions, at what level, in what sequence, etc. We have learned some things. We have shared much of this in the preceding pages. At least we have moved beyond the beginning. You are most welcome to continue the journey with us."

Teaching for Moral and Civic Education: In-Service Training Implications

Edwin Fenton
Carnegie-Mellon University

The research of Lawrence Kohlberg and his colleagues in the area of cognitive moral development has implications for in-service education. While these implications apply most directly to teachers of social studies and English, in less direct fashion they touch the entire faculty and administration of any school that undertakes a comprehensive program of moral education.

Kohlberg's research indicates that thought about moral or ethical issues takes place on three levels (preconventional, conventional, and principled) each of which has two stages. According to Kohlberg, each of the six stages represents an organized system of thought that a person uses consistently to think about moral or ethical issues. These stages are seen as natural steps in the development of ethical thought, not as something contrived or artificial. People pass through the stages in invariant sequence, never retrogressing to a lower stage of thought once a higher one has been attained. A person's thought process may become arrested at any stage, however, for one of three major reasons: the lack of basic cognitive skills (such as capacity for formal operational thought); the lack of role taking abilities; or the lack of experiences that set up cognitivie conflict inducing stage change.

According to Kohlberg, people generally prefer the highest stage of moral thought they can comprehend, and most of us can comprehend one stage higher than the one we customarily use. Hence, being exposed to one-stage-higher arguments in meaningful contexts can produce stage change, often over a period of several years. The stage of thought a person uses can be determined through content analysis of an interview based on three moral dilemmas using a scoring system that Kohlberg has been perfecting for twenty years.

Higher moral stages are better than lower ones, Kohlberg argues. They are better cognitively because they are more differentiated, more integrated, and more universal. Moral philosophers lend independent support for the quality of thought at Stage 5 and Stage 6, and our most fundamental civil documents, the Constitution and the Declaration of Independence are based on Stage 5 thinking. In addition, problems for which there are no solutions at lower stages can be solved at higher stage reasoning. Kohlberg contends that society should intervene to facilitate stage change. He argues that people who think at a higher moral level reason better and, according to his research findings, act in accordance with their judgements more frequently than less developed thinkers.

Deliberate attempts to facilitate stage change in schools through educational programs have consistently been successful. Within the last decade, more than a score of investigators have attempted to facilitate stage change by leading moral discussions in elementary schools, junior and senior high schools, and on the college level. Although results vary in detail, one generalization about this research stands out: compared to the students in control groups, students in experimental groups, who participate in moral discussions, show significant increases in the stage of moral thought they commonly use.

In these programs, Kohlberg and his colleagues use hypothetical moral dilemmas to trigger moral discussions particularly in social studies and English classes. The dilemmas–should a man steal a drug to save his dying wife–present situations for which the culture lends some conventional support for a number of actions the protagonists could take. Teachers present dilemmas in a variety of forms: orally, written, on recordings, sound tapes, film, videotape, or as skits or role playing exercises. The discussion leader then attempts to get students to confront arguments one stage above their own. This confrontation takes place either when students who think at contiguous moral stages discuss each other's reasoning or when the teacher poses a higher level argument through a probe question or a comment.

In 1974, the Harvard group began a second type of intervention known as a Just Community School. This school-within-a-school, located in Cambridge High and Latin School (just a few blocks from Harvard) is composed of about seventy students and their teachers. Staff and students together drew up a constitution. They make decisions through community meetings in which each person has one vote. Many of the issues that come up in community meetings, such as what to do about a student who has cheated on a test or stolen from someone else, involve real-life moral dilemmas. It is hypothesized that processing these real life dilemmas should lead to stage change on the Kohlberg scale. (Data is currently being analyzed).

If school administrators decide to institute a program of moral development based on Kohlberg's research, these are some of the problems that are likely to turn up:

1. Few people in the school will have heard of Kohlberg's work, and those who have, will not know enough about it to lead a staff development project.
2. Many teachers will insist that their job is to *teach,* not take major responsibility for a program of ethical and moral development. Or they may be unwilling to devote twelve or eighteen classes a year to moral discussions if this means cutting out a corresponding number of hours from their regular classes.
3. Many teachers will lack the discussion and leadership skills essential in conducting such a program; they may not know how to develop sound moral dilemmas for classroom discussion or how to integrate moral discussions with other class work. Appropriate social studies and English courses for just community schools may not be readily available.
4. Teachers will not know how to evaluate the success or failure of a program of moral and civic education based on Kohlberg's research.
5. Community opposition may develop because many people believe that values education is not a proper function of public schools.

The two school systems in which Kohlberg and his colleagues piloted their program faced most of these problems. The Danforth Foundation had decided to support two projects in moral development, one in Cambridge and Brookline (based at Harvard) and the other near Pittsburgh (based at Carnegie-Mellon University). Kohlberg and Ralph Mosher, head of Boston University's program in guidance education, headed the Harvard effort, and I joined them for a year as preparation for starting the program in Pittsburgh. Kohlberg took chief responsibility for the development of a Just Community School in Cambridge; Mosher headed a project designed to introduce a program of moral education into the Brookline schools.

Brookline's Superintendent of Schools, Robert Sperber, helped set the in-service work there in motion. He met with Kohlberg and Mosher to plan the project and helped Kohlberg persuade the Brookline School

Committee to approve the project for the fall semester of the 1974-75 school year. Kohlberg made a public presentation to the Committee, and he and Sperber answered questions. Sperber also helped persuade the high school principal and the directors of social studies, independent studies, and English to lend their support.

Brookline has an unusually good school system with an exceptional faculty. Most of the guidance counselors and most of the social studies teachers had already known about Kohlberg's research before the project began. The project staff decided to begin work with a group of twenty-five persons from the social studies and guidance staff at Brookline High who volunteered to attend workshops after school during the fall semester. The workshop met twice monthly from October through January, 1975. It had three objectives: to acquaint teachers with the major research findings of Kohlberg and his colleagues; to examine curriculum materials for moral education in social studies and psychology; and to begin to create new moral education curriculum materials. Teachers were not paid to attend the workshop nor did they receive university credits.

The participants did some reading in preparation for each workshop session. Kohlberg presented his theory and answered questions about it. Demonstration videotapes illustrated the teaching process and introduced teachers to the skills they and their students would need to conduct moral discussions. Teachers examined the existing materials carefully and spent a session or two critiquing moral dilemmas that they had developed for their own classes. In January, about two-thirds of the participants committed themselves to continue work during the Spring, and the School Committee unanimously endorsed the continuation of the project for the following two-and-a-half years.

During the spring semester, Mosher and one of his graduate students (Paul Sullivan) continued the bimonthly workshops for social studies and guidance teachers, assisted from time to time by Kohlberg. Through this process, moral education materials were incorporated into ten social studies and psychology courses. The consultants, in increasing demand as teachers tried out new techniques, critiqued dilemmas written by the staff, taught demonstration classes, observed teachers conducting moral discussions, and analyzed teaching recorded on videotape. They also conducted three sessions for elementary school teachers interested in moral discussions.

The project continued during the summer of 1975. Sixteen teachers worked from a week to a month each to develop courses of study. They were paid $40 per day from the Danforth grant, a standard summer pay at Brookline for curriculum work. The materials on which the Brookline teachers worked are now being classroom tested in about ten social studies, psychology, and English courses, and will be made available through the project to other school systems in the near future.

The Brookline project has undertaken several new programs this fall. Mosher and two colleagues continue to consult with the teachers who worked during the summer. Kohlberg and two teachers have begun biweekly workshops for teachers from the Brookline middle schools, and they will conduct another workshop for interested parents. The staff is also helping an already existing School-Within-a-School to set up a community government modeled after the work in the Cambridge Cluster School.

As this work progressed in Brookline, another educational intervention was taking place in Cambridge High and Latin School, a traditional school with a thoroughly heterogeneous student population. A group of parents, whose children had not been able to obtain entrance to an already existing school-within-a-school, asked school officials to open another alternative school unit. The officials turned to Lawrence Kohlberg in the summer of 1974, and he agreed to become a consultant. Although he had the full support of the superintendent and the high school principal, most of the faculty members were not familiar with his work.

About seventy students were recruited for this school-within-a-school that became known as the Cluster School. Eight faculty members volunteered and were accepted without screening. They had a variety of academic backgrounds (science, physical education, social studies, counseling, and so forth) and within the Cluster School, they conducted the community meetings and taught the social studies and English courses. On the whole, they were unprepared for these tasks. None of them had ever led a community meeting or conducted a moral discussion, none was familiar with Kohlberg's research, and most were not trained in either English or social studies.

Early in the school year, the staff and the student body drew up a constitution setting forth a set of rules and a method of carrying them out. Each person in the school community, staff and student alike, had one vote on the adoption of the rules, and each had one vote in the community meetings. Long discussions in which everyone participates precede any action by the community. During these discussions, students and staff alike constantly encounter real-life moral dilemmas: How should you punish a student who has broken the rule against stealing when you know that other students have also stolen and were not caught? Should you suspend a member of the community who constantly disrupts classes but who has found his first real home in the community?

Students have only their social studies and English courses in the Cluster School; they take the remainder of their academic work in the wider Cambridge High and Latin School. Because the staff of the Cluster School had had no time to prepare a new curriculum in social studies and English, they decided to teach mini-courses partly in response to what students requested.

This situation presented an in-service education task of frightening proportions. Kohlberg acted as the consultant, and was assisted by two young graduate students and occasionally by some of his colleagues. His experience with Just Communities had been gained in a women's prison in Connecticut where he had worked as a consultant for several years. He had never been a high school teacher nor had he developed curricular materials for English or social studies courses. He and the staff of the school were immediately faced with the task of getting the community organized and the governance structure set up.

Kohlberg attended the weekly community meetings throughout the fall. The student body was divided into small counseling groups that met to discuss issues scheduled to come before the community meetings. After these sessions, the entire community met in a single room under the leadership of either a staff member or a student. Much of the in-service training took place in these community meetings as staff members learned by doing. In addition, Kohlberg conducted long staff meetings each week to discuss what was happening in the school to help to build skills. He used recordings and transcripts of community meetings as the basis of many discussions in staff meetings. After a chaotic beginning, the community meetings slowly took form, and by the end of the year, ran very well.

In the meantime, the formal curriculum in social studies and English was not faring well. Teachers had no time to prepare interesting mini-courses because each of them taught a full load (two classes in the Just Community School and three outside it) and now had the new responsibilities of community meetings. Nor did they have time to learn how to lead moral discussions in their classes. Hence, the formal curriculum of the courses and the informal or hidden curriculum of the governance structure never merged to become a single educational experience.

During the summer of 1975, the faculty of the Cluster School worked on a new curriculum in English and social studies. Each person was paid to attend a week's workshop, and Kohlberg brought in several consultants. The group decided to purchase multiple copies of several texts to form the core of each course rather than try to develop entirely new courses. They incorporated moral discussions into the curriculum. School opened that year on a much more placid note than it did in 1974. Most of the staff returned as did most of the students. This year, Kohlberg and Mosher will run a workshop for teachers in Cambridge High and Latin School to introduce them to the theory and practice of moral discussions and to build a support base for the Cluster School. Since Brookline is opening a Just Community School, it is clear that the two systems have exchanged their particular field of experience to build two coherent programs of moral education each of which will have both a governance structure and a series of moral discussions built into the formal curriculum.

Much has been learned from these experiences. Kohlberg and Mosher have been conducting a careful program of research to test the effectiveness of these programs. Until these research results are in, I can offer you only hypotheses about similar programs of moral education. Here are some important ones:

1. A program of moral education needs the enthusiastic support of the chief school officer. Only this person can mobilize resources, enlist the support of the community, and cause things to happen. If opposed to a program, the chief school officer can kill it quickly.
2. Educators should involve the wider community in order to avoid trouble. The School Committees in both Brookline and Cambridge have been kept informed, and each has endorsed the program. A parent workshop was held in Brookline to help enlist parent support. So far, no one has complained.
3. Consultants must get teachers involved and enthusiastic by treating teachers as colleagues and by joining them in classrooms and community meetings. Without enthusiastic, voluntary teachers, no such project can succeed.
4. A successful program of moral education can develop only over a long period of time. (The Brookline and Cambridge projects run for three years.) Teachers need time to learn a sophisticated rationale, to internalize techniques required to lead moral discussions, to learn how to write moral dilemmas, and to learn how to live as a member of a community where a teacher must share authority with students.

5. A program requires careful, long-range planning and substantial financial resources to pay for consultants, materials, and curriculum work during the summer. A knowledgeable and dedicated consultant or group of consultants who know developmental psychology and curriculum theory are absolutely indispensable for success.
6. Programs should be evaluated as soon as possible to help determine the future direction of the program and furnish evidence that a program is valuable enough to be continued. (The staff of the Cluster School is using a participant observer supplemented by information derived from moral interviews and from interviews with students). Once a new curriculum has been developed, the staff should probably use standardized tests for basic social studies and English skills to assure parents that these vital elements are not missing from the program.

The staff of the Social Studies Curriculum Center at Carnegie-Mellon University has joined with five school districts in and near Pittsburgh to begin a new in-service program during the present academic year. A twenty-week Staff Development Seminar beginning in January will precede the openings of two units (to be called Civic Education Schools) in each of the five high schools beginning in September, 1976. The core staff consists of myself (half-time), a full time consultant on social studies curriculum, a full time consultant in English curriculum, and several graduate students. A teacher from each of the five schools works for the project full time. The Danforth Foundation has provided financial support that is supplemented by a grant from the Commonwealth of Pennsylvania under Title IV. The project has already been approved by the Chief School Officer of each of the five districts involved, and a round of meetings with school faculties has been conducted.

Each high school will choose between ten and twelve volunteers to attend the Staff Development Seminar. They will include social studies teachers, English teachers, counselors, an administrator, and parents or school board members. The seminar will meet for two hours each week. Participants will not be paid, but they will receive graduate credit from Carnegie-Mellon University, and graduate credit can be used to obtain a salary increment. At the end of the seminar, participants should know enough of Kohlberg's theory to understand the principles behind Civic Education Schools, to be able to lead moral discussions to the satisfaction of the core staff, be able to develop moral dilemmas as the basis for moral discussions, and know how to run community meetings. The members of the core staff visit teachers on request in their classes during the period the Seminar meets. At least one person from each school will spend a week during this time visiting the Cluster School in Cambridge and the School-Within-a-School at Brookline.

A curriculum development program will take place parallel to the staff development program. During their first year, each Civic Education School will enroll all of its students (an equal number from grades ten, eleven, and twelve) in the same social studies and English courses. These courses were carefully designed for the full context of a Civic Education School. The core staff people are mainly responsible for providing materials and an organizing theme, and work closely with members of the seminar. Each school will have a full-time representative to do curricular work and adapt the new courses to the particular needs of individual schools.

The first social studies course in the series is an extremely flexible course built around a number of units that can be used in various orders according to special needs. The Community Meeting itself will be an integral part of the course, the heart of civic education in the school. The remainder of the course is designed to help students understand what a community is all about and to learn how to run a community meeting. The following are some possible units.

The Meaning of Community. An investigation by committees of a variety of voluntary, blood-related, geographic, or economic communities to find who joins, what benefits they receive, what obligations they have, and how the communities treat members who fail to meet their obligations. Individual papers should analyze what students learned from the unit that applies to their community.

Deciding How to Organize a Community. Based on the research of Joseph Adelson, this unit would use a questionnaire with ten-year olds, community members, and adults to determine how they think a new community would perform such functions as choosing leaders, punishing rulebreakers, making laws, and so forth. Comparing returns will teach basic data processing skills, reveal the developmental nature of political thought, and provide rich insights into how to organize a community in a school.

Deciding How to Punish Rulebreakers. In this unit, committees could study and report about ways in which a variety of societies have handled rulebreakers—trial by ordeal in the Middle Ages, trial by the mob during the French Revolution, trial by a single judge, trial by jury, and so forth. This unit should help students to examine alternative ways to handle rulebreakers in their own community.

Choosing Decision Makers. Committees can study and report on a variety of ways to choose decision makers as they think about how they want to choose decision-makers for their community. These ways can be organized around case studies such as choice by lot in ancient Athens, choice by co-option in the Soviet Union, choice by seniority in Congress, choice by election in democratic societies, and so forth.

The Decision Making Process. Again working in committees, students can study and report on the ways in which decisions are made in institutions as diverse as the Society of Friends, the United States Army, a New England town, a traditional society, or the American Congress. They should apply what they learn to their own community.

Becoming a Member of a Community. In an attempt to establish criteria for choosing new members of their community, students could study and report about ways in which organizations develop a system for choosing new members and inducting them into the society. They might study a confirmation or Bar Mitzvah, becoming a United States citizen, joining a sorority or fraternity, joining a religious order, or undergoing puberty rites in a traditional society.

The Aims of the Community School. This unit should introduce students to the theory behind the organization of community schools. Students should learn basic information about developmental psychology and civic education. As a final exercise, class members should draw up a set of goals for their own community.

Running Community Meetings. A nuts-and-bolts unit, this part of the course should help students to learn rules of order, study ways to control distracting individuals, and assess practical ways to conduct business.

During the spring semester, each high school will make plans to open two Civic Education Schools. Each Civic Education School will consist of roughly sixty students drawn in about equal numbers from grades ten, eleven, and twelve, and representing a cross section of the wider student body. They will study only English and social studies in separate classes, taking the remainder of their courses in regular sections of the high school. These students must be recruited, and must enter the Civic Education Schools as volunteers.

When these Civic Education Schools open, they should be well staffed with trained people. They should have carefully prepared formal courses in social studies and English. Each staff should have worked out a school philosophy and a set of objectives. A member of the CMU core staff will be assigned to each school as a full-time colleague during the initial year of work. During the same year a second Staff Development Seminar will be held to prepare a new set of teachers for the second year courses and test the format of the staff development seminar before it is exported elsewhere. We also intend to stay in close touch with our colleagues in Cambridge and Brookline so that the three projects can learn from each other and share materials.

In the immediate future, most schools should not make preparations to establish multi-unit Civic Education Schools. Educators should wait until the Harvard and CMU groups have developed new courses, put together successful staff development programs, and provided research results for school personnel to assess. In the meantime, many school systems want to incorporate modest programs of moral discussions into their ongoing social studies and English programs. Larry Kohlberg and I want to provide materials for the in-service work implied by that goal. We have made arrangements with Guidance Associates to publish materials for a six-hour teacher workshop and two sets of moral discussion materials for high school social studies, one in American History and the other in Civics/Problems of Democracy. I shall describe these materials with some hesitation because I distrust in-service "packages," even ones I have put together myself.

We have in mind a kit containing four sound filmstrips and a variety of printed materials. The audience for which we intend these materials is composed of average and above average social studies teachers, although teachers from any discipline should be able to use them with profit. We intend to design the materials so that they can be used by an individual teacher or, preferably, in a workshop with a trained leader.

We will begin such a workshop by having its members take part in a moral discussion. One of the sound filmstrips will contain three moral dilemmas designed for classroom use. We will play one of these dilemmas and then lead a discussion based on it with all of the members of the workshop taking part. A debriefing will follow in which participants will be asked to write a list of adjectives describing how they felt as they discussed (conflicted, involved, angry) and to identify the skills that the teacher and the students must have in order to carry on a good moral discussion.

Next we will play a sound filmstrip on which Kohlberg explains his findings. It will contain two lock grooves so that participants will be able to react to what they have been seeing and hearing on a worksheet that will accompany the recording. Then, in order to help participants grasp the idea of a stage, we will distribute envelopes containing slips of paper on each of which is written a response to the moral dilemma that the participants have already discussed. We will provide a dozen responses, two or three at each stage from one through five. Then we will divide the participants into small groups, asking each group to arrange the responses by stages and to be prepared to report on their classification scheme. This exercise will have an incidental benefit because it will familiarize participants with typical responses at several stages to a dilemma they can use in class. Knowing what responses may be forthcoming helps a teacher prepare for a moral discussion with some assurance.

We will follow this exercise with another sound filmstrip, again with lock grooves, which will explain the principles of leading a moral discussion. It will get at grouping students, asking probe questions, and similar techniques. Exercises designed to develop each essential skill will follow in dittoed form.

The last item in the kit is another sound filmstrip. It will contain a discussion among several teachers about how to get started in a program of moral discussions. They will explain how to obtain dilemmas, how to incorporate moral discussions into ongoing course work, and similar subjects. They will also explain how to use two self-evaluation instruments we have been working on. One is an adaptation of an interaction analysis system specifically developed for moral discussions. The other traces through a recommended teaching process to help a teacher assess areas that may require additional work. We will recommend that teachers use these instruments on videotapes of their classes or that teachers observe each other using these instruments. In closing, the teachers on the sound-filmstrip will suggest that teachers should use the moral dilemma that they have discussed in the workshop as the basis of the first moral discussion in their own classes. They will already be familiar with the dilemma and hence be more likely to succeed.

All of us know that a one day experience will not make skilled leaders of moral discussions out of typical teachers. We will try to be of additional help in several ways. We will leave with each teacher a copy of the April, 1976 issue of *Social Education* that is devoted entirely to moral education in the social studies. The new sets of sound-filmstrips from *Guidance Associates* in American History and Civics/Problems of Democracy will provide tested materials. Providing self-assessment materials should also be helpful, even though these materials require substantial skills to use. In addition, we want to organize a follow-up procedure using videotape. Members of the staff of CMU's Social Studies Curriculum Center have contracted to follow up three workshops that we will run this fall by analyzing videotapes sent to us by teachers. We intend to develop an efficient and nonthreatening system design to improve instruction by providing useful feedback at relatively small expense to a school system.

We have one additional idea for in-service work in this field. We wish to establish Mid-Career Internships of one semester at CMU beginning in September, 1976. To these internships we hope to attract experienced teachers, possibly teachers on sabbatical leave. We want to give them an intensive one-semester experience that will enable them to become leaders of in-service work in moral and civic education in their own schools. In the meantime, we have plenty to do in order to make sure that what we have to share with them will be first rate.

Mediated Instruction and In-Service Education of Teachers

Bruce R. Joyce

Stanford Center for Research and Development in Teaching

Media use in schools has fluctuated widely in the past two decades. The relative hunger for the use of effective media is indicated by the fact that 23 percent of elementary schools made some use of "The Electric Company" programs in their first year of operation. Many of the nation's schools are well-equipped with television sets, projectors of various kinds, tape recorders, and the capability for language laboratories. In addition, a wealth of materials has been produced utilizing media of all kinds, including television.

There are two sources of data and ideas relative to in-service teacher education and mediated instruction.[1] One of these is the study of the behavior of teachers when they are using media or when they are involved in man/machine educational systems. The second is the theoretical and empirical study about the nature of the media. In this article, I will draw from both sources to discuss some of the studies that give us insight about teachers and media. Although there is, incredibly enough, no decent body of literature on the roles of teachers in mediated systems, there does exist literature that deals with mediated systems and there are a few outstanding studies about the reciprocal roles of teachers. With these we can improvise a framework on which we can base a stance for in-service education. I will attempt to squeeze meaning out of those small bodies of literature that exist, and to generate a set of propositions for in-service work in mediated instruction with teachers

1. Instruction that utilizes print, audio, or visual media or a combination thereof as important components.

based on this literature and on my personal experience with various media.

In examining the literature related to media and education, it is clear that teachers are interested in using media, and that the equipment is available. Unfortunately, the literature is incredibly weak with respect to the behavior of the teacher when dealing with media. Reports about the utilization of "Sesame Street" are often cited. In fact, almost half of the media/education literature currently stored in ERIC deals with "Sesame Street" or "The Electric Company." But a recent view of "Sesame Street" points out that children learn about as much when they watch "Sesame Street" in classrooms or at home by themselves as they do when they watch in the presence of a parent or a teacher.[2] However, we *cannot* conclude from this that the teacher is unimportant with respect to media or even that he or she might not be important in mediated instructional systems. The "Sesame Street" programs were designed to be self-administering (self-viewing) and no specific roles were planned for teachers or parents. In addition, the objectives of "Sesame Street" were measured on the program's terms (and had to be). Teachers may have generated their own objectives and carried out procedures relative to them, but the evaluation of "Sesame Street" could not possibly have taken this into account. We will return to "Sesame Street" after reviewing some earlier studies that also examine the relationship of teachers to media.

The best study of the use of media is the Guba and Snyder study, "Instructional Television and the Classroom Teacher."[3] This is an exemplary study that has not been followed-up by the kinds of cumulative investigation it should have generated. No investigator or group of investigators has developed a cumulative line of research on teachers and media; consequently, we have relatively little depth of data to go on as we talk about the problems of in-service education in a media context.

Egon Guba and Clinton A. Snyder examined teachers' uses of television programs broadcast from an airplane over the Midwest during the early 1960s. They asked a variety of questions: Do teachers who incorporate instructional television into their classrooms differ in

2. Samuel Ball and Gerry Ann Bogatz, "Sesame Street Summative Research: Some Implications for Education and Child Development," (Princeton, New Jersey: Educational Testing Service). Paper presented at the American Psychological Association Annual Meeting, Washington, D.C., September 7, 1971.

3. Egon G. Guba and Clinton A. Snyder, "Instructional Television and the Classroom Teacher," *A-V Communications Review,* 13, (1965) pp. 5–27.

their instructional behavior from teachers who do not use television? What patterns of utilization of television exist? Do the patterns of utilization recorded by teachers actually using instructional television differ from the patterns of utilization that nonusers imagine they would adopt? Do teachers using instructional television generally have a more favorable attitude toward new instructional media than do non-using teachers? Do teachers using instructional television generally have a more favorable attitude toward instructional television than do nonusing teachers?

Guba and Snyder studied 72 elementary schools believed to be representative of the 316 elementary schools that, in late 1962, were members of the IMPATI system. They studied 56 schools that were using IMPATI and 46 schools that were not using IMPATI but that were matched with members of the 56 schools. The sample of teachers eventually included 322 users of IMPATI and 275 nonusers.

They concluded from their attitude survey that nearly all the teachers felt relatively unprepared to use instructional television, or more particularly, to understand the goals of television vis-a-vis classroom instruction and the special uses they should make of television. The teachers who used television generally developed more favorable attitudes toward it than teachers who had no experience with it. The teachers who did not use television were much more concerned that it might usurp the teacher's role. The nonusers also expected that there would be more unusual uses of television and teachers' roles with respect to it than did the users, who found that television really did not have as much of an impact on their general behavior as they had expected that it might.

The most important information from the study concerns the behavior of teachers when they attempt to use the IMPATI programs. The most important conclusion is that the classroom teacher's role is affected very little by the introduction of instructional television. Part of this may have been because most of the programs were relatively straightforward lectures with the "talking face" of the lecturer being presented to the viewers. The "talking face" is not as much of an intrusion into the norms of the classroom situation as, for example, simulation games.

The second conclusion from the Guba and Snyder study is that "the patterns of utilization of instructional television are conventional and stereotypic." The television shows were used "heavily as a replacement for the telling and showing function, at least for the content covered in the lesson. . . . There is a lead-in and a follow-up, but the studio teacher does the major teaching job. The classroom teacher follows up, building upon what has been in the lesson." The television face simply provided some of the kinds of functions that teachers ordinarily provide and the teachers followed it up much as they might their own lectures. The important thing here is that the television intervention did not make much of a break in the kinds of patterns employed by the teachers.

What surprised many people at the time was the *relative unimportance* of the television programs. "The televised lesson, whatever it may be, is often seen as an interlude or break in the usual routine of the classroom. Following its completion, the teacher returns to whatever it was he or she was doing before. As one respondent put it, 'We were interrupted by the telelesson.' " This is probably not surprising since teachers must consider their own interactive teaching role in a much more complex way, psychologically, than they do an external intervention around which they build their behavior and that of the students. Quite clearly, television had relatively little impact on those classrooms and was not particularly disturbing to the patterns of behavior either of the teachers or the students before television came along.

Another study of the same period was conducted by Sydney Eboch along with Egon Guba and Wesley Meierhenry.[4] Although it does not deal specifically with television, it provides us with a good deal of information about the impact of media on the classroom situation. The Eboch, Guba and Meierhenry study was carried out through the Ohio State Research Foundation in 1966 and was supported by the United States Office of Education. It was an evaluation of Project Discovery, which was instigated by the Bell and Howell Company and Encyclopedia Brittannica. These companies conceived the idea of placing 500 motion pictures and 1000 filmstrips plus an assortment of projectors in a series of elementary schools in order to determine what kinds of uses teachers would make of such media and to study how their roles would be affected. One of the schools was in Shaker Heights, Ohio, one in Daly City, California, one was an inner city school in Washington, D.C., and there were three elementary schools and two high schools in Terrell, Texas (this comprised the entire school district).

The materials mentioned above were placed in each one of the schools. Participant/observers spent a full year in each site interviewing

4. S. C. Eboch, ed., with E. G. Guba and W. C. Meierhenry, *Novel Strategies and Tactics for Field Studies of New Educational Media Demonstrations* (Columbus: The Ohio State Research Foundation, 1965).

principals and teachers, giving questionnaires to teachers and students, making observations in the classroom, and assisting the teachers in making records of the use of the materials. In the five elementary schools involved during that year, there were more than 13,000 uses of the materials, or about one hundred thirty per teacher, which amounts to two uses in every three school days. The median uses of the films alone per teacher ranged from thirty-three to eighty-five, and the range across all teachers in the study was from ten to one hundred eighty-seven. That is, one teacher used the materials as few as ten times during the entire school year, and one teacher used something nearly every day. The teachers vastly preferred films to filmstrips.

With respect to teaching styles, the study found that the teachers usually worked with the children in a whole group situation about three-fourths of the time. The discussions were generally teacher-oriented and prescriptive, and the questions asked were, by and large, convergent. The teachers generally did the summarizing. Discussions of key points or points of clarification were initiated by the teachers about twenty times to each time the students initiated such discussions. It was relatively rare that a student raised a question that was responded to by a teacher in a clarifying manner. The teachers tended to select the points they thought should be clarified and dealt with those. The same was true with respect to assignments. When media were used, assignments were given about 40 percent of the time and student-initiated assignments occurred only about one-twentieth as often as teacher-selected assignments.

On the whole, the teachers did not integrate the films and print media, but treated the media as supplementary. Eboch, Guba, and Meierhenry concluded that generally the teachers went on doing what they usually did and that the project did not result in innovations in teaching styles or strategies. But the project apparently met the real need of teachers to have plentiful supplies of materials at hand. They were delighted with the materials and expressed high satisfaction with the project. They had very little difficulty adapting the media to their normal modes of instruction and, rather than inventing new modes of instruction to accommodate the media, generally went on doing what they had been doing and found ways of fitting the media into their normal patterns of instruction. Instruction, as far as the teachers were concerned, was technically easy, and they almost literally gobbled up the media that were available and asked for more when the project was concluded.

From these studies, one would have to conclude that media had a relatively small impact on the teaching and learning styles of the classroom, and that normal modes of teacher and student behavior appeared able to assimilate media on their own terms rather rapidly. One could also conclude that if it were felt desirable for teachers to use teaching strategies that were uniquely adapted to the requirements of media, then extensive in-service teacher training would probably be necessary. The teachers were comfortable both with television and with the films and filmstrips, but either did not feel that they needed special teaching strategies for using them or did not have these special teaching strategies in their repertoire.

Although the studies by Samuel Ball and Gerry Bogatz of the utilization of "Sesame Street" and "The Electric Company" were not nearly as extensive with respect to teacher behavior, essentially the same pattern appears to emerge.[5] Teachers were glad to incorporate both types of programs into their classrooms and appeared to deal with them in much the same way they dealt with other kinds of materials. Often teachers would orient the students to the programs, would interrupt the programs for clarification, and would summarize or generate follow-up activities. On the whole, those programs were not integrated into the larger programs of instruction but were permitted to stand on their own terms. Teachers were much more positive toward "Sesame Street" and "The Electric Company" than they were about the IMPATI programs. Perhaps this is because times have changed and teachers are more comfortable with television and other media in general. It may also be because facilities for receiving televised programs have become much better over the years. (There seems to be little doubt that this is true; the facilities in the early 1960s were not at all good and current facilities are very, very good in many cases.) Finally, the programs are a lot better today than they were then. The "talking face" appears less often and, especially in the case of the programs produced by Children's Television Workshop, a variety of media uses, such as animation, are incorporated into the instructional systems.

It must be said that the Children's Television Workshop did not design its programs to incorporate teacher roles directly into the mediated system. Both "Sesame Street" and "The Electric Company" are self-contained instructional systems, and "Sesame Street" especially was very effective on its own terms. Essentially, the role of the human

5. Ball and Bogatz, "Sesame Street."

training agent in such systems is primarily to help the children have access to the programs and to follow up as the children initiate a need for clarification or understanding. The programs simply were not designed around major models of teaching that provide specific roles for the teacher integrated into the roles occupied by the mediated material. Thus, the teacher has no planned instructional role.

Nearly all of the outstanding programs in recent years have been self-contained instructional systems of this sort, which is no doubt one reason why there is so little literature on teacher utilization.

MEDIATED SYSTEMS BUILT AROUND STRATEGIES THAT INCORPORATE TEACHER ROLES

Although there have been relatively few examples of mediated systems that have been deliberately planned with respect to the teacher role, the few are significant. Most common are the highly structured instructional systems such as Individually Prescribed Instruction (IPI), but other kinds concentrating in one subject area such as social studies have also been developed.

IPI was built around particular curriculum areas, with its most notable development concentrated in reading and arithmetic. However, it was designed around an instructional strategy that incorporated specific teacher roles and also made provisions for aides and other personnel. Schools using IPI to make the curriculum change needed differentiated roles among its staff. Under the reorganization plan, teachers and aides play specific roles and relate to the materials-based instruction in prescribed ways. IPI also included training systems to help prepare the teachers and aides to operate the system and to accommodate to the new roles that were required of them, recognizing that teachers would need training to fill their new roles.

The Foreign Policy Association and the Twenty-one Inch Classroom in Boston generated a program known as "Cabinets in Crisis" several years ago that was built around the concept underlying game-type situations. In the television studios, performers played the roles of members of the United States Cabinet at particular crisis times. The program classes could communicate to the studio the kinds of things that they thought particular cabinet members or the cabinet in general should do. The cabinet members could then respond to these instructions in such a way that the consequences of the changed actions could be seen. For example, if a cabinet member was instructed to behave in a certain way, it was easy to see how the other members of the cabinet would respond to him as a consequence of this change in behavior. Thus, "Cabinets in Crisis" was an integrated man/machine system in the sense that there were roles for teachers and students, as well as for the television portions of the instructional system.

Even more complex, and with even more explicit attention to the teacher role, was the "Operation Moon Vigil." "Operation Moon Vigil" was also a simulation beamed largely over broadcast television. The instructional system consisted of several components. One of these was the broadcast program in which actors simulated the functions of "Mission Control." Mission Control announced to the students (who simulated the crew of a spaceship) that their craft, which was about to leave the moon for earth, had malfunctioned, and they would be required to stay on the moon for an undetermined period of time while attempts were made to enable the ship to return to earth. Instructions were given to organize themselves into groups and to look in their specially prepared packets for further instructions about what to do to preserve their life support systems and maintain contact with mission control. The notion was that the communication between the spaceship and earth had been broken except for period broadcasts by mission control. The crew of the spaceship could not communicate to earth and had to receive the instructions and information solely through the television set. The packets that were used in the classrooms organized the students into teams that were responsible for tending to various aspects of the life support systems. The roles of the students were so constructed that some students had relatively prominent roles while others had relatively routine and wearisome ones. In addition, decisions had to be made about the conservation of resources. This process was organized in such a way that students could feel the problem of dividing scarce resources and placing the authority for that division in the hands of a relatively select group of people. The result was an interesting dynamic, and once the operation was successfully completed and the spaceship had returned to earth, the teachers debriefed the students about the patterns of interpersonal relations that had developed in the course of the simulation. These patterns almost always brought the students to an awareness of the dynamics of conflict and cooperation and problems that arise from status differentiation. The simulation used the media to create a very realistic situation, used packets of print material to generate an interesting interpersonal situation, and developed the role of the human teacher around the function of human relations trainer. With this kind of organization the teacher's role was very important and, in addition, he was doing what the human teacher could do best, while the media were being used to create realism and set problems to the students that would be very difficult for the human teacher working alone. "Operation Moon Vigil" combined television, print material, and the role of the human teacher simultaneously and intelligently, using an appropriate curricular strategy. Under these conditions, the teacher has an important role for which he may well need (and be happy to receive) training. When the mediated system has no place for the teacher then there is little basis for orienting training and, in addition, teachers have little reason to feel benign about either the media or training.

PROPOSITIONS FOR ACTION

It is incredible to this observer that the literature does not contain many more examples such as "Operation Moon Vigil" and "Cabinets in Crisis" (although they are not the only representatives of the use of complex teaching strategies to organize instructional systems). There are simply relatively few cases where the human teacher is used effectively in relation to the capability of the media. The bulk of the programs beamed over television have been self-contained instructional systems, with the teacher playing the role of introducer, summarizer, and drill-master in relation to the media. This does not make maximum use either of the television, which is being expected to carry a bigger instructional load than is appropriate, or the teacher, who is seriously underutilized. It is important to develop a comprehensive set of strategies that can integrate various forms of media and appropriate teacher roles.

This section offers, therefore, a series of propositions in two areas. One of these areas is the relationship between media-related roles and the functions of the human teacher. With respect to the development of media-related roles, it appears that television can be used with respect to a variety of types of roles. Much of the literature either assumes that the teacher is not an important part of the educational scene and that he or she should be in the hands of an instructional system along with the students, or it assumes that media are relatively helpless with respect to the life of the student and that all instruction should be in the hands of the teacher. It would appear wiser to develop a set of multiple roles. The second area deals with the media substance to be taught, an area addressed in the theoretical literature but almost totally neglected in the practical literature. The important 1973 Schramm volume deals with almost everything related to the use of media except the teacher, although it is implicit that the human agent is an important part of any mediated instructional system.[6] The extensive 1974 yearbook on "Media and Symbols in Education" also deals very little with the teacher.[7] It is small wonder that teachers may feel alienated by the introduction of media. "Why shouldn't they?" we may ask, when the literature ignores them as totally as it does.

Proposition One: Instruction Mediated Through the Teacher. A teacher's role can be developed in relation to a course that is primarily mediated through television or another form of media. With that type of media use, the teacher role becomes that of facilitator, supporter, and helper. The outstanding example of this is the English open university that uses print instructional systems, television courses, and tutors. The tutors help the students to master the course that is presented in the media. The tutor knows that this is his task and has to accept it wholeheartedly. The teacher did not construct the course, develop the television programs, or write the material; what the teacher is expected to do is help the student learn how to study, help the student solve problems, and help the student with information that he or she finds difficult to acquire.

Proposition Two: The Media/Teacher Interactive Curriculum. The examples of "Cabinets in Crisis" and "Operation Moon Vigil," as well as the IPI system, are developed with a comprehensive strategy in mind, a strategy that provides roles for the media and the teacher that capitalize on the unique capabilities of each. There are a variety of types of models that can be used to generate interactive systems such as these, and there is no reason why a great deal more mediated instruction could not utilize interactive strategies.

Proposition Three: Media as a Resource to the Student. The following discussion is based on some of my own work in building data banks for children. Data banks for children provide mediated instruction in which technology is used to integrate material in the learning environment, not merely to provide an external addition (such as showing a film).

6. Wilbur Schramm, ed., *Quality in Instructt Television* (Honolulu: The University of Hawaii Press, 1972).
7. D. R. Olson, ed., *Media and Symbols: The Forms of Expression, Communication and Education*, the Seventy-third Yearbook of the National Society for the Study of Education (Chicago: University of Chicago Press, 1974).

Whenever we bring information to a student, we *edit* it. That is, we put some things in and leave other things out. We also *structure* it. We organize it in certain kinds of ways that reflect our frames of reference and that are limited and extended by the present state of our vision. *Our focus is on creating information systems for students in which both editing and structuring are minimized or are controlled in known ways that can be made apparent to the student so that he knows how editing and structuring affect the information sources with which he is brought into contact.* How we should go about this task is the subject of our work.

Strategy for Initial Exploration

In approaching the problem of creating information systems for students, it is necessary to conduct two kinds of work more or less alternately and in conjunction with each other. One kind of work is to create information systems according to particular specifications and principles that seem to have known characteristics with respect to editing and structuring what is offered to the children. The second is to conduct research on children's utilization of those systems, exploring the effects of features of the systems on the children's behavior. Then, after the interaction of the children with the system has been studied, elements of the system can be recreated and the empirical work repeated until gradually a set of principles begins to emerge. These principles form the first fluid edge of a technology for creating information systems for young children and for teaching them in a setting characterized by random access to large quantities of information. Because the first data banks were developed to bring information to children about communities representing various world cultures, we use those communities as referents in the description of our beginning work. Most of the referents are derived from a Pueblo community that served as the information source for the first extensive data bank.

Initial Operating Principles of Data Banks

Our developmental work began with the definition of a set of five principles by which information would be edited and structured in known ways. These principles guided the development of the information system and provided a focus for the first set of research studies.

Principle 1: *Use a defined and very broad category system for searching for data for the banks.*

One of the ways in which we edit the world for students is by choosing the data that we bring to them. We can describe a community, for example, *only* in terms of its economic system, or only in terms of the things people wear, or from a perspective of art, politics, or family life. In order to reduce the editorial effect of the search for information one can select a very broad category system that covers many aspects of a community. By using this broad category system to obtain information to be stored for children, one obligates oneself to study many aspects of the community rather than just a few sides of it. Logically, the more aspects of the community that are studied as information sources, the smaller one's bias probably becomes. The more *defined* the category system used, the easier it becomes to specify its framework in order to make it obvious to the student that he is not faced with information that has been edited by an unseen hand. Also, the defined system provides a point of departure. Alternative category systems can be compared with it and studied in relation to it. *No category system can entirely eliminate editing.* The broadest system cannot eliminate editing *within* the categories nor do we know of any system broad enough to eliminate *any* bias.

Hence, our first task was to select an exceedingly broad category system and use it to study the communities that were to be the sources of the data banks for children. At the suggestion of David E. Hunt, Professor of Psychology, The Ontario Institute for Studies in Education, we began with the index to the Human Relations Area Files.[8] This index contains more than 700 categories and 629 subcategories. For example, the major category "geography" is subdivided into seven subcategories: location, climate, topography, soil, mineral resources, fauna, and flora. The general category "demography" is broken down into eight subcategories: population, composition of a population, birth statistics, morbidity, mortality, internal migration, immigration, emigration and population policy. Under "interpersonal relations" we found social relationships and groups, friendship cliques, visiting and hospitality, sodalities, etiquette, ethics, ingroup antagonisms, and brawls and riots.

Collection of Data Sources Relating to the Community

Principle 2: *Use original sources as much as possible.*

A second principle was to fill all possible categories of the search system with information from the many firsthand sources available in order to build the information system as close to the real life of the

8. G. P. Murdock, et al., *Outline of Cultural Materials,* 4th revised ed. (Human Relations Area Files, Inc., 1961).

Pueblo as could possibly be done. We engaged in the following procedures with respect to the Pueblo culture. A Pueblo community (henceforth referred to as "La Stella") was selected as content for the first data bank because a great deal of information was available on it and the other Pueblo communities; it is a relatively easy place to get to from most places in North America; and yet it is not a typical American community. Its multicultural aspects (the influence of Indian, Spanish, and Northern European culture) made it attractive as a source for the first bank because many possible types of children's inquiry would be possible and the first investigations could thus explore more aspects of children's use. The atypicality of the community was also desirable: because so few eastern American children have more than superficial knowledge of Pueblo life, learning experiments could be designed to determine what the children learned about the culture as a result of the experience within the data system.

Transformation and Classification of the Documents

The major developmental efforts were transforming the material into a form that children could use in classifying the transformed material into the area file categories. A serious problem appeared to be that material was available in vastly different quantities for various historical periods. At length, we decided to attempt to provide documents for the area file categories in four periods of the Pueblo's life:

1. the prehistoric period, before the Spanish influence, with evidence from archeology
2. the period of the "early anthropologists" from about 1865–1895, after the Spanish influence but prior to much contact with English America
3. the early twentieth century, when English-American influences can be discerned and the contact between the cultures was intensifying
4. the contemporary period

These groupings would, hopefully, enable children to explore processes of cultural interchange and contemporary problems, but would keep the data bank from becoming impossibly complex. As it was, we were attempting to fill four "observation periods" for each of the 600 subcategories of the area file, or more than 2400 subcategories altogether. Since the system was in a continuous state of revisions, the number of categories for which documents were available varied. At peak, over 70 percent of the categories contained at least one document. The documentary evidence about Pueblo life consisted of pictures, written material, graphs, charts, and maps. This material was culled, reworked, and classified into area file categories: written material was rewritten, statistical data was formed into charts, and written passages were constructed to accompany pictures, charts, and maps.

The process is most easily described through examples, for instance, in the "animal husbandry" category. The material for this area is built around several pictures. The pictures are accompanied by a recording or descriptive written material. For example:

> Picture Number 2202: The village of La Stella is in this land. There isn't very much rainfall here. The horses and cattle of the people who live in the villages have to go a long way to find grass to eat.
>
> Picture Number 2054: The Indians of the village of La Stella have fenced in their fields for their animals. The fencing in this picture is wire. When a field is fenced in, it is called a corral.
>
> Picture Number 2266: The horses of the village of La Stella are used many times for celebrations. Here a horse is being led onto the field. It will be a part of the show the people are putting on.

Storage and Retrieval

At this point the entire mass of material was photographed and reduced to 35-millimeter slides. All written material for each area file was then tape-recorded. The slides were placed in storage trays, and the tapes were numbered consecutively and placed nearby. Large maps of La Stella, displays of pictures and artifacts, and posters were prepared. Carrels large enough to write in were built to hold tape recorders, slide projectors, a small projection screen, and a small map.

Principle 3: *Store the information in such a way that the students will have maximum random access to it.*

To help us in the task of storing this information in modules that could be retrieved by the student in accordance with questions that he might ask, we again utilized the Human Relations Area File, which provides a very broad index system. It enables students to retrieve information at many of the possible points for entering the study of a culture. Its chief disadvantage probably lies in its complexity and, therefore, the difficulty of teaching it directly to the students (some uses would undoubtedly require knowledge of the index by the user). In other words, a broad, intricate system helps the learner obtain exactly what he wants and reduces the amount of unwanted information that is retrieved in response to a request. However, it may bring the most benefit to a sophisticated user who can comprehend the classification system and learn how to use it to further his own ends. Students used the data in the following manner.

1. To get information, students simply asked a question. The question was translated by an adult attendant into an area file category.
2. The student took the number of the category to the storage center, where he located and retrieved slides and tapes and carried them to his carrel.
3. In the carrel, he showed himself the slides and listened to the tapes, seeking the answer to his question. When finished, he returned the material and asked another question, beginning the cycle again as his new question was translated into an area file category.
4. Each individual student was permitted to ask questions for several hours (working one hour at a time) and then was asked to make a tape recording describing the Pueblo. He was also interviewed to obtain impressions about what he had learned, difficulties he had working with the system, his understanding of the task, and other procedures.

Principle 4: *Store the information in modes that can be readily defined and manipulated.*

Our initial strategy for accomplishing this mode of storage was to include wherever possible both pictorial and written information within the categories, and to make tape recordings of all written material so that a student who could not read the material could listen to it. Hence, a student could extract data from pictures, written material, auditory tapes, and, in many cases, from charts, maps, and graphs as well, and the modes available to him could be varied to explore the effects of each.

Principle 5: *Organize the information system in such a way that the structure of the conditions under which the students use it is known; the structure can be varied and its effects ascertained.*

Such organization enables the conditions under which the students use the sources to be manipulated precisely so that optimal use of conditions can be identified, and alternative teaching strategies can be investigated. This enabled us to study a large number of teaching strategies.[9] The following means were used to control the structure of the environment:

1. Tasks presented to students were varied in terms of content, complexity, and the restrictions placed on students. For example, the "free-inquiry" task simply asked the students to learn about the culture until they felt ready to teach another child about it. The student could select his own content, level of complexity, and restrictions. On the other hand, a task asking the student to explore a certain social science concept with respect to the culture ("Find out if this is a matriarchal or patriarchal society") determined the content focus, the intellectual complexity, and placed restrictions on the search behavior of the student.
2. Control over the selection of information categories was varied. For example, the student might be free to select his own information, or he might be presented with it, or he might be presented with the option of selecting more.
3. Input to students in addition to system use was varied. A task might be preceded by instruction in social science, or an "advance organizer," or other tasks or instructional programs.
4. Association with other students was varied. A student might work alone, or in groups, and leadership patterns might be specified.

The teacher and student can shape the resources of the data banks in a variety of ways and could do this equally well with banks and television programs. The astonishing thing to us was the extent to which teachers differed in their effectiveness using the resource. Many otherwise facilitative teachers, for example, depressed the inquiry of students by careless use of praise. Others depressed the levels of questioning. We became convinced that teachers do not naturally use open-ended resources effectively but that much training is needed to help them make optimal use of open-ended mediated materials.

Needs surveys of teachers could help to provide a basis on which to select the kinds of storage systems to build, and studies of teachers' utilization of such resources could, as in the case of the Eboch/Guba/Meierhenry study, provide us with information about the impact of the media on the role of the teacher and the kinds of help he or she would need in order to utilize them properly.

With such a differentiated concept of the possible relationships that teachers can have to media, it is possible to build a typology of teacher

9. B. R. Joyce and E. Joyce, *Data Banks for Children* (New York: Teachers College Columbia University, 1970).

roles and to estimate the amounts of in-service training that are necessary in order to play each of the roles. When the teacher is simply a surrogate to an already existing course, relatively little in-service training with respect to pedagogy should be necessary, although much may be necessary with respect to substance. With the media/teacher interactive curriculum, teachers need to learn the substance and the roles they are to play and how to mesh their work with the capability of the media. Finally, resources provide teachers with a wealth of opportunities for use, and if we can judge adequately from the single instance of the Eboch/Guba/Meierhenry study, on the whole, teachers would use such media resources in conventional ways, and in-service training would be necessary in order to expand the possibilities that they see both for media utilization and for the utilization of themselves.[10]

MEDIA AS CONTENT TO BE LEARNED

It was my pleasure to participate in the construction of the 1974 National Society for the Study of Education Yearbook on "Media Symbols and Communication." A major theme of that book was that media contain the possibility for various kinds of coding systems. Ordinarily in school we teach students to use the coding systems of the print media, but fail to teach them the processes of encoding and decoding information that are made possible because of the nature of other media. For example, a given kind of message can be encoded literally or metaphorically in print, and literally or metaphorically in film, but the language of print and the language of film are not identical with one another.

Much needs to be done to develop an understanding of the nature of the content of media, but I became convinced that while we should not necessarily take McCluen or Langer's positions literally, there really *are* different coding systems and these are teachable. If we can orient in-service instruction around the symbolic nature of media, teachers will be better able to assist students in comprehending what is presented to them through media, enrich their perceptual fields, and insulate them against a subtle intrusion of knowledge or propaganda made possible because of their lack of understanding of the techniques that are being used. This topic is in itself much too complex to be dealt with

10. D. E. Hunt, B. R. Joyce, J. Greenwood, J. E. Noy, R. Reid, and M. Weil, "Student Conceptual Level and Models of Teaching: Theoretical and Empirical Coordination of Two Models," *Interchange*, 5, no. 3, (1974) pp. 19–30.

here, but it is extremely important. In-service education needs to focus on helping teachers to learn more about the nature of symbol systems and to help teachers learn how to facilitate children learning to "read and write" in nonprint as well as print media.

References

1. Ball, Samuel and Bogatz, Gerry Ann. "Sesame Street Summative Research: Some Implications for Education and Child Development." Princeton, New Jersey: Educational Testing Service, 1971.
2. Eboch, S. C., ed., with Guba, E. G. and Meierhenry, W. C. *Novel Strategies and Tactics for Field Studies of New Educational Media Demonstrations.* Columbus: The Ohio State Research Foundation, 1965.
3. Guba, Egon G. and Snyder, Clinton A. "Instructional Television and the Classroom Teacher." *A-V Communications Review,* 13, 1965, pp. 5–27.
4. Hunt, D. E., Joyce, B. R., Greenwood, J., Noy, J. E., Reid, R., and Weil, M. "Student Conceptual Level and Models of Teaching: Theoretical and Empirical Coordination of Two Models." *Interchange,* 5, no. 3, 1974, pp. 19–30.
5. Joyce, B. R. and Joyce, E. *Data Banks for Children.* New York: Teachers College Columbia University, 1970.
6. Murdock, G. P., et al. *Outline of Cultural Materials,* 4th revised edition. Human Relations Area Files, Inc., 1971.
7. Olson, D. R., ed. *Media and Symbols: The Forms of Expression, Communication and Education.* The Seventy-third Yearbook of the National Society for the Study of Education. Chicago: University of Chicago Press, 1974.
8. Schramm, Wilbur, ed. *Quality in Instructional Television.* Honolulu: The University of Hawaii Press, 1972.

The Consolidation of Formal and Informal Education: Some Essential Teaching Strategies

Louis Rubin

University of Illinois

The concept of informal education has recently ascended to a level of high fashion. As is frequently the case with new movements, and with older movements that have been rescued from retirement and freshly refurbished, purpose and intent are sometimes confusing and occasionally misleading. Informal education has sometimes been used to designate the kinds of learning that occur in the classroom when specific objectives have not been established in advance; on other occasions, it has been used to distinguish between the formal instruction of the schools and the more informal learning that occurs elsewhere in the child's environment. Therefore, informal education can be taken to mean either unstructured or extra-curricular learning.

FORMAL AND INFORMAL EDUCATION

As extra-curricular learning, informal education consists of attitudes, information, and knowledge acquired in the home, the church, and the community, as well as with those acquired by television, popular music and peer culture.

As unstructured learning, informal education includes: (a) knowledge obtained as a by-product of participation in teacher-directed activities (incidental-ancillary learning); and (b) insights that develop when children are allowed to explore ideas and materials without specific teacher direction, so that they are free to follow the dictates of their curiosity and pursue their own inclinations. The virtues of this kind of informal education, not surprisingly, are a matter of issue: some theorists contend that such learning constitutes the highest form of education, while others argue that schooling is much too important an issue to be left to the child's momentary whim or caprice. These disparate viewpoints are nurtured by conflicting ideologies, but our concern here is in another direction, so a thorough consideration of the dispute would be a needless digression. However, it should at least be noted that, as I judge matters, informal education, as self-initiated discovery learning, should take place only under specified conditions: (1) it should complement rather than replace the formal; (2) it should be restricted to purposes that are unsuitable to more structured learning situations; and (3) it should be used to facilitate individualization, heighten self-awareness, and accommodate the learner's idiosyncratic nature.

The premises then, on which my subsequent propositions are built are as follows: (1) formal and structured instruction is an indispensable ingredient in good general education; (2) within particular constraints, informal education–in the shape of unstructured, self-directed intellectual exploration–can usefully be joined with formal instruction; (3) teaching strategies that ease the integration of formal and informal learning are of considerable benefit; and (4) students acquire information, develop perceptions, and form values as a consequence of their out-of-school experiences.

The odds are good, in this regard, that adept teachers already make use of imaginative tactics for connecting the formal with the informal. Whether or not the connection is attempted depends in large measure on the individual teacher's pedagogical convictions. In schools where exposure to traditional bodies of knowledge is seen as the classroom's principal business, it is likely that little attention will be given to anything else. In contrast, where a teacher assumes that a student's behavior is based on personal notions–irrespective of how or where these notions are acquired–the teacher may see fit to counteract the more deleterious aspects of either formal or informal education. Thus, if a number of integrating strategies are already available and in use, the problem is not so much a matter of invention as one of clarification and dissemination.

TEACHING AND LEARNING

Unfortunately, the present state of practice, in this regard, is difficult to assess. In addition to the teacher's own professional ideology, constraints within particular community expectations, parental attitudes, and other social forces such as peer and popular culture, influence the kinds of activities that occur in the classroom. Although it is impossible to generalize about the prevailing situation, if one judges by the peripheral clues, it may well be that we give too little attention to what is learned informally—both in and out of school.

For example, we sometimes fail to recognize that the way assignments are made can be as instructive to the child as the assignments themselves; that the emotional climate of a classroom is often as significant as the subject-matter at hand; and that what teachers personify through their actions is sometimes more important than the teaching method they deploy. Moreover, we frequently ignore the unanticipated, detrimental aspects of seemingly good instruction. One may teach a Shakespearean play in such a fashion that the play is learned, but the student may, at the same time, develop a permanent dislike of drama, Shakespeare, or both.

All in all, much of current practice reflects little understanding of the ways in which incidental-ancillary learning occurs. And perhaps of greatest consequence is the fact that many practitioners regard the learnings that take place outside the school as beyond their sphere of interest.

It is also probable that the integration of informal-formal learning will be affected by the rising mood of conservatism. The school's public image, at the moment, is not a healthy one and, as so many times in the past, people may once again succumb to two counterfeit beliefs: first, that schooling is responsible for society's malaise; and second, that educational changes of one sort or another will cure society's ills. If this is the case, a curricular reversal may be in the offing. The continuing decline in achievement scores on standardized tests, the recent National Assessment of Educational Progress report indicating that a large percent of students lack basic information and skills that are essential in everyday activities, and the growing conviction that the schools have failed to inculcate responsible citizenship, are all likely to fuel the conservative trend.

It is worth noting, if only parenthetically, that much could be lost if the conservative trend is allowed to dissipate recent gains. The efforts, for example, to humanize the classroom environment, to balance cognitive objectives with affective ones, and to extend instruction's relevance for children, could all be destroyed by excessive regression. Much of the danger stems from the unnecessary dichotomy that has unfortunately emerged with regard to fundamentals and other educational goals. The basics *are* basic and public expectation deserves to be satisfied. It is conceivable, of course, that with a potent program of public information and clarification, parental attitude regarding what knowledge is worthy might be altered. Until this happens, however, the existing demands will not go away. In any event, it is most unlikely that what we euphemistically call the 3 R's will be relegated to a place of secondary importance. It is also unlikely that parents who have found benefits in more humanistic programs will take kindly to the tyrannies of old.

Salvation seems to lie in an instructional program that attends to cognition as well as to affect, that emphasizes knowledge as well as heuristic skills, and that offers both structured and unstructured learning opportunities. There is a time and place for drill and memorization, for the nurture of healthy values, for the pursuit of essential general education as well as subject-matter of more personal interest, and for teacher-controlled and student-controlled learning.

It is possible that most schools will endeavor to do something about shrinking scores on standardized tests. The problem has been dramatized and publicized to such an extent that to do otherwise would be to court overwhelming antagonism from a sizable portion of the public. Nonetheless, it is interesting to speculate as to what useful gains may have been accomplished as verbal and mathematical achievement have slightly diminished. The tests, after all, measure only a portion of education's ambitions. They tell us nothing about the school's success or failure in developing social awareness, in deepening the future generation's perspective of the human condition, in permitting the student to acquire a set of values by which to live, in enhancing self-awareness and self-esteem, or for that matter, in teaching the young to cope with all of the human problems not directly associated with mathematical and verbal skills. In view of the findings of the National Assessment of Educational Progress, it may be that schools have relied too much on unstructured exploratory experiences for the provision of commonplace skills, or that the equilibrium between formal-informal learning is out of kilter, and realignment is necessary. Realignment, however, is one thing; the impetuous rejection of everything other than the 3 R's is quite another.

It is clear that incidental learning, particularly that which occurs during the out-of-school experiences of students, can be both positive and negative. The child who watches television, for example, may learn from daily news programs, be stimulated into vicarious fantasies by soap operas, and perhaps be harmed by the violence depicted in crime shows. Similarly, an hour spent in the library with a piece of literature that the student understands, may evoke considerable benefit whereas time spent with material that is inadvertently misinterpreted may work to the student's disadvantage. It follows, therefore, that the integration of formal and informal learning will require in-school activity that sometimes reinforces and sometimes rebuts learning derived from the child's out-of-school experiences. In other words, since the school cannot possibly control the kinds of experiences that accrue during nonschool hours, it must deal with both the good and the bad of these experiences. The front page of a newspaper may provide an effective way of dealing with current events yet, advertisements for pornographic films on another page may exert a negative effect. As a consequence, four specific teaching functions are essential: first, teachers must learn something about the out-of-school experiences that affect their learners; second, they must make judgments as to the constructive or destructive aspects of these experiences; third, they must try to offset the experiences that are corrosive; and fourth, they must seek, wherever possible, to bolster the experiences that are constructive.

COMMUNITY-CENTERED EDUCATION

It might be observed, in this connection, that precisely the same kinds of problems are inherent in the recent drive for increased community-based learning. There is no way we can guarantee that all of the "reality" learning that occurs in a community setting will be completely wholesome. A craft can be learned in a factory but so can goldbricking. It seems clear that strategies needed in the integration of formal and informal learning–strategies, moreover, about which altogether too little is known–involve techniques through which the effects of out-of-school experiences can be judged and interpreted. We are thus brought, fullcircle, back to the dilemma posed by low standardized achievement scores. Teacher time spent in identifying and assessing the educational consequences of children's out-of-school experiences is, of necessity, time that is not used for improving verbal and mathematical skills. Choices must therefore be made.

But, as long as parents find little virtue in a school that seeks an intelligent fusion of all learning experiences that affect their children, and as long as they overlook the fact that some nonschool experiences (like some school experiences) are educationally counter-productive, we face an uphill battle. On the other hand, if parents' concerns regarding their children's mastery of fundamentals can be allayed–or if the mastery can be assured–they are less likely to look askance at efforts to integrate the formal and informal aspects of their children's education.

Since much of what passes for educational theorizing often consists of suggestions for possible improvements, without tangible indications of how such improvements can be accomplished, there is perhaps an obligation to strengthen the preceding arguments in somewhat more concrete terms. It seems obvious that to catalogue and code all of a child's nonschool experiences would involve complexities bordering on the impossible. A fragmentary conversation in the street, a casual experience in a bus depot, an episode in the supermarket and similar incidents are sufficiently random as to defy a manageable bookkeeping system. Furthermore, even if such cataloging were possible, the task of discriminating between good and bad experiences, and of determining cause and effect in the consequences growing out of a particular experience, would be equally problematic. Thus, some form of generalization is imperative.

THE EXTERNAL CURRICULUM

If it can be argued that experiences produce knowledge in the form of perceptions, beliefs, attitudes and values, it may be possible to deal with these secondary effects rather than with the raw experiences themselves. Such effects are obviously far easier to assess. Insofar as we are less interested in cause than in effect, it does not matter how, when or where a given idea or belief has its genesis. When children act in particular ways, they rarely distinguish between school-learned and community-learned conceptions. Rather, they tend to respond in terms of their particular experimental gestalt. In fact, it is because of the difficulty of discriminating between the various influences on an individual's learning that the evaluation of schooling is made so vexing. Thus, if we concern ourselves with students' knowledge, beliefs, and attitudes on important issues, we will, as a matter of course, touch on whatever has been informally learned.

Suppose we had assessment instruments with which to evaluate the attitudes, beliefs, values, and substantive knowledge of students on a variety of significant matters, particularly those indigenous to the informal learning environments of students: Could we then assess the effects of out-of-school experiences and prescribe in-school corollaries?

The makings of such assessment devices are already in progress. Their fabrication would pose no special difficulty and they would be relatively simple to administer, score, and interpret. Because they would focus on issues and ideas generally outside the existing curriculum, the ubiquitous tendency of students to fulfill teacher expectations and preferences would be minimized.

Admittedly, we would be unable to differentiate between in-school and out-of-school learning. Yet, the distinction would be unnecessary because the intent would not be comparison but rather the derivation of clues to desirable instructional content. To note a medical parallel, when a physician gives a child an annual physical examination he seeks to appraise the child's general state of health, not the factors that may cause disease or malfunction. It is only after such an evaluative appraisal that correctives are considered. What we are after, here, in a sense, is a kind of annual intellectual examination encompassing informal learning, i.e., extracurricular learning. It is difficult to see how—without such evidence—we can make any serious effort to consolidate formal and informal learning, compensate for the misconceptions that students reach outside the school, or plan their general education with prudence and wisdom.

I do not mean to argue that such assessments represent the only strategy, or even the most desirable strategy, but rather that an assessment strategy of this sort would have considerable utility. The assessments, if they could be managed, would permit us to overcome inconsistencies between school-based instruction and peer-culture influences. They would also provide direction in the extension of relevance and in the reduction of important voids in the instructional program. Above all they would point the way to educational readjustments designed to lessen the cognitive dissonance and the mixed messages frequently conveyed by the school and the out-of-school environment.

Educators have long been confounded by the contradictions between the lessons of school and the child's functional beliefs. For example, some years ago, Remmers and his colleagues discovered that many high school students believed that people who were critical of government practice should not be allowed to express their views through the media. More recently, researchers have discovered that many young people regard marijuana as totally harmless while others are convinced that the authorities should censor the mail of anyone who acts in a suspicious manner. Similarly, an extraordinary number of secondary school students (like many of their elders) assume that if immoral behavior is commonplace it is justifiable. It is hard to assume that such ideas were taught in schools. Most likely, they were learned through other experiences. Yet, if worthy citizenship remains an educational ideal, these misconceptions must be rectified, irrespective of where they were acquired. The essential point of departure in such rectification, presumably, lies in the experiential context of these misconceptions. Thus, the need to assess is critical.

EDUCATION FOR THE COMMON GOOD

We are in a time when renewed concern has developed over the values of the younger generation. It seems fitting to observe that it would be folly to presume that whatever values not taught by the school will not enter the minds of students. And it would be equally senseless to suppose that, if schools teach the right things in the first place, wrong things would not be learned outside. Thus it is in the area of values education, particularly, that the integration of formal and informal learning is most germane.

My own suspicion is that the arguments regarding a so-called value-free curriculum are essentially nonsensical. While, to be sure, values differ, and not many are universal, there are some that are generally respected, and it is these, I believe, that the schools must convey. It is the public character of education that makes it imperative for educators to be preoccupied with the common good. The schools must be committed to a democratic ethos and a set of cultural beliefs that are passed from generation to generation. No teacher who really teaches can avoid expressing what he or she regards as important and it would be absurd to seek teachers who are indifferent to the kinds of attitudes engendered in the young. Consequently, the values students develop out of their life events are the common ground between formal and informal learning.

The implications of all this for the continuing professional education of teachers are not peculiar to the bridges between community and school; rather, they penetrate the very heart of sound pedagogy. Good teachers, if only intuitively, have always strived to fuse the events of the classroom with those in the learner's other milieu.

The dominant teaching requirements are: (1) an awareness of the things that go on with students while they are away from school; (2) a capacity to relate the established teaching content to outside circumstances and, conversely, to blend the external forces with the content;

(3) a willingness to go beyond the subject-matter itself to the learner's general development; and (4) a faculty for influencing the students with whom one works. It is this influencing ability, more than anything else, that tends to distinguish the good teacher from the mediocre one.

In reaching into the learner's outside experiences, we are less interested in the substantive aims of the organized course of study (although these are sometimes implicit) than in the learner's overall intellectual, social, and emotional well-being. Spelling, chemistry and the intricacies of grammar are not usually learned outside the schoolroom. While the skills and concepts encountered in the curriculum are frequently reinforced by outside experience, the informal education lessons of greatest significance are concerned with attitudes about what is important and trivial in life, with convictions about how one lives, with the privileges and responsibilities of citizenship, and with personal esteem and worth.

A great deal of the thought on in-service education has dealt with the methods question. There is a widespread assumption that one teaching technique will invariably produce better results than another. When the facts are carefully reviewed, however, this does not seem to be the case—particularly in such endeavors as the fusion of formal and informal learning, where the teaching content is nebulous and subject to great variation.

INSTRUCTIONAL METHOD AND MYSTIQUE

Methods, in and of themselves, do not make a definitive difference. The connection between teaching and learning is still far from clear, and, as a general rule, when the student's incentive to learn is reasonably high, one method seems to work as well as another, at least with respect to test scores. This is not to suggest that good methods and poor methods do not exist; it is to suggest, instead, that, given the motivation to learn, students are able to neutralize the consequences of a particular method. Logically, good teaching techniques are more efficient and more powerful than bad ones. However, by expending greater time and effort, students can overcome the limitations of poor methodology. It is as if two men each had the task of unloading a truck. One man, because of greater experience and adeptness, might unload his truck in a shorter time with a smaller expenditure of energy. But the other man, albeit less skillfully and more slowly, will also unload his truck.

It is entirely possible that with further research and development, we will come upon teaching methods that do make a decisive difference. For the moment, however, other variables in the teaching-learning process are sufficiently powerful to offset the impact of any one method. There is, therefore, one other point that is germane: the integration of formal and informal learning need not await the invention of arbitrary teaching techniques—good techniques are more likely to come from efforts to attack specific instructional problems.

In a broader sense, it may well be that the place of methods has perhaps been distorted in the theorizing that has gone on in regard to teacher in-service education. We know that good techniques are essential, but what constitutes a good technique is subject to great variation. There are instances, for example, where authoritarianism works better than permissiveness; instances where the deductive is more effective than the inductive; instances where lecture provides greater benefit than discussion; and instances where stress, failure, and the ultimate overcoming of failure are indispensable to the educational process. Indeed, it could be argued that the school that teaches the child coping strategies essential to the survival of failure is far more valuable than the school that insulates the child from failure. Life, alas, is not failure-proof.

The choice of optimum method, moreover, depends heavily on the individual teacher's personality. Style evolves out of personality and—in teaching—it is the stuff of life. As teacher developers have long known, there are many useful techniques that cannot be used by a given teacher simply because they are incompatible with the teacher's personality. The connecting tissue between style and personality, in fact, is so strong that we have come, in our most recent theory, to assume that it is far better to adjust to the teacher's natural mode than to try and change it.

Most teacher developers approach their task with a fixed conception of what constitutes good teaching and good teaching techniques. Consequently, it is hardly surprising that a good deal of havoc has been perpetrated by trainers whose insistence on a particular brand of pedagogy has caused the teachers with whom they work to feel hopelessly inadequate, perverse, or out-of-step. The character of good teaching varies with the subject, with the learning environment, with the characteristics of the learner, with student and community expectation, and with the organization for instruction that exists. These too, then, must be respected in designing strategies for the welding of formal and informal learning. Relatively few teacher trainers, whether preservice or in-service, approach their task by inquiring what sort of teacher is most appropriate to the specific situation, what instructional procedures are likely to be most workable, and what teaching priorities are dominant.

The roads to good teaching are many. It is, moreover, the very diversity of teacher behavior that contributes significantly to the richness of school experience. One could easily make a case, in fact, for the argument that if all teachers functioned in precisely the same way, used precisely the same techniques, and acted on precisely the same pedagogical impulses, learners would lose a great deal. Hence, true artistry in teacher in-service education is a matter of fashioning expert performance out of the raw materials inherent in the teacher's personality.

Teachers must be competent, but the competencies of greatest utility in the blending of the formal and informal will vary from situation to situation. One does not have to look far or long to find a rigid or didactic teacher who, all things considered, does his or her students a great amount of good. Similarly, although dogmatism may not be a particular virtue in teaching, dogmatic teachers sometimes achieve excellent results. It would seem, therefore, that while rules, conventions, prescriptions, and models have their place, considerable allowance must be made for exceptions. For if any one thing in teaching is certain it is that a given learning objective can be accomplished in multiple ways. While some of these ways, at times, are better than others, nothing, apparently, is absolute. Each teacher must adapt to his or her circumstance. Hence, the sine qua non of healthy teacher in-service education is to adapt to, rather than obliterate, individual difference.

We have, in an informal experiment, been working toward this end and, in the process, have developed a tentative system for the continuing professional education of school faculties. Among the more significant aspects of the system are the following: professional growth procedures occur during the school day; they respect the premise that one can learn while one teaches; they center on a particular objective that has to do with technical skills, attitudes, or teaching knowledge; they are completely individualized in their architecture; and they are oriented towards the cumulative evolution of a personal style in teaching.

It is in-service characteristics of this sort, I suspect, that are necessary in the integration of formal and informal learning. Teaching style, teaching subject, and teaching objective are unusually powerful variables and each exerts a profound impact on the situation. Where the end goal is that of more efficiently fusing teachings that are acquired in the child's different worlds, the array of potential mechanisms is virtually infinite. One ploy will work best for the English teacher in an inner-city school, and another will be better for the science teacher in a rural community. It follows, therefore, that the teaching coach, or staff development specialist, who can kindle desire, demonstrate potential, and unfetter the teacher's creative imagination is likely to make the greatest contributions.

Accountability and Teacher Performance: Self-directed and External-directed Professional Improvement

Ralph W. Tyler
The Center for Advanced Study of Behavioral Sciences

At first glance, accountability, teacher performance, and self-directed and external-directed professional improvement may not seem to be directly related to each other. Nevertheless, the connection is significant, although somewhat roundabout. If teachers are to be held accountable for their professional performance, then the entire fabric of their preservice and in-service education must provide a solid, continuing network of supportive and evaluative procedures to help them become more effective in performing their professional tasks. Accountability can be viewed positively only after teachers have been provided with adequate opportunities for professional growth. The following discussion presents both an overview and practical examples of methods that contribute to improved teacher performance.

ACCOUNTABILITY

Since 1965 both oral and printed educational discussions have stressed accountability in education. Many educators viewed this as a new demand placed on teachers and school administrators, and some resented it. However, those employed to provide important public services have always been accountable, teachers no more or less than policemen, firemen, postmen, and sanitary engineers. The difference between today and earlier periods is not in accountability or lack of it, but in what teachers are considered accountable for. When my grandfather became the head teacher (principal) of a Fort Wayne public school, he replaced a teacher who had been dismissed for his inability to maintain order and discipline in the school. When I was in the seventh grade, a teacher in our school was dismissed because she could not explain long division to her pupils. In 1956 discipline was the major task of the elementary school teacher. Many years ago discipline was an important issue because sixteen- and seventeen-year-old boys were not interested in school. They came when they were not needed on the farm and began each term where they had previously stopped, continuing their studies until their parents put them back to work again. There were no grades, and pupils were grouped in terms of their progress through their books. Hence, sixteen-year-old boys were often grouped with 10-year-old girls. This stimulated revolt and disorder. The public anticipated less learning on the part of those who could spend only a few weeks a year in school, but they expected the school to be orderly and quiet so that pupils could concentrate on their work. Teachers were held accountable for maintaining these conditions.

Fifty years later orderly classrooms were taken for granted, but public attention was then directed to such matters as the teacher's knowledge of the subject he or she was expected to teach. School committees and boards of education often conducted oral examinations in which teachers were quizzed on the fine points of arithmetic (such as long division and extracting square root), spelling, and facts of history and geography. A teacher was sometimes asked to read a classical literary selection so that the committee could check on his or her reading competence. The public's notion of schooling at that time was the passing on of information from teacher to pupil. The teacher's acquisition of certain skills demonstrated and exemplified the skills pupils were expected to learn.

It was assumed at that time that if the teachers knew their subject, presented it accurately, assigned practice exercises, and firmly required the pupils to fulfill their assignments, the process of schooling was satisfactory. If pupils did not learn in such classes, it was the pupil's fault. They might be lazy, stubborn, hostile, disinterested, or inherently uneducable. It was too bad that such students did not get an education, but neither the teachers nor the schools were considered responsible.

The situation has changed now. Uneducated persons are usually unemployable. Consequently, they may become welfare recipients. Their chances of engaging in criminal behavior are greater than those of educated youth. They are likely to be poor citizens, inadequate parents, and persons who have not realized their potential. Furthermore, the current work of neurologists and psychologists, as well as that of teachers in learning clinics, seems to show that every child who is not brain-damaged can learn what the school has to teach. Today the public expects all children who are not seriously handicapped to learn. The schools and the teachers are considered accountable for the educational achievements of their pupils, not merely for ensuring that order in the classroom is maintained.

This shift of public expectation has also affected teacher education institutions. In the past, accrediting agencies and the public alike focused on such criteria as the academic degrees possessed by college or university faculty members, the quality of the courses offered, the range of facilities, and the like. The public and many educators are now concerned with the competencies of graduating teachers and in-service teachers.

TEACHER PERFORMANCE

The current stress on competency-based, teacher education programs has, in many cases, resulted in a simplistic view of just what education can contribute to a teacher's effective performance. It is not too difficult to identify the tasks or activities of a teacher, lawyer, doctor, or member of any other profession, but it *is* difficult to answer the following questions: (1) What can or should a student learn in order to perform these professional tasks or activities? and (2) Which of the things that a student needs to learn can or should be the responsibility of the college or university curriculum or of in-service education?

A profession differs from a trade. Presumably, a student learning a trade practices its essential skills, guided by the traditional rules of the trade until these activities have become habitual. A professional, on the other hand, deals with many complex, idiosyncratic, and consequently unpredictable tasks. A doctor cannot safely follow a fixed set of rules if he or she is to help a particular patient overcome an illness. The differences in patients, in the nature of illness, and in situations make a set of invariant rules patently absurd. Neither can a lawyer follow a legal formula if he or she is to effectively serve the individual needs of his or her clients. The differences in clients, the legal peculiarities of a case, and its particular circumstances also make following fixed rules ridiculous. For similar reasons, the teacher, also a professional, cannot follow a prescribed formula for stimulating and guiding the learning of students. Differences in students, in educational objectives, and in particular situations make a set of invariant rules unworkable if not absurd.

Over the centuries certain characteristics of a profession have been widely accepted throughout the world. A profession is an occupation that assumes responsibility for some tasks too complex to be guided by specific rules. Professionals perform these tasks by the artistic adaptation of general principles, that together with a code of professional ethics, guide their work. In order for professionals to perform these tasks competently, they must internalize a "cognitive map" of the phenomenon with which they are dealing. They must learn to follow certain procedures in analyzing and interpreting the situations they encounter. They must develop an understanding of the objectives of their professional tasks and internalize the ethics of their profession. They must also be able to apply general principles relevant to the situation, to devise courses of action, and to follow them, guided by the principles and the ethics of their profession. Although not complete or universally valid, this list serves to show that the primary aim of a professional curriculum is to help in the development of the intellectual tools of a profession, for it is impossible to teach particular answers to unknown future problems. Professionals must learn how to work out appropriate answers for individual situations.

Some teacher educators argue that the teacher's tasks are not as complex as those of a physician or a lawyer, and they further assert that the objectives for teacher education are simply to develop certain skills, such as lecturing, questioning, discussing, and disciplining. They claim that competence in these skills provides an adequate base for the teacher. It is certainly true that some of the tasks of the teacher are not professional, but this is also true of other professions. Many student teachers learn what the schools seek to teach them without requiring much professional help. Many sick people get well with little or no professional medical attention, but others do not. And there are many pupils who do not make significant progress in school except when their learning is individualized. Teacher education in America has been assigned to colleges and universities because the value of teachers as professionals, as opposed to routine workers, has been recognized.

Viewed in this light, the special role of the college or university in the education of the professional is to assist students to draw upon science and scholarship in dealing with their professional tasks. Helping them develop the skills of practice is not the primary role of higher education. Apprenticeship and other kinds of on-the-job learning are better places to emphasize skill development. The statement that the college or university has a primary responsibility for bringing its scholarly resources to bear in educating the professional is not meant to suggest, however, that theory and practice are to be separated. I shall touch on this subject later.

The above comments should indicate that the educational objectives of a professional can be determined by an analysis of the competencies needed in performing professional tasks, and by taking an additional step, that of determining *how* professionals carry on each major task, and what internal resources they use. From the results of *this* inquiry, judgments of what the professional needs to learn can be made more rationally. Over the past forty-five years while working with medical and engineering schools, schools of nursing, social service administration, agriculture, and education, I have found that the professional leans heavily on the internal resources mentioned earlier.

The professional has learned to perceive a professional problem in the setting of his or her cognitive map. For example, as physicians work with their patient, they keep in mind their cognitive map, the general functions and structures of the human body, and the various factors that may impair or facilitate the functioning of the organism. On this map, as it were, they put relevant information, obtained from observation and questioning, about the patient. As they analyze the patient's situation, they may seek more information from tests or other observations, but they lean heavily on their cognitive map to guide their inquiry and interpretations. Similarly, professional teachers have a cognitive map of important factors in the development and learning of children. They see children as dynamic organisms, learning what they think is necessary to achieve their purposes at home, in school, and elsewhere. Against this map, the teacher obtains and interprets relevant information about an individual student's progress and problems in learning.

Professionals have learned certain procedures they follow in analyzing and interpreting the particular situations they encounter. They have developed special procedures appropriate for their work, but these are generally of the problem-solving type. They understand not only the central objectives of their profession, but the particular goals of an individual problem. A central objective of the physician's profession is to help the patient effectively maintain his or her own health. Although the physician may be treating a heart attack, he or she develops a long range plan of treatment consistent with this central goal. In the same way, the professional teacher understands that a central objective of teaching is to help the student become an autonomous learner. Seeking continuing education, he or she simultaneously works toward more immediate, short-range goals, e.g., learning phonetic rules for attacking unfamiliar words.

Professionals have internalized the ethics of their profession. This means that they not only understand the ethical principles and can apply them appropriately to the situations encountered, but they have also accepted them and use them as one set of guides in their work.

Professionals have learned a number of important principles that explain and predict the phenomena with which their profession deals. They understand and use them in seeking to clarify the problems they encounter and in working out solutions.

Finally, professionals devise courses of action in dealing with their tasks. These courses of action may be unique in that they differ in some respects from previous courses, but they are not arbitrary. Professionals are guided by their professional ethics, principles, and procedures. In this way, a physician's work with an individual patient can be different from any he or she has followed before, but it is nevertheless consistent with relevant medical principles. In similar fashion, the professional teacher devises courses of action to facilitate the learning of the whole class, a group of students, or an individual who requires assistance that is unique in some respect.

This list of inner resources, and the tools the professional employs in the performance of his or her functions, may not be complete, and others may find different ways of categorizing them. But in general, these are the kinds of things a professional learns, and they are quite different from the lists of specific behaviors often formulated to represent the objectives of education for an occupation. The highly specific lists take no account of the ability of human beings to generalize and thus to surmount the limitations of learning that focus on specific items to be remembered, specific rules to be followed, specific solutions to specific problems, and specific, inflexible skills and habits.

PRESERVICE AND IN-SERVICE EDUCATION

When lists of resources employed by the professional are compiled, the curriculum makers face two other problems. First of all, time is not available in the preservice program for students to learn all of the concepts that could be helpful in the development of their conceptual maps or to learn how to use them in their professional work. This same time limitation makes it impossible for students to complete their learning of the other helpful inner resources. The second problem is the likelihood of continuing change in the society, in the profession, and in the body of relevant knowledge. Even if there were enough time in preservice education for students to acquire all the tools they presently need, there would be a need for new skills and capabilities in the future. Some of the things professionals need are not recognized or have not been developed by the time they enter the profession.

In consideration of these two problems, the objectives for the preservice education of professionals need to be formulated as the substantial beginning of a life-long program of professional education. The point of view to be emphasized with students is that what they are learning in preservice education is only a beginning. The concepts, principles, and practices of the profession are matters for continuing, life-long inquiry. As time goes on they will be able to elaborate more deeply and more comprehensively. Their professional work should stimulate reflection, and study both their experience in practice and their efforts to understand relevant theory.

THE CURRICULUM FOR THE EDUCATION OF A PROFESSIONAL

This view of the education of a professional implies that the initial step in establishing objectives for preservice education is to select a small number of elements in each kind of inner resource. These elements should have wide applicability and serve as a guide for the beginning professional in his or her tasks. For example, the initial cognitive map for teachers may be composed on only twenty or thirty concepts, but these can be selected to furnish a basic way of perceiving learning situations for children in and out of school. With only a small number of concepts to learn, the students have time to internalize these important and useful resources and to use them in a variety of practical situations. Too often now the theoretical part of the professional curriculum includes more than students have time to adequately comprehend, interpret, and relate to actual practice so that they become part of their habitual behavior. Once a smaller number of concepts, values, principles, and techniques of inquiry and problem-solving have been internalized, others can be gradually added to the list of educational objectives.

As mentioned above, the primary consideration in the selection of these elements is their helpfulness as inner resources that professionals can use in guiding their performance of professional tasks. In most professional fields these concepts have been drawn from a number of disciplines. In medical education, concepts and principles are drawn from anatomy, physiology, and biochemistry, as well as from fields of clinical medicine. More recently, medical educators have found concepts and principles from the behavioral sciences helpful. In teacher education, concepts and principles have long been obtained from psychology and philosophy. Only recently has the helpfulness of elements from anthropology, sociology, political science, and economics been recognized. The curriculum development process is a continuing one in which all possibly relevant disciplines are investigated in order to discover those elements that will be helpful in guiding the practitioner.

But this growing list of disciplines from which helpful elements can be drawn creates a problem in making a rigorous selection. Learning requires time. New things to be learned cannot be internalized by the student unless adequate time is provided. In general, this means that the selecting of a new element requires the elimination of an older one. It is often difficult for a professor to eliminate something from his or her course, but it is usually necessary if the curriculum is to maintain its contemporary vigor.

It is easier to deal with this problem of selection when it is recognized that what the professional can helpfully use from another discipline is only a small part of that discipline. For example, what the physician finds highly useful from among the concepts, principles, and methods of inquiry in anatomy is only a small part of that subject. Selecting that part required continuing judgments about each element and its helpfulness in guiding the physician in his or her professional tasks.

Another problem is relating elements taken from one discipline to those in another. Scholarly disciplines have not generally been integrated. Each discipline, in order to make its study manageable, has selected certain phenomena for study, has worked out assumptions that help to limit the scope of its inquiries, and has developed concepts and principles that help to make its functions interrelated and cumulative. These separate disciplines cannot be added together to achieve a simple unity of science and scholarship. Practitioners can use elements from several disciplines by treating each discipline as a different lens through which they can view the phenomenon with which they work. This multifaceted view of a professional event gives them a greater understanding and awareness than could be provided by a single discipline. The physician, for example, who perceives a patient's illness in terms of those principles developed by the discipline of physiology can obtain an added view through the lens of sociology, which uses concepts such as "family stress." The teacher who perceives a student's learning problem in the terms developed by the discipline of psychology can obtain an added view by using the anthropological lens with concepts such as "culture conflicts." The professional curriculum objective is to use these different inner resources in ways that guide effective performance. It is not to develop a unified integrated science, nor is it to provide the elementary courses for persons who are to become specialists in the discipline.

In summary, with regard to educational objectives, the emphasis on competency-based education of the professional results in a selection of "what is to be taught," which differs in many respects from the usual collection of courses in the disciplines thought to be relevant. Not only can this approach result in substantial changes in objectives, it can also influence the means of professional education, that is, the learning experiences made available to students. When the elements to be learned are selected because they can provide helpful guidance in the performance of professional tasks, it is easier to plan learning experiences in which the situations professionals encounter in their work are used. These learning experiences can, on the one hand, serve to explicate the theoretical concepts, principles, methods of inquiry, and the like, and on the other hand, illustrate the application of these elements in ways that help to guide the performance of professional tasks. This makes clear to the student both the relevance and the meaning of these elements, and greatly reduces loss through forgetfulness and misdirected energy wherein students try to memorize rather than practice these elements.

There are numerous examples of the change in learning experiences that occur when the elements are viewed as tools rather than objects to be known for their own sake. For example, a number of medical schools now have their freshman students work part time each week with a physician so that they can see the relevance of important elements from anatomy, physiology, and biochemistry—subjects commonly taught in the freshman year—and can practice using them. In the sophomore year, students participate in clinical conferences in which the patient's problems are reviewed by professors from several relevant disciplines. The students grasp the meaning of these elements more clearly and easily than they did before and gain further experience in applying them to professional practice. Both of these innovations were first developed by the Medical School at Case Western Reserve University in its effort toward CB Education.

These illustrations also suggest possible effects on the organization of learning experiences as competency-based curricula are developed.

The common placement of the basic subjects in the early part of the program and the professional subjects in the later part is often replaced by concurrent learning, which is necessary if the meaning and helpfulness of these disciplines are to be understood and internalized by the students. Furthermore, the criteria for effective sequence in the professional curriculum is the provision of elements that become increasingly more complex and applicable to the professional tasks the student encounters. Additional elements of the inner resources are introduced from time to time so that the student gains a larger set of intellectual tools as the professional tasks become more complicated.

EVALUATION OF PROFESSIONAL EDUCATION

The process of evaluation in the operation of a competency-based curriculum is not simple. Unfortunately, some institutions appraise the students' performance of the professional tasks rather than the degree to which they are guided by relevant inner resources that the institution has been helping them to learn, internalize, and apply. In many cases, in the early development of a professional, one who works by rule of thumb or has acquired certain practical skills can perform the task more effectively than a novice who is gradually acquiring the professional tools. If the student is to be encouraged in becoming a professional, and if the appraisal is to help in assessing the effectiveness of the curriculum, the evaluation should focus on what the student is supposed to have learned. It should indicate the elements he has internalized and uses in guiding his performance of the task. In an appraisal program that does not do this but simply assesses the apparent competence in performing the task, the trade school type of student rather than the professional will often get higher marks. As time goes on and the professional acquires skill and experience, he should be able to handle the simple cases—the trade school type—as well as the more difficult ones.

This view of evaluation is also appropriate for the appraisal required for professional certification and for periodic relicensing. Several studies have shown that as professionals become more experienced, a majority take shortcuts, that is, they depend upon their success in what appeared to be a similar case in the past and use the same course of action in the present case without collecting enough information to determine the real extent of similarity. Thus, some doctors take a look at the patient, decide that he or she has a certain infection and prescribe penicillin without an adequate diagnosis. Some teachers observe a few fragments of a pupil's behavior and decide that his or her problem is lack of motivation and prescribe accordingly. Although a majority of these cases turn out well, these practitioners have ceased to be professionals. They are now performing as trades people. Their investment in professional education is lost.

The evaluation program for certification and licensing should involve the professional's use of important inner resources in dealing with examples of practice. The focus should be on their internalization and use of accepted professional procedures and principles to identify problems, to bring relevant concepts to bear (including those of professional ethics), and to design appropriate courses of action, rather than to assess solutions to problems in terms of their correspondence with those of the judges. If the licensing is periodic or continuing, an outline of a sequential, in-service program of continuing education should be developed both to guide the individual's self-improvement and to serve as a basis for licensing evaluations after a certain number of specified years of practice.

FUNCTIONS OF IN-SERVICE EDUCATION

A good deal of time has been spent discussing the problems of preservice education rather than in-service education in particular. A general perspective is essential in order to see more clearly those issues that may be peculiar to in-service education. As mentioned above, the primary function of preservice education is to help the individual develop a rough cognitive map of the phenomena of learning, teaching, and professional ethics, and to give him or her some practice in using the map so that they can get the feel of professionalism. Most students are not expected to have a well-developed cognitive map by the time of graduation, nor will most of them be skilled in its use. They will, however, have internalized some essential features of the map and will be able to use much of what they have learned in practice. It is important, then, for the graduates to be employed in situations where they can continue to develop their map and gain increasing skill in its use.

Accepting this purpose for preservice education, we can easily identify four functions of in-service education: (1) remediation; (2) developing the competence required to deal with particular problems; (3) helping the individual learn what is needed to attain his or her own professional goals; and (4) furnishing the stimulation and learning opportunities that counteract boredom and lowered professional performance.

REMEDIATION

Not all who complete programs of preservice education and obtain teacher's certificates have learned to perform as professionals. Some have acquired specific skills and fixed habits as their modes of operation in the classroom. Others follow specific rules in presenting instructional materials, guiding pupil practice, and establishing discipline. Many of these do not encounter difficulties that challenge the adequacy of their performance, because most of their students are able to direct their own learning and do not require professional assistance. Some of these teachers have not acquired initial professional competence and do not recognize the inadequacies of their practice, because they assume that the difficulties of their pupils are due to such factors as low intelligence, which teachers can do little or nothing about. Nevertheless, there are other in-service teachers who want to develop professional competence and participate in educational programs that have the same objectives as those outlined above for preservice education.

Programs designed for remediation require an assessment of the needs of involved teachers, inasmuch as their reactions to their teaching experience are highly individualistic and may result in different cognitive maps and guides to practice. From this assessment, objectives for the remedial program for individuals can be formulated and group needs can be identified by collating individual formulations. The learning experiences for remedial programs will usually be somewhat different from those used in preservice programs because of the greater experiences of in-service teachers and the particular opportunities they have had, both for gaining concrete understanding of the concepts, principles, and problem-solving procedures of the professional, and for applying the professional tools they are seeking to internalize.

DEVELOPING THE COMPETENCE REQUIRED FOR PARTICULAR PROBLEMS

As mentioned above, many children require little or no assistance in guiding their learning in school. Interviews with school children reveal a number of cases in which children able to guide their own learning have constructed their own sequences for learning when neither the teacher nor the writer of instructional materials had consciously planned a sequence. But children who are unaccustomed to building their own order out of unordered experiences are commonly overwhelmed by a mixture of simple and complex skills, basic ideas and illustrative examples, and the prescriptive rules and principles that explain them. They require a planned sequence to enable them to move step by step in their learning.

Furthermore, children who have learned how to learn are usually able to determine for themselves what the objectives of school assignments are, that is, what they are expected to learn from carrying out the assignment. On the other hand, many other children have no idea what they are expected to learn and therefore do not focus their attention on the desired outcomes. When in doubt about the purpose of an assignment, they try to memorize the assigned material rather than analyze it, apply it to problems, and/or compare and contrast it with other points of view.

Because many middle-class students learn without being told what they are expected to learn, many teachers have not recognized that for some children to succeed in their school work, the teacher or someone else needs to serve as a role model, to be a live illustration of what the children are expected to become. This is understood in the learning of sports. In golf, for example, we must see someone–a guide–playing golf. In learning how to make a long drive, novices are greatly aided by observing someone making a long drive. So, as teachers, we should realize that childen must also be able to observe examples of the kind of behavior they are expected to learn.

Other teaching procedures that are differentiated for different children are those involved in reinforcement and feedback as students practice the behaviors they are trying to learn. Each successful practice effort should be rewarded and unsuccessful efforts should be aided with the kind of information that will contribute to future improvement. Unfortunately, our common school practice has been to give higher grades or rewards to those who already know or can do, and to discourage those who need help by giving them lower grades. Few efforts are devoted to helping students correct unsuccessful behavior. Consequently, those students who need help in learning are not likely to receive much assistance.

These illustrations delineate the need for new policies and procedures to meet the new problems that schools are now facing, problems arising from the expectation that all children, regardless of backgrounds, will gain a basic education and that many more students now than in the past will be going beyond high school. There is also a need for new practices that will be appropriate for the several new educational objectives schools are expected to attain, such as learning to analyze controversial issues by a variety of different but equally valid views, learning to formulate alternative courses of action in social situations and appraise the probable consequences of each of them, and learning to make decisions in harmony with accepted values and evaluate their consequences. The knowledge and skills students need to learn in order to attain these objectives is not that well understood, and there is even less experience in implementing them. Effective teaching requires the learning of many new things: new and different policies and procedures for different situations.

Schools support in-service education in order to help teachers learn these new phenomena. However, the shotgun approach to in-service education is an ineffectual and inefficient use of the schools' resources. Since a school's effectiveness in solving its educational problems depends upon teachers gaining the necessary competencies, the school has a stake in encouraging and supporting in-service programs that clearly focus on these new and critical issues.

To obtain this focus, school districts should identify their critical problems. In most school systems, 70 to 85 percent of the children are making substantial progress in learning. In these situations, there is little need for schools to invest heavily in continuing education, but in the case of the 15 to 30 percent of the children who have learning difficulties there are likely to be some serious problems. For example, in most large cities there are critical problems in the inner city. Children who come from homes where the parents have not had much education and/or may lack experience in living in modern urban centers are having the greatest learning difficulties, as is the case with those who recently arrived from the Mississippi Delta, where they lived in a very different society. The education of disadvantaged children is generally recognized today as a common problem in inner cities and in certain rural areas. Most schools have two or three critical problems that reduce the overall effectiveness of their educational efforts.

The next step is to work out possible solutions to these problems, or, more commonly, promising strategies for attacking them. In the case of the primary education of disadvantaged children, at least two different strategies are being employed in different schools. One of these is to extend the educational efforts to include the parents and other concerned groups in the community in order to build a background of influence to support and aid the work the school is doing. The other is to devise and use a learning system that specifically provides for the conditions known to facilitate learning, including such things as clear examples of what students are to learn, immediate rewards for successful performance, ample opportunities for practice, sequential organization of learning experiences, and opportunities for students to move at a pace they are able to handle and to master each unit before proceeding to the next one.

The application of either of these strategies requires new attitudes, new understanding, and new skills on the part of many of the persons involved. For example, the first strategy requires both principals and teachers to perceive of the home and community as partners in the education of children in subjects such as reading and language arts, arithmetic, and social studies. These subjects have traditionally been viewed as the school's exclusive responsibility. The first strategy also demands that school personnel understand ways in which the home and community can furnish situations where children can use reading, practice more effective language, employ arithmetic, and use concepts and values from social studies. School personnel are also expected to know ways in which the home and community can arouse children's interest in these areas and provide the encouragement, time, and place for study. Finally, this strategy requires that school personnel have the skills of observation, listening, and communicating that are necessary to work effectively with parents of disadvantaged children and others who live in low-income neighborhoods. They must perceive the inadequacy of school programs that result in sorting instead of universal learning. They must understand the essential conditions for learning and the varied ways in which these conditions can be met. Finally, they must develop the skills required to work with children in a "mastery type" of situation and to manage learning systems that involve varied activities and the use of aids, student tutors, electronic technology, and the like.

These illustrations should make it clear that the solution of some of the critical educational problems encountered in a school requires the acquisition of new attitudes, knowledge, and skills on the part of the persons involved. To acquire them, in-service education is necessary. Furthermore, to learn just a few of these things requires a good deal of time, effort, and guidance. Hence, an effective and efficient program must first determine what those involved want to learn and then provide them with the necessary support and activities. From this point of view, school systems planning to attack their serious educational problems must simultaneously plan for continuing education programs that will furnish opportunities for teachers to acquire what they need to support those strategies adopted by the school.

ASSISTING INDIVIDUAL PROFESSIONAL DEVELOPMENT

Both remediation and providing the means for developing special competence are two ways of helping teachers perform their present jobs more effectively. In addition, some teachers want to learn other things that will aid them in attaining their individual professional goals. Some seek upward professional mobility and want preparation for jobs they see ahead, while others are primarily interested in developing professional competencies to use in their present positions, that is, they aspire to superior performance.

Society benefits from social mobility because it encourages personal and professional development and usually brings a wider variety of people into the higher echelon of society, thus counteracting the tendency toward limited views and sterile performance, two characteristics of a monolithic culture. Organizations like school systems benefit from upward mobility for the same reasons. Hence, it is proper for educational institutions to encourage teachers to learn those things that will help them achieve this upward movement. However, since a job at a higher echelon usually involves an increase in salary, it is not necessary that this function of in-service education be heavily subsidized.

On the other hand, the school benefits directly from the teachers' acquisition of those skills and insights that contribute to his or her superior performance. Hence, a program for their acquisition can be justifiably planned and supported by the school system.

COUNTERACTING BOREDOM

Follow-up studies of the professional performance of graduates from several different professional schools indicate a common tendency for a majority of practitioners to reach a plateau of development within seven to ten years after graduation. More than half of the graduates decline in effectiveness during that period. Interviews with graduates indicate that when they do not participate in some form of continuing education experience, they find their work routine and boring after a while. As one doctor said, "Now I can handle my work so easily I put my effort into golf where I find fresh challenges." These studies also show that two kinds of circumstances are important in determining whether or not graduates maintain a high level of professional performance. One of these relates to the attitudes and practices of colleagues with whom they are working. For example, if young physicians go into communities where the older, respected physicians use shortcuts in lieu of careful diagnoses and are scornful of the "impractical theories" of the medical schools, they are likely to lose much of their drive to become master diagnosticians. Instead, they are greatly tempted to emulate the shortcuts used by the older and seemingly successful colleagues. As another example, Becker studies the induction of new teachers. The neophytes were told not to make a big job out of teaching. If they maintained discipline in class and gave textbook assignments, they would succeed as teachers. "Don't take wild-eyed ideas seriously," they were told.

Situations like this suggest the desirability of furnishing in-service education programs that help teachers see new facets to their work, new challenges to be met, and new resources to be developed and utilized. Some of the most successful programs of this sort are often called action research. In these programs teachers and consultants identify, through inquiry and problem-solving procedures, significant educational problems on which they can all work.

SELF-DIRECTED AND EXTERNAL-DIRECTED PROFESSIONAL IMPROVEMENT

Thus far the discussion has dealt with accountability, teacher performance, and preservice and in-service education. The last two terms in the title of this paper are self-directed and external-directed professional improvement. Is this an important distinction? Most of the preceding comments dealt with the schools' needs and the use of their resources. Only brief attention was given to the goals and needs of the individual teacher. There is a real threat in a mass society that planning and operating mechanisms will lose sight of the individual and, consequently, will stifle initiative and encourage conformity. Yet, a society seeking to be democratic sets up as a goal the autonomous individual, one who has a good deal of control over his or her own life, one who has a wide range of choices and knows enough about the probable consequences of each major, possible course of action that he or she can make an informed choice. In this sense, autonomous persons are the masters of their fate, not merely people buffeted about by forces outside their control.

There is danger that a school system, like some other bureaucracies, will be planned and operated in such a way that teachers have little or no autonomy. Under such conditions the only apparent choice is either to submit to the pressures of the system or to sabotage them. Fortunately, this is not a necessary characteristic of even a large school system. The autonomy of teachers can be preserved and actually augmented by appropriate programs of in-service education. By being one of the responsible participants in identifying educational problems, selecting or devising strategies for their attack, identifying the new attitudes, knowledge and skills required to carry out the strategies, and selecting or designing possible means for acquiring them, teachers develop the necessary background for not only broadening their range of choices, but for making more informed choices.

The Eight-Year Study of the 1930s provides an excellent illustration of the significance of teacher participation in task forces working on curriculum improvement. Inasmuch as high school graduates could not find jobs during the Great Depression, teachers in the study were given the freedom to build a curriculum that might better meet the needs of students who were currently enrolling in secondary school. Many teachers did not want to make any changes in curriculum or instruction. It was hard for them to perceive of anything very different. Some said, "We are successful teachers. Why should we mess up what we now do well?"

Task forces, which included teachers, were established to study the problems facing the new kinds of students, investigate their abilities, interests, and needs, and obtain data on the larger social context that had changed so markedly during the lean years. When teachers confronted these problems, they recognized the need to acquire new attitudes toward youth and the role of the school, a new understanding of contemporary society and youth problems, new knowledge and strategies as a basis for planning instructional units, and new skills in teaching problem-solving and in participating in pupil-teacher planning. Recognizing the need for workshops through which teachers would have the opportunity to learn these things, they established them, and they participated in them thoughtfully and vigorously. The fact that they had a clear understanding of the serious problems on which they were working bolstered their resolution and reduced their discouragement when they discovered that it took more effort and time to plan and carry out the new strategies than they had anticipated. They were not honestly able to plead, "Why did we get ourselves into this hard work when we were getting along very well before?" because they knew that there were serious problems that must be solved.

Teachers need to see a larger picture than that which is provided by their immediate situation if they are to have real autonomy in working on their continuing education as a means of career development. Such a picture will help them recognize the educational problems to be solved, the in-service opportunities available to them, what things they need to learn if they are to render these services, and the ways in which they can learn them. They need information about the rewards that will come to those who can carry on the strategies adopted by the school. Rewards include satisfactions such as the following: a sense of greater professional competence; knowledge of having aided pupils to learn important things they have not been learning before; greater responsibility in the school organization; greater respect and esteem from colleagues or the public; and greater financial remuneration. Participation in problem-solving task forces is one means by which an individual teacher can outline this larger picture and be able to make decisions about his or her own development with fuller understanding of the available choices and the probable consequences of particular courses of action.

Autonomy also requires alternative ways of learning. We can find many illustrations of continuing education programs that provide a variety of ways for autonomous teachers to learn. Under Louis Rubin's leadership, the Center for Coordinated Education in Santa Barbara conducted a project in cooperating school systems to demonstrate the ways in which one teacher can help others to identify and acquire the skills necessary for teaching controversial issues. Several state medical societies, having surveyed their membership to identify the knowledge and skills they wish to acquire, have made tape decks that physicians can play in their cars while they drive from place to place, thus learning new techniques, getting new ideas. The College of Dentistry of the University of Illinois has made video-tapes that can furnish dentists with a clear, close-up demonstration of new techniques. Questions raised by the video presentation can be followed up by telephone at hours when specialists are available for consultation. Herbert Thelen and his colleagues have devised ways in which teachers can learn some important things from their pupils. The teacher says to the children, "Will you work with me on this task? I am a dud at it. Can you show me what to do?" The thought that pupils can teach the teacher arouses great interest in most children. These are only a few of the many possible examples of in-service education programs that are not college or university courses. Teachers should not feel they are in a narrow alley with only one way to go to acquire greater professional competence.

Many opportunities for autonomy arise in the early months and years of teaching experience. Teachers may see gaps between their standards of teaching and their own performance and choose to gain more training in order to do a better job. They may begin to identify educational problems not previously recognized and choose to learn more about these problems and possible means of attacking them. They may join a task force–if one has been established–to deal with important problems faced by the school, and acquire the competencies necessary for that particular role.

Other opportunities for autonomy arise when there is available a variety of learning opportunities, varied both in educational objectives and in the means of learning. Under such conditions, teachers may have a chance to learn new skills, gain new understanding, and form new attitudes and perspectives. Furthermore, they will have to choose which objective to work on at a given time. For example, some teachers may want to acquire the skills of operant conditioning needed to conduct the Engelmann program for young children. Others may choose to develop the skills required to stimulate and manage programs of inquiry learning. Still others may want to learn how to guide high school students in the study and discussion of controversial issues. Others may wish to develop the management skills needed to operate educational activities that involve the community. The availability of these options and information about the probable consequences of different courses of action enables teachers to be autonomous in the choice of objectives for their continuing education.

In each of these choices teachers have a further opportunity to choose the means, that is, the kind of educational activities they can carry on in order to attain these objectives. The illustrations presented earlier are only a few of the many possible means for learning what is or can be made available to teachers. Clearly, the school should seek to provide at least two or more ways for teachers to learn each of these different kinds of behavior so they can choose the ones that seem more appropriate for their particular circumstances and style of learning. Feedback should be built into every program in order to facilitate further choices by teachers, to indicate unwise decisions made earlier, and to guide their efforts for continuing improvement. This feedback to individual teachers should tell them how well they are doing, where they are having difficulty, and suggest a number of ways to correct errors, overcome difficulties, and make improvements.

SUMMARY

This paper has emphaszied four themes. Those responsible for the education of in-service teachers are accountable for helping them become truly professional problem-solvers guided by concepts and principles, and directed by an ethical code appropriate for our contemporary, democratic society. There are four accepted functions of in-service professional education. From the functions, clear objectives can be derived to take the place of the vague goals of the shotgun approach. The in-service education of teachers can be planned and carried out in a way that greatly increases the effectiveness of the school, particularly in dealing with its serious problems. By enlisting the enthusiasm, initiative, intelligence, and energy of teachers in program development and execution, continuing education can be a means for promoting autonomy in teachers rather than pressing for conformity.

Section III

Other Voices: Other Opinions

Their Hearts Were Young and Gay: The In-Service Needs of an Inexperienced Teaching Force

Martin Burlingame

Universit o Illinois

Many of our conventional wisdoms about the in-service needs of teachers are not based on data. For example, the newest of the conventional wisdoms argues that in the 1970s, throughout the entire 1980s, and into the early 1990s, the teaching work force will become less mobile, less prone to exit and reentry, and more aged and experienced. This wisdom implies that these more experienced and aged teachers will be a major source of societal concern because: (1) they will be less willing to experiment with or develop new educational methods; (2) they will be more prone to seek security for themselves rather than intellectual excitement for their clients; and (3) they will be increasingly provincial in their orientations toward the needs of American youth and toward new means of enhancing the American educational system.

Nonetheless, much of this new conventional wisdom rests on insecure or unexamined information about the present age and experience structure of the American teaching work force. The task of this paper is to describe the current work force of teachers in the State of Illinois. Such a description suggests that the in-service needs of this work force are more properly oriented toward the inexperienced rather than the aged, even in the next decade or so. We begin by inspecting the teaching force of the State of Illinois from 1951 to 1975. After this numeric overview, several implications for in-service education will be dis cussed.

ILLINOIS TEACHERS, 1951–1975

The materials we will be discussing are summarized in Table 9–1. The discussion briefly reviews the rapid growth in size and inexperience of the Illinois teaching force from 1951–1975.

Turning first to the question of sheer numbers, from 1951 to 1975 the number of teachers in the State of Illinois increased 275 percent (37,518 to 102,569). An inspection of Table 9–1 indicates, not surprisingly, that this rapid increase produced a less experienced teaching force. For instance, in 1951 36 percent of all teachers had twenty or more years of teaching experience. In 1975 only 13 percent of Illinois teachers had this amount of experience. It is interesting to note that the actual number of teachers who had twenty or more years of experience increased only slightly over this time span. On the other hand, an inspection of the less than four years of experience column, makes it clear that since 1951 those with such limited experience have doubled

Table 9–1 Percent and number of active Illinois teaching service for selected years by years of teaching experience

		Years of Experience					
Year		0–4	5–9	Total Less Than 10	10–19	20 or More	Total
1951	%	20.97	14.99	35.95	27.91	36.14	100.01*
	n	7,867	5,622	13,489	10,471	13,558	37,518
1955	%	30.18	13.94	44.12	23.46	32.41	99.99
	n	12,270	5,665	17,935	9,537	13,175	40,650
1961	%	35.27	17.22	52.49	19.82	27.68	99.99
	n	19,917	9,723	29,640	11,194	15,632	56,466
1965	%	38.37	19.46	57.83	21.10	21.15	100.08
	n	26,167	13,269	39,436	14,390	14,421	68,197
1971	%	48.25	17.44	65.68	19.38	14.94	100.01
	n	46,341	16,747	63,088	18,618	14,346	96,052
1975	%	39.36	25.84	65.20	21.47	13.33	100.00
	n	40,369	26,507	66,876	22,018	13,675	102,569

*Errors due to rounding.

Data compiled from selected year *Report of Examination: Public Employees' Pension Funds.* Springfield: Department of Insurance, State of Illinois. The figures represent all full-time members of the teaching service and most administrators in the state, except some district superintendents. The experience category includes *only* experience in the Illinois teaching service. This table does not contain data for the Chicago city schools. However, informants suggest that the Chicago and Illinois state data are compatible on the general trends discussed in this article.

in percentage, but in terms of actual numbers have increased nearly six fold.

One way of summarizing this information is to compare the columns of less than ten years experience, ten to nineteen years experience, and twenty or more years of experience. In 1951, for example, roughly one of every three teachers had less than ten years of experience. Equally, one of every three teachers had twenty or more years of experience. By 1975 these figures had changed dramatically. In that year, nearly six of every ten teachers had less than ten years experience. The number of teachers with twenty or more years of experience, however, was only slightly more than one in every ten.

It is possible also to ascertain from this table the beginnings of the aging process. For example, in 1971 nearly one half of all teachers in the State of Illinois had less than four years teaching experience. By 1975 that figure had dropped to four out of every ten teachers. The actual numbers in the category of five to nine years experience have grown sharply over that short period of time. However, if we were to wipe out magically the category of less than four years teaching experience in 1975, reducing in force nearly 40 percent of all Illinois teachers, the number in the five to nine year category would still be larger than either of the experience categories remaining on the chart. While such a dramatic reduction in force is unlikely, the contemplation of such a tragedy highlights the relative inexperience of the Illinois teaching service.

Finally, although evidence is not presented in this particular table, the comparative youthfulness of the Illinois teaching force must be recognized. For example, in 1951 23 percent of all teachers in Illinois were under the age of thirty-five while in 1975 63 percent of all teachers were under thirty-five. At the other end of the age spectrum, in 1951 48 percent of all female and 40 percent of all male teachers were forty-five years of age or older. In 1975, by way of contrast, only 29 percent of all female and 12 percent of all male teachers were over forty-five.

What has happened over the last twenty-five years in Illinois has been a marked transition from a teaching force whose membership was composed of nearly equal shares of relatively inexperienced, moderately experienced, and experienced, to a teaching force dominated by young and inexperienced teachers. Hence, while the 1950s were a period of Illinois educational history in which schools were dominated by an older and experienced teaching force, the 1970s appear to be a decade in which youth has captured the educational work service. We now turn to some implications of these statistics for in-service education in Illinois.

IN-SERVICE NEEDS OF INEXPERIENCED TEACHERS

While no one can discount the vitality and energy that inexperienced teachers can bring to classrooms in the State of Illinois, there appear to be significant differences in the training needs of inexperienced teachers that must be met in any in-service educational program. These needs are for: (1) enhanced formal training in the area of linking colleges of education to schools; (2) emphasis on the basic skills of teaching; (3) efforts to provide multiple information sources to inexperienced teachers; and (4) development of prestige systems to enhance the status of inexperienced teachers.

College/School Linkage

Much has been said of the failures of colleges of education to link systematically with school systems. Many critics have suggested that the medical model of an intensive and deeply practice-oriented internship needs to be analyzed closely for suggestive parallels. While often immediately satisfying to those who seek to become teachers, the usual experiences of student teaching rarely provide either a strong intellectual basis for continuing growth in such areas as analysis of teaching. With the increased demands on colleges of education to find activities for professors as student enrollments decline sharply, many professors might become available to work closely with school district personnel in the development of more vital and stimulating clinical experiences for beginning teachers. These clinical experiences should focus not only on the necessary vocational skills, "the tricks of the trade," but also provide beginning teachers with useful insights drawn both from the behavioral sciences and from modes of criticism concerning the aesthetics of teaching styles. (These aesthetic modes might rest heavily on analogies drawn from the arts such as ballet, drama, or literary criticism.)

As they are conceived, these in-service activities would not be for just a short period but would extend over at least the first three years of teaching. This time commitment would mean that novice teachers would have lighter teaching loads and less class contact time with students. Their teaching schedules would provide opportunities to meet with other practicing teachers and professors who are interested in working with these inexperienced teachers on a variety of practical and scholarly problems.

Teaching Techniques

A second focus of much of this initial in-service training for inexperienced teachers has to do with the development of the basic skills of teaching, rather than with those esoteric concerns that confront older teachers. Clearly, teachers pass through various stages of development and need as they move through their careers. In their early years, those from student teaching through three or four years of experience, young and inexperienced teachers face many of the problems of coping with a group of students. They lack, for example, a catalog of teaching tricks or teaching games that can be used to enrich and deal with classes. They are perplexed by many of the organizational demands schools make upon their time and energy. Novice teachers must learn not only classroom management but the management of their own time and energy. These youthful teachers confront social demands that many of them have thought little about, such as "crushes" by their more senior students. They confront, and must resolve, their own agenda of issues about what a career in education might look like. These new and inexperienced teachers face a very different set of problems from teachers who have five to nine years experience, or those with experience of ten to nineteen years, or twenty or more years experience.

What must be underscored is the notion that in-service training needs should be specifically oriented towards the stages of experience of various cadres of teachers. Programs cannot be spread willy-nilly over all teachers. Programs must be tailored and pertinent to the different needs of clusters of teachers at particular stages of their careers. In Illinois, for example, at least one third of the 1975 teaching force needs programs designed for novice teachers.

Information Sources

A major need of a youthful and inexperienced teacher is for various sources of information. At least three such sources deserve mention. First, individual teachers must develop tools for extracting from their own experiences in classrooms meaningful insights into student behaviors and their own teaching styles. These observational skills can be abetted by professional and peer support but they are the paramount skills that inexperienced teachers must develop. The category schemes and the various frameworks that the individual develops in these early stages of teaching can either provide significant springboards for more insightful analyses of issues at later stages or become crippling blinders that inhibit their development as teachers.

A second source of information is the peer culture. Mechanisms must be developed by which teachers are enabled to gossip systematically with other teachers. The popularity of many of the so-called teacher centers seems to rest on the ability of teachers to visit with their peers about what they do. Such visiting often provides useful tidbits of information and important exchanges about various techniques. What is often lacking in this type of exchange is a sense of intellectual recognition that permits teachers to crystallize, then analyze and generalize their experiences.

Much in-service work with teachers needs to concentrate on the development of a common language for discussing teaching events among peers. This language could allow teachers to indicate clearly when differences in style and taste mark them off from their colleagues. This lack of a common language leads to many muddles. Teachers often argue about issues upon which they would find fundamental agreement if they could observe each other's work. Much of this common language will rest upon exchanges that follow the observation of the classroom teaching activities of others. Such an empirical base could provide the grounds of a language of commonplaces for teachers.

Other sources of information for teachers are to be found in the disciplines of education and the behavioral sciences. These language systems, frequently developed by professors, facilitate the communication of common information about a multitude of activities. For instance, work done concerning small group activities, analyses of socially approved or disapproved behavior, explorations of various kinds of linguistic systems, or understanding of the emotional and physical development of children and adolescents all provide rich vocabularies for teachers.

Teacher Status

The final need that most inexperienced teachers face is the need for enhancement of their own status and prestige. Many of the earlier devices discussed for in-service training are aimed at the enhancement of both the self image and the skills of inexperienced teachers. Much can be done to enhance the personal and organizational prestige values that accrue from clinical experiences, the development of language systems for the analysis and improvement of practice, and the scientific advancement of practice. Such social inventions provide the groundwork for the augmentation of personal and professional status. However, the goal of such activities is not enhancement of an aura of professionalism but rather improved service to the clients of the schools. It is the contention of many that such improvements in practice will lead to improved accomplishment by the clients of the school. These clients will, in turn, become important advocates for a more prestigious and better prepared teaching force.

SUMMARY

To summarize, we are able to use teaching service statistics about the experience and age of our teaching force to suggest important strategies for improving in-service education. Second, if we inspect closely the needs of an inexperienced teaching force, we find at least four needs that are important and need attention: the need for clinical training, for training content to be focused on problems of inexperience, for access to various information sources, and for enhancement of individual and professional prestige.

If the teaching force in Illinois does become less mobile, less prone to exit, and more experienced and elderly over the next few years, we can accommodate this change in teacher population. However, the relatively great group, nearly two of every three teachers in Illinois, who are *not* now experienced and who have special in-service needs must not be overlooked. In-service training plans should be developed now to answer the needs of all teachers.

An Overview of Critical Issues

James F. Collins
Syracuse University

It may strike the reader as senseless, and even futile, to set forth a statement on in-service education that is no more than a recital of issues. I do so, not out of perverseness, but out of a long-standing conviction that a summary of points in dispute provides an effective means of conceptualizing problems. Administrators, it may be argued, have a penchant for creating problems but devote relatively little energy to finding solutions. While the indictment may have some legitimacy, my years in administration compel me to believe that the identification of problems often has its virtues.

The in-service education of educators is not a new consideration. It has, however, become prominent in a rather unusual time—one when commonplace educational pursuits have been questioned—and it is now viewed as an old procedure in need of fresh provisions. In such times of reevaluation, there is always a danger that problems will be oversimplified and excessive reliance placed on convenience and simplicity. An effort, therefore, to define the issues and to compare a range of alternatives may be useful.

It might be noted, in fact, that while a few readers will find the issues elementary and reach a conclusion regarding their solution without undue difficulty, there nevertheless is likely to be a considerable disparity of opinion. Views will differ as to the importance of issue as well as its optimum resolution. As a result, a taxonomy of problems and issues not only defines the existing situation but it can also help in major points of contention. For these reasons, the following synthesis may not be entirely without merit.

1. Defining In-Service Education
   What is In-Service Education?
   Should it include:
   - postemployment, degree and/or nondegree-oriented study
   - certification-oriented activities
   - curriculum development activities
   - personal development of the professional
   - self-directed study
   - activities essential to the maintenance of the individual's position
   - only activities that improve the effectiveness of practicing educational personnel

   As professionals, how much individual diversity and autonomy can we tolerate?
2. Governance–Management–Decision-Making
   What constitutes governance? Who should govern in-service education?
   What constitutes management? What should distinguish the governance and management aspects of in-service education?
   What are comparative advantages and disadvantages of in-service that are:
   - state controlled
   - district controlled
   - school controlled
   - university controlled
   - professional organization controlled
   - partnership–limited joint control
   - consortium–multiple control

   What are the effects of unilateral decision-making and collaborative decision-making on program credibility, acceptance, and impact?
   Do collaborative or consortium governance mechanisms guarantee parity of decision-making?
   What functions should a governing body, as opposed to a managing body, perform:
   - policy making
   - program development
   - operation and management
   - grievance hearing
   - facilitation
   - monitoring and evaluation

- dissemination
- research
- acquiring and allocating resources
- information exchange

What degree of independence should partners and consortium members have?

Should a consortium be attached to a "parent" institution?

Should consortium members be self-governing?

What is the appropriate role and function of state agencies in the governance and management of in-service education?

Are state plans for in-service education desirable?

3. Organization of In-Service Programs

What are the dominant incentives for participating in in-service education?

- credentialing
- salary increments
- professional advancements
- personal satisfaction
- personal development
- social/political benefits

What are the primary program objectives?

- staff development (professional and/or personal)
- curriculum development
- improvement of instruction
- program advocacy
- professionalization

What are the optimum modes of delivery?

- school designed courses/workshops
- college or university designed courses/workshops
- district or state designed courses/workshops
- teacher center programs
- in-school programs
- individualized activities
- group activities
- professional improvement experiences
- other-directed professional improvement experiences

When should in-service education be offered?

- before school

- after school
- weekends
- evenings
- summers

Who should develop, direct and teach in-service programs?

- teachers
- district administrators
- supervisors
- university professors
- consultants
- principals

What are the special advantages of teacher centers in delivering in-service education?

- participant sharing
- theme focus
- access to materials
- inter-school collaboration
- cost efficiency
- pedagogical experimentation

Should in-service education be:

- voluntary
- mandatory
- based on teacher-contributed time
- based on teacher-compensated time

4. Criteria and Processes for Assessing and Evaluation

Should evaluations focus on attainment of:

- individual goals
- group goals

Should evaluations be based on:

- student performance
- teacher performance
- teacher opinion
- administrator opinion
- consultant opinion

Should evaluations utilize:

- fixed criteria
- flexible criteria

What are the roles of the participants in evaluation?

- self-evaluation
- peer evaluation
- group evaluation

Who should determine the evaluation format?

- state departments
- district administrators
- building administrators
- teacher organizations
- participants
- evaluation specialists

When should program evaluation occur?

- during programs
- at the conclusion of programs
- at some subsequent point
- all of the above

5. The Development and Implementation of Multi-Cultural In-Service Programs

What should multi-cultural in-service education include?

- crisis and conflict resolution
- techniques for enhancing social consciousness
- strategies for reducing racism, sexism and other forms of social prejudice
- techniques for extending multi-cultural sensitivity
- orientation to diverse cultural values
- processes for improving human relations in the classroom
- identification and development of multi-cultural curricula

Does multi-cultural education require:

- conventional teaching methods
- adaptations of conventional teaching methods
- special teaching methods

How can stereotypic thinking among educational personnel be eliminated?

- through admonition
- through modeling
- through precept
- through behavior modification

6. Financing In-Service Education

Are effective programs:

- low cost
- moderate cost
- high cost
- variable

Should in-service education be paid for by:

- federal government
- state government
- local boards of education
- business and industry
- foundations
- participants
- institutions of higher education

Should existing funds be redirected by:

- reducing the budget for outside consultants
- assigning supervisors responsibility for in-service education
- assigning state college and university professors responsibility for in-service education
- assigning principals responsibility for in-service education

Other issues, of course, could be noted. Similarly, other potential solutions to those listed could be suggested. My intent has been to paint a picture that was representative rather than comprehensive. Moreover, many of the issues will, I suspect, engender political as well as intellectual debate. We are faced, in short, with conflicts that reflect self-interest as much as commitment and belief. Such disagreements, however, are inevitable and in keeping with our way of doing things.

My hope is that the six sets of issues outlined above will serve as a springboard to further reflection and discussion. In the last analysis, it may not matter which resolution (or group of resolutions) we choose—since one panacea frequently may be made to work as well as another—but what will matter is our ability to invent programs of professional improvement that are of genuine benefit to all of the actors in the educational drama.

An Aptitude-Treatment-Interaction Approach to In-Service Teacher Training

Lyn Corno
Christopher M. Clark
Stanford University

Declining school enrollments and low teacher turnover have intensified the interest of teacher educators in the in-service training of teachers. Educators agree that traditional methods of in-service training–graduate coursework and school-based workshops–have outlived their utility. The search is on for new and better in-service techniques. So far, this effort has produced an abundance of promising ideas, many represented in this volume. Few of these suggestions and recommendations, however, derive from theoretical research. Most research and development efforts in teacher education have focused on innovations in preservice practice. Novel, research-based techniques, such as microteaching and minicourses, were initially devised for preservice programs and later adapted to in-service needs. Innovations designed specifically for in-service training on the basis of research on teaching and learning have rarely been considered or implemented.

There is one area of considerable research in education and psychology that we find particularly relevant to in-service teacher training–Aptitude-Treatment Interaction (ATI). While the philosophy of ATI is not new (cf., Lewin 1956; Whitehead 1929), the concept has only recently been accepted and reviews of the research have only recently appeared (Hunt and Sullivan 1973; Cronbach and Snow 1976). The principles and findings of ATI research therefore, are not commonly known, and implications for educational practice are even less evident.

This paper has benefited from personal communication between Lyn Corno and Professor Robert Calfee of Stanford University.

It is our intent here to describe ATI as it applies to in-service teacher training, and to recommend its approach as a method of continuing research on teaching and teacher education.

In its most general form, ATI is a technical term related to the individualization of instruction. "Individualization" is itself a catchword concept widely applied and generally acknowledged as desirable, though difficult to achieve. Proponents believe individualized instruction to be the best way of attending to individual needs and abilities. In practice, however, resources are inadequate to insure one-to-one teacher-pupil or pupil-computer relationships. Individualization of instruction then becomes a matter of homogeneous ability groupings, various sorts of programmed seat-work activities and methods of supplementary and remedial instruction. All are at best, practical adaptations, and at worst, questionable dilutions of the original concept.

In contrast to the one-to-one aim of individualized instruction, the hope of ATI is that groups of people can be found who respond similarly to the same general instructional approach. More experienced teachers, for example, might benefit from group discussions, but not from role-playing techniques. If it proves workable, the ATI approach is an eminently more practical and, possibly, more simple method of attending to individual differences than complete individualization of instruction. Thinking about in-service training in an ATI way implies that teacher training take into account characteristics of individual teachers—their background experiences, learning aptitudes, present situations, personal preferences, and specific needs. Teachers in urban schools with slow learners have different needs from rural teachers of average students. An ATI approach would seek to design in-service training in accordance with these diverse teaching situations in order to capitalize on available teacher resources and experiences.

Such practice seems to us exceedingly sensible in dealing with in-service teachers. These people are mature and experienced in their profession; they are not the same as preservice teachers and should not be treated like novices learning a trade. Effective in-service training must reflect the fact that teachers' preferences and needs are important and that they know many of the things they need to improve upon. There is, of course, an implicit assumption that continuing education motivates concern for attaining the highest standards of professional performance. This assumption is not always present in the more general process of schooling (that is, in the usual teacher-learner situation, where it is all too readily accepted that the adult knows what's best for the child). An approach that considers preferences and needs is uniquely appropriate for adult training situations.

What would a program for training teachers with an ATI strategy look like? A successful ATI approach to in-service teacher training must match teacher characteristics (person), teaching situations (context), and training programs (method). The prime source for developing a matching process should be research literature on ATI. But even the best research offers only limited information. Cronbach and Snow point out that much of the ATI research conducted to date suffers from methodological flaws, and that "no ATI's are so well confirmed that they can be used as direct guides to placement."[1] Put differently, no specific learning environments have been found to be consistently more beneficial to students of different personalities or abilities, although positive outcomes have been observed in many individual cases.

One strong general conclusion has resulted from ATI research—the degree to which general intellectual ability (usually defined by intelligence test scores) affects student academic achievement varies with the mode of instruction. Learning depends more on general mental ability when the student is required to do less initial information processing, and is given more directed instruction.[2] What this might imply for in-service training, is that brighter teachers can be expected to accommodate reasonably well to even the worst of training conditions, but less bright teachers will need an especially well-organized program, at least at first. While this is a fairly common sense solution, it has not been considered recently, nor has it been thoroughly supported by research. Thus, despite the fact that more research is needed before specific matching procedures can be recommended, there are some general ways of approaching the in-service training problem based on what we do know. Proposals for using our knowledge to date can be potential vehicles for research by teachers and teacher educators on their own classroom transactions and training techniques.

What we know about teacher aptitudes and training procedures at this time can be summarized by two principles and their resultant implications for in-service training:

1. Aptitudes (broad characteristics that affect learning such as interests, habits, and skills) are not necessarily fixed at birth, but rather, change with time and experience. Aptitudes may develop as a result

1. L. J. Cronbach and R. E. Snow, *Aptitudes and Instructional Methods: A Handbook for Research on Interactions* (New York: Irvington Naiburg Publishing Corporation, 1976).
2. Ibid., chapter 14.

of learning, as well as forecast learning success. Since aptitudes for certain tasks can be expected to develop and change with use and instruction, no mode of training should be permanently considered most appropriate for a given group of teachers. In-service education should be an on-going, information-seeking cycle of placement, training, assessment, revision, and reassignment. Placement decisions should be based on teachers' common aptitude profiles; training should be keyed to these teacher sub-groups; additional aptitude information should be obtained periodically for each teacher; and training should be revised and teachers reassigned as their aptitudes change.

2. An ATI approach will be functional only if different forms of training can be shown to be more or less effective for different kinds of teachers. Present methods of delivery comprise so many variable procedures, in such broad and abstract forms, that nominally different approaches frequently use many of the same techniques. Computer and programmed methods, and demonstrations and videotapes, for example, so shade together in procedure that user effects are remarkably equal.[3] Only through fine conceptual analysis—analysis that specified trainee skills, styles, and prerequisite knowledge, as well as training process variables—will actual distinctions among methods become evident.[4]

It follows from the above principles that steps must be taken to devise different ways of presenting similar training topics; that possible topics should encompass more global teaching strategies and styles, as well as specific skills; that training materials should include pretests over the content to be taught and any prerequisite knowledge, in addition to multiple means of aptitude and criterion assessment; and that training should be of sufficient duration for teachers to grow accustomed to the method so that their responses will be both stable and practically informative.[5]

A similar, but more restrictive, approach to teacher training has been proposed by David Hunt. Hunt's conception of a Matching Model for Teacher Training seeks to match trainee "skill level" (present knowledge) and "accessibility characteristics" (ability variables) with specific training techniques.[6] If a trainee is deficient, for example, in capacity for structuring the classroom environment, he will receive

3. D. Jamison, P. Suppes and S. Wells, "The Effectiveness of Alternative Instructional Media: A Survey," *Review of Educational Research* 44 (1974): 1–59.
4. Cronbach and Snow, *Aptitudes and Instructional Methods,* chapters 1 and 5.
5. Ibid., chapters 2, 6 and 14.
6. D. E. Hunt and E. V. Sullivan, *Between Psychology and Education* (Hinsdale, Ill.: The Dryden Press, 1973), p. 54.

training on structuring techniques in a form that defines capacity for structuring the environment in terms of "conceptual level"—a cognitive construct on which most of Hunt's research is based. While the matching model is limited in that the research is restricted to a single ability variable, the approach is based on ATI principles, and is very likely the only one of its kind presently in use. Examination of the Hunt model may be a good place to begin in efforts to generate ATI hypotheses about in-service. In doing so, however, additional interest, and other ability variables not considered by Hunt should be put forth as potentially important for training effectiveness. For example, Orme found the effectiveness of microteaching to vary according to the teacher's experience: whereas inexperienced graduate students dramatically changed their teaching behavior as a result of microteaching, tenured education faculty members did not.[7] This finding implies that microteaching is not a useful technique for more experienced, less flexible teachers, and points up the necessity for examining trainee variables in assessing the effectiveness of training.

When this more general, but adaptive, information-seeking method of training is adopted, several important benefits become evident. First, training will be appropriate to individual teacher needs, yet will not require total individualization of instruction. Second, valuable information about the teaching-learning process, as well as the training process will be gained along the way. And third, by dealing explicitly with a flexible, ongoing cycle of renewal, such training realizes the ideal embodied in the concept of continuing education of teachers.

To summarize, greater attention should be given in the in-service training of teachers to the more meaningful kinds of teacher competencies that form the core of everyday classroom life: teacher planning, classroom decision-making, process analysis of classroom transactions, and other maintenance techniques. Teachers should be given the tools with which to become investigators of their own teaching effectiveness. They should be encouraged to experiment with new methods and creative ideas of their own. Perhaps more importantly, in-service training should assist teachers in conducting these experiments by providing a program of continued guidance and consultation. Such a program would capitalize on the fact that in-service teachers know what many of their needs and interests are, and would utilize that knowledge to design training suitable for similar groups of teachers. The ATI ap-

7. M. E. J. Orme, "Microteaching Strategies for the Improvement of College Instruction," paper presented at the Joint Council on Economic Education Conference, Indiana University, Bloomington, Indiana, 1973.

proach is an eminently useful way of renewing in-service training because it explicitly deals with unique in-service needs. Revising preservice techniques for in-service ignores the singularity of the practicing teacher, as well as the operational constraints not present in preservice. Only when in-service training is specifically designed to serve the system of which it is a part will it begin to pay the dividends we have been expecting of it.

References

1. Cronbach, L. J. and Snow, R. E. *Aptitudes and Instructional Methods: A Handbook for Research on Interactions.* New York: Irvington Naiburg Publishing Corp., 1976.
2. Hunt, D. E. "Matching Models for Teacher Training." In B. R. Joyce and M. Weil. *Perspectives for Reform in Teacher Education.* Englewood Cliffs, N.J.: Prentice Hall, 1972.
3. Hunt, D. E. and Sullivan, E. V. *Between Psychology and Education.* Hinsdale, Ill.: The Dryden Press, 1973.
4. Jamison, D., Suppes, P., and Wells, S. "The Effectiveness of Alternative Instructional Media: A Survey." *Review of Educational Research* 44(1) (1974): 1–59.
5. Lewin, K. *Field Theory and Social Science.* New York: Harper & Bros., 1951.
6. Orme, M. E. J. "Microteaching Strategies for the Improvement of College Instruction." Paper presented at the Joint Council on Economic Education Conference. Indiana University, Bloomington, Indiana, 1973.
7. Whitehead, A. N. *The Aims of Education.* New York: The Macmillan Co., 1929.

Teacher Education—The New and Radically Different State Expectations

Joseph M. Cronin
State Superintendent of Education

What state education officials wanted and needed from colleges and universities during the 1945-70 era is not what they want and need today. The needs have changed dramatically since 1970, and teacher training institutions ignore these new developments at their peril.

After World War II, public school enrollments grew enormously in the aftermath of the great baby boom that followed fifteen years of depression and war. Large increases in the number of teachers were required in most states and a serious shortage of fully qualified teachers existed from about 1948 to 1971 in fields other than English and social studies at the secondary school level. Hardly anyone noticed that in 1959-1960 the birth rate leveled off and by 1965 actually began to decline in a trajectory similar to that of the increases of the 1950s. By 1970 the effects were visible in the lower grades, and by 1975, high school and university officials were ready to acknowledge the likelihood of a full decade or more of enrollment decline.

THE RADICAL NATURE OF THE SHIFT

Demography accounts for only the most visible reason for radical changes in teacher education. The drop in student enrollment from 1970 to 1984 in a state such as Massachusetts will exceed 200,000; in Illinois, 400,000 or more. Parochial school enrollments will drop as well as public school enrollments. At best, 100 school buildings will close down in each of two dozen states.

The other great shift is in employer retention of teachers. In the 1950s and 1960s, according to W. W. Charters, Jr. and others, 20 percent of the new teachers left teaching at the end of their first year until by the fifth year only one in four remained in the profession. (No other occupation above the clerical level except nursing has had to train so many to accommodate such a turnover.) But by 1975, the teacher dropout rate in Illinois had plummeted to 9 percent per year, with future declines likely. The old familiar attrition explanations of marriage, maternity, and mobility have faded along with the large family. Divorce and the day care center are just two of the new forces helping to keep women in the classroom longer or returning earlier than anyone expected. Teachers of both sexes benefited enough from collective bargaining wage settlements from 1965 to 1975 to reduce even the attrition of heads of households from teaching.

As a result of these two convergent trends (fewer pupils, more teachers staying) higher education no longer needs to produce, every five years, 100 percent of the number of teachers employed in American schools.

Even now, many teacher education administrators bristle at the thought of curtailing the number of new teachers prepared. Never mind the rising frustration of thousands of unemployed or underemployed teachers, they seem to say. Why not cut class size again, some suggest, ignoring the substantial cuts made already in virtually all schools, or the rather soft research data supporting smaller classes, or the frightening increase in cost (reducing class size by just one pupil in each Illinois classroom could cost as much as $100,000,000). The ration of professionals to pupils, thanks to new special education programs, dropped from 24:1 in 1970 to 20:1 by 1975. The point is that many states during the remainder of the 1970s will continue to train two or three times the number of teachers as will be needed in the work force that year.

The surplus will be cumulative. The most dedicated or persistent of last year's teachers will compete with the current crop. Joining them will be hundreds of previously trained married teachers whose children are now in school or college. Soon even teachers with tenure will find that their services are no longer needed, and will try to find a new job in a more secure school system ten or twenty miles away from home. During the Depression unscrupulous school officials in more than a dozen citites demanded kickbacks and favors from those desperate for jobs. These scandals could reappear in the late 1970s.

The realities of the chronic teacher shortage, the steadily dropping class size and the growth of the American high school have required of state school officials considerable patience and the deferment of emotions such as pride in the quality of the work force. Most states, California being one exception, suffered these indignities for two decades:

1. Almost any college or university had to be allowed to offer major or minor programs in teacher education such as would lead to a teacher license or certificate. States had to accept "credit hour" counts as surrogate indices of minimum competence, a great leap of faith.
2. Most college graduates were allowed to teach some subjects on a provisional or emergency basis, at least if they agreed to take a few methods courses part-time or summers to qualify for a teaching credential in due time. This was especially true of science and math teachers during the years of great concern about Sputnik.
3. Most of the larger colleges or universities, right through the 1960s, ignored birth rate trends and planned future growth, especially at the graduate level for those who would train even more teachers, counselors and school administrators. California, on the other hand, mandated fifth-year programs of study for prospective teachers at the secondary school level.

Of course, education can still correct its excesses. Responsible educators do not want a version of Gresham's Law under which the merely persistent drive out the competent. Education *can* adjust to a downward shift in the demand for new teachers.

QUALITY, NOT QUANTITY

The drop in the need for new teachers gives us a glorious opportunity—we can expect our new teachers to be quality teachers. What is a quality teacher? One who knows the subject, enjoys working with children, and can engage the two effectively. How many of us have endured personalities or subjected our own children to teachers who fall short of either of these two dimensions?

Education has suffered in the vain hope that a given number of credit hours can attest to the necessary knowledge of either a subject to be taught or to competency in teaching. I do believe in requiring a major concentration in the subject taught at the secondary school level and sufficient breadth in studies for the elementary school teachers—including literature, art, music, health, and work in history, government, and economics. Teachers at both levels benefit from courses in the sociology of education and should demonstrate awareness of basic issues in the philosophy and history of education. Psychology of education courses should stress styles of learning, motivation, and the special problems of exceptional children and of adolescents. All teachers should know how to teach reading (especially in the middle and upper grades) at least in their specialized field or discipline and should know about testing and evaluation.

I also believe that the ability to relate effectively with children can and must be demonstrated prior to acceptance into a student-teaching program. For a quarter of a century we have settled for on-the-job learning. Many teachers discovered either on-the-job or during practice-teaching (student teaching) that they were not cut out to teach or that they could not handle children. This was almost too late. States can now ask candidates for a preliminary proof of probable success with children shown as early as sophomore year in college but in off-campus settings. Many practical tests exist, including volunteer or paid work at camps, youth centers, coaching, community service programs, scouts, 4-H clubs, or other alternatives.

The state could also endorse such programs as the one the American Federation of Teachers feels all urban teachers need—a paid, carefully supervised internship in the classroom for at least a year. Massachusetts now issues an interim certificate and will not grant a full teaching certificate until the candidate has completed two successful years in the classroom and has had a full review by both teacher peers and administrators. Each of these requirements should contribute to the rising quality of teachers for the next twenty-five years.

NEEDED: A REDUCTION OF THE SURPLUS

At the University of Illinois Conference in Chicago I proposed an application of the old soil-bank program. Perhaps we should pay universities for training fewer teachers! Another alternative may also come from agriculture: that we export to the many dozens of developing nations our surplus teachers. This second option is a serious one, an adaptation of the original Hubert Humphrey-John Kennedy concept of an overseas Peace Corps. The United States currently staffs dozens of dependent schools for the Department of Defense and other government children and also helps a network of private American schools succeed in many countries. The need for world literacy is well-established. Unfortunately, however, nine out of ten prospective teachers seek a job close to home or at least in their own state. A tour abroad is just that, and not really a permanent solution to domestic overpopulation.

Another approach is the one taken by such universities as Boston University, Northwestern and Northeastern, Illinois State University, and Southern Illinois University. They have cut back initial teacher education programs by as much as 35 to 50 percent rather than contribute to the great crush of candidacies for few vacancies. These universities actively counsel students into other growth careers such as adult education, community education, police and protection work, consumer and environmental education (much of it out of school), diagnostic and counseling careers and other related social services.

Many teacher-educators say "courses in education" can help anyone–future parents, policewomen, nurse supervisors, businessmen. Fine! But, this is the right moment to limit the number of persons who are admitted into student teaching or internship programs and to eliminate the unqualified or marginal contenders. We don't need any more mediocrity in education. We no longer need the vast numbers of almost-ready teachers. We want the best prepared and the most enthusiastic to have a chance to teach. What a great gesture, an advance gift to the twenty-first century!

THE RENEWAL OF TEACHERS NOW IN SERVICE

Doctors now attend annual seminars on new medicines, surgical procedures, and other developments. Lawyers and engineers attend similar programs in their fields. Teachers, however, are rewarded for advanced study even in fields other than those they teach. Teachers in most Illinois counties, for example, attend a one-day teacher institute with a guest speaker or two or three short sessions on special topics, in which a briefing on teacher retirement benefits somtimes competes effectively with seminars in new ways to teach about ecology.

A more appropriate format would be short, concentrated workshops (two or three days or ten to twenty clock hours) on such emerging issues as metrication, the inevitable conversion to measurement systems used elsewhere throughout the world, and mainstreaming, the new way of returning moderately handicapped and even mildly disturbed children to their nearby schools–with resource rooms within the schools for emergencies.

If we believe the futurists, each year will bring new pedagogical and scientific advances to master. As a young principal I planned a special workshop on teacher-made visuals for the overhead projector, only to find out that three of the thirty veterans had never been shown how to thread a 16mm film projector. What new technology?

Who teaches the social studies teachers the meaning of concepts such as infra-structure, stagflations, cost-benefit analysis or the critiques of national health programs or United States policies? The emergence of teacher centers in many parts of the United States has great potential for revolutionizing elementary education; but neither states nor universities have thought enough about how to motivate and compensate high school teachers for necessary life-long learning. Some of the most effective approaches were developed by the National Science Foundation whose success should be more closely evaluated by state decisionmakers.

The Continuing Education of Teachers of the Arts

Martin Engel
National Institute of Education

THE PRESENT PROSPECT

Although today's educators have become aware of the importance of the affective domain to the educational curriculum, budgetary knives are cutting a wide swath into just that area. Researchers are discovering interrelationships between the various modes of symbolization and knowing, and between doing and knowing. Arguments demonstrate the importance of the arts, of sensory perception, of aesthetic discrimination not only as self-evident values, but as integral dimensions of learning. Yet almost every state has reduced expenditures to the schools for special instructional services in the arts. While school budgets for the arts plummet, both private and federal support increase for programs *outside of the schools*—community arts, extension arts, and similar programs reflecting the dissatisfaction with school based arts education. There has not been quality education in the arts available in our elementary and secondary schools to enhance the artistic/aesthetic capacities and potential of our students. The schools remain an unimportant source of creative stimulation in our children's development. Nor are they a viable source for information about the arts or activities that lead to enhanced artistic appreciation.

It is not only the low level of effective instruction, but the divisiveness and separateness of the arts and nonarts at the elementary level, that have proven harmful to the education of every child. Part of the problem stems from the nature of our educational system where the human experience of reality is fragmented into "subjects" made teachable by discreteness and compartmentalization. When the vast sweep of the arts is fractionated into units of instruction, manageability has been achieved at the cost of comprehensiveness and legitimate experience. Such curricular destructuring may lend itself to packaging and lesson plans with measurable outcomes, but only at the cost of sterility. The corrective burden falls upon the development of curricula for the general classroom, and the development of general classroom teachers who can deliver that curriculum to the students. This is what in-service education in the arts should be about.

TEACHING TEACHERS TO TEACH THE ARTS

What does staff development mean?

1. It means that nonarts teachers, in the elmentary and secondary schools, be taught one or more art (music, dance, theater, visual arts, etc.), the aesthetics of perception and the importance of aesthetic judgment.
2. It means that the present cadre of teachers of the arts, who themselves have had art training, significantly improve their skills, learn about other art forms and about aesthetics as theory and instructional content.
3. It means that professional organizations of arts education develop priorities that strengthen the professional behavior of their membership. This means greater competence in the arts themselves, in conceptual and intellectual understanding of the theory and foundations of aesthetics and education in the arts, and in interpersonal skills with young people. Professional organizations can set standards and determine qualifications for the teaching of the arts.
4. It means that institutions that train teachers reorganize themsleves so that enrollments consist less of new teachers and more of experienced classroom teachers already in the field. This means that colleges of art, music, theater, and dance open their doors to a different student body; provide a more realistic curriculum, tempered and proven through experience in the schools; offer mini-courses, external degrees, workshop formats, in-service training on the job, and itinerant faculty who will leave their college classrooms to join the teacher in the field–in the elementary and secondary school classroom.

In-service education as nothing more than greater quantities of art courses and workshops for art teachers in each of the arts misses the issue. The market for in-service education in the arts includes general classroom teachers in the lower grades and subject-specialists in the upper grades.

For those teachers who already have background and training in the arts needed for their artistic foundations, in-service education in the arts will not constitute a refinement of existing skills and knowledge. Instead it can be an introduction to a whole new discipline. The content of in-service training can include a new set of skills in seeing, hearing, thinking, and doing, an introductory experience in the fundamentals of aesthetic perception.

The teacher can be encouraged to become a doer. The mind in the body and in the hands can be as well developed aesthetically as the mind in the head. If the classroom teacher can already play the piano, she should receive reinforcement to practice and enlarge her repertoire of enjoyment through music (likewise to any other art practice). In-service education can foster a greater commitment to, and involvement in, the practice of art by the general classroom teacher.

THE IN-SERVICE ISSUE

The contention here is that the arts in education should pervade all the classrooms. The principal and his staff, the art teacher and the supervisors of art education must understand that experiences in the arts need to extend beyond a twenty-minute class period; experiences in the visual arts can be more than a series of crafts lessons; music more than memorizing key signatures and words; drama more than an annual Christmas pageant; and a field trip—to museum, concert hall or theater—more than an outing. Experiences in the arts will be meaningful experiences to the students when they are woven into a comprehensive and continuous program.

The vehicle for redress of the distorted curriculum can be in-service creative arts education for all teachers. The art specialist in the schools can work closely with the general classroom teacher so that in-service training becomes stage one of a two-stage instructional program in which arts specialists *train teachers rather than students.* Institutions that provide professionals in the arts, colleges of art and music, can be intimately involved in creative arts education in the schools. Teachers Centers can be ideal vehicles of contact between learner-practitioner and teacher-professional. Residential Artists-in-Schools programs can be set up to work closely with and for teachers. Classroom teachers can be encouraged to teach the arts as a far more integrated activity, woven into the fabric of the total curriculum, rather than the specialist-adjunct that it now is. Perhaps the creative arts will gain recognition through involvement in schools. Attendant reversals in the budgetary picture for arts specialists could follow.

There are more questions than answers.Who will assume initiatives for enhancing skills of arts specialists in elementary and secondary schools? What is the best role for colleges of art and how can they relate to education colleges? How can a rigorous and meaningful training program in the arts and aesthetic education be given to the general classroom teachers in the elementary schools? How should training be paid for? How can training stimulate curriculum development at the teacher/classroom level? What is the role of the administrator/supervisor in the arts? Can production/performance, appreciation/criticism/analysis awareness, knowledge acquisition and creative process be taught as a unified whole?

The teaching profession has the obligation to pull the arts and aesthetic perception from its peripheral and expendible place in the curriculum, into the core of education as basic and essential skills. Nonverbal expression is as important to human growth and development as verbal. Research suggests that the functions of the right hemisphere are as significant as those of the left and that they are mutually interdependent. That means new and different valuations and skills for all classroom teachers. It means new behaviors and measures. Teachers must demand it and the education community must provide it. The basic resource for revitalizing the creative arts curriculum could very well come from the artistic community now outside education.

Law: A Curriculum for all Students

Louis Fischer and David Schimmel

University of Massachusetts

Teaching about law has become one of the most important and popular new dimensions in American education and a major growth area of in-service teacher training. According to the American Bar Association, there were less than 100 programs in law-focused education in 1970; six years later there were more than 400, with more than half of these focusing on in-service education. The purposes of this article are: (1) to outline the goals of law-focused education and some of the reasons for its rapid growth; (2) to describe the major curriculum materials, teaching strategies and in-service models; and (3) to suggest where educators can get additional help in starting or expanding programs in this field.

THE REASONS

Why have law studies become popular? The reasons are complex and interrelated: they include the need, the times, and the changing attitudes of lawyers and educators.

The Need. Law pervades our individual lives—from birth, through compulsory schooling, marriage, the purchase of a home or car, divorce, and death. Law is also an element of almost every major problem we confront as a people: the way we select our president, the energy crisis, abortion, busing, crime, welfare, taxes, and corruption in business or government.

Despite this, the *New York Times* noted in 1976 that "not more than one percent of pre-college students are exposed to law-related courses."[1] An equally small percentage of teachers have had pre-service preparation in law-related subjects. Since law plays a crucial role in our personal and public lives and since there is massive legal illiteracy among students and teachers, the need for in-service programs in law-related education is clear.

The Times. With the spiraling rates of juvenile delinquency and adult crime, with periodic revelations of government corruption, and with decreasing faith in our law and public institutions, voters during the 1970s have become increasingly concerned with, and critical of, the school's role in developing good citizens.

Studies during the past decade indicated that traditional civics courses not only failed to instill respect for the law but succeeded in alienating students both by their method and their content–platitudes, chauvinistic statements and unrealistic descriptions of how our legal and political institutions function. One recent survey reported that such courses "have little impact at the time and virtually none afterwards. The most lasting effect may well be an *increase* in the student's cynicism and alienation."[2] In earlier generations, pious lectures about the virtues of our country and obedience to the law might have encouraged good citizenship. But in this post-Watergate era, when many students are skeptical about all of our institutions, solemn exhortation does not work. And we cannot afford another generation of legally illiterate citizens–young people who are uninformed, apathetic, and perhaps hostile to our democratic system. Thus both recent events and scholarly studies have made an increasing number of parents, teachers and administrators realize that something must be done–our traditional curriculum is not meeting the challenge of the times.

Help from the Legal Profession. In the past, the study of law was left largely to lawyers because of the popular belief that law was a specialized field that could only be understood by individuals with years of expert training. Lawyers did little to dispel this belief. Today, however, the American Bar Association clearly acknowledges that "law is too important to be left to lawyers."[3] In fact, the American Bar Associa-

1. *New York Times,* "News of the Week in Review," 26 February 1976.
2. American Bar Association, Special Committee on Youth Education for Citizenship, *Law-related Education in America: Guidelines for the Future* (St. Paul, Minn.: West Publishing Company, 1975), p. 1. For a review of these studies, see Ronald A. Gerlach and Lynne W. Lamprecht, *Teaching about the Law* (Cincinnati, Ohio: W. H. Anderson Company, 1975), pp. 13–17.
3. Joel Henning, "What are Law-related Studies?" *Social Studies Review* vol. 14, no. 1, (Fall, 1974): 5.

tion is now actively encouraging state and local bar associations to cooperate with schools and colleges to ensure that "legal literacy" becomes as central to public education as reading or math.

GOALS

Programs in law-related education vary in their focus. Some emphasize "street law," legal knowledge about matters of immediate and practical interest to students. Others emphasize broad legal concepts and critical thinking. While their priorities may differ, the goals of most programs are to provide students with: (1) information about the law; (2) an understanding of the legal system; and (3) problem-solving and analytical skills.

Information About the Law. Many programs believe law studies can and should respond to student demand for "relevance," for information that can have practical and immediate value. Laws about crime, drugs, student rights, the family, the consumer, and the environment are some of the areas that relate directly to the lives of students. The purpose of providing such legal information is not to train "schoolhouse lawyers," or to create an illusion of legal expertise. Rather, the idea is to begin where the students are, with the legal questions that currently concern them, and thus to make the schools become places to make sense of real-life experience.

Understanding the System. In most programs, teaching young people about their rights and responsibilities as students, consumers, or possible defendants is just the beginning. Of critical importance is helping them understand how our legal system functions and why it operates the way it does. Thus law-focused courses examine: (1) the role, the value, and the limits of laws, lawyers, and judges; (2) why laws, contracts, and legal procedures are often complicated; (3) how the law is developed and applied in their school and their community; and (4) why our legal system sometimes seems to break down and what can be done to improve it.

Analytical Skills. By learning to analyze cases, students can develop problem-solving skills and critical thinking abilities that can be applied to other social and political problems. In studying actual cases, students can be taught to find out: (1) the causes of the problem, the arguments on each side, and the values that are in conflict; (2) the laws or legal principles that would be used to handle the problem; (3) the alternative ways the controversy could be resolved and the costs and benefits of each; (4) the way the conflict was actually settled, the reasons for it, and its significance to society and themselves.

There is a triple payoff for students who learn such an analytic, case-study approach—they are better able to apply general concepts and principles to real-life situations; they tend to have more positive attitudes toward the law and our legal system; they are more tolerant of diversity and recognize that most important legal controversies are not simple cases of right against wrong but of legitimate rights in conflict.

Other Benefits. In addition to knowledge, understanding, and analytical skills, students in law-related programs may gain several additional benefits. Followers of Harvard Professor Lawrence Kohlberg believe that the discussion and analysis of legal controversies can enable students to clarify values and develop moral and ethical reasoning ability. Others see these programs breaking down such legal misconceptions as "there is a solution for every legal problem" or "law is simply a tool for the rich." In addition, law-related programs can teach an approach to responsible citizen action by showing how law has been successful in grappling with many important problems and how it can continue to be used as a tool to resolve societal conflicts and to affect change without violence.

CURRICULUM MATERIALS

Because of their technical and complex nature, most legal materials designed for lawyers and law students are not suited for use in social studies or civics courses. During the past decade, however, several law studies projects have developed excellent law-related materials for the public schools. These materials assume no prior legal knowledge, cover many aspects of the legal system, and enable teachers to choose those most suited for their own classrooms. This section will discuss a few of these materials and will mention several others.

Law In A Free Society: In-Service Materials is the only project that has developed materials primarily for use by in-service project coordinators and teachers. Sponsored by the California Bar Association, the L.F.S. curriculum focuses on eight concepts: authority, justice, freedom, participation, diversity, privacy, property, and responsibility. It has prepared four booklets on each concept: an In-

Service Course Guide, a Casebook, a Curriculum (objectives on each concept for students, grades K–12), and a set of sample Lesson Plans.

The in-service materials are designed to give teachers an understanding of the subject-matter and methods needed to present effective lessons at their grade levels on each concept. The Casebooks are especially good compilations that include actual court cases, hypothetical cases, news stories, and excerpts from historical and sociological literature that examine the concept from different viewpoints. Although the Casebooks were designed primarily for teachers, they can also be adapted for student use in secondary classrooms.

Under a grant from the National Endowment for the Humanities, L.F.S. is now developing student materials that will parallel those already published for in-service programs. Designed for students K–12, the curriculum will include a student resource book, filmstrips, audiotapes and teacher's guide on each of the eight concepts.[4]

Law in American Society Foundation: Material for Grades 4–12 has developed the "Trailmarks of Liberty" series consisting of three supplementary texts (and teacher's guide) to enrich history and social studies courses from intermediate grades through high school. Based on important constitutional issues, the series is designed to encourage (1) an acceptance of value conflict as a normal part of our pluralistic society; and (2) a commitment to reason and compromise through the judicial process as the best way to resolve conflict. The texts focus on legal concepts at three levels: upper elementary (*Law in the New Land*), junior high school (*Great Cases of the Supreme Court*), and senior high school (*Vital Issues of the Constitution*).[5] Emphasizing the case method, these books explore the constitutional aspects of social problems in their historical context and as they exist today. Rules of law are seen "as the values which our American society has selected as important enough to enforce . . . as a power tool for settling real-life conflicts." The constitutional cases are all presented in an open-ended fashion followed by discussion questions for the students. The Supreme Court's solutions to the problems are found in an accompanying teacher's guide or *Decision Supplement.*

L.A.S.F. also developed a series of six paperbacks entitled *Justice in Urban America* designed to provide a full course in legal studies for

4. More information about any of these materials can be obtained by writing to Law in a Free Society, 606 Wilshire Boulevard, Suite 600, Santa Monica, California 90401.

5. Robert H. Ratcliffe, ed., "Law in a New Land" (1972); "Great Cases of the Supreme Court" (1971); "Vital Issues of the Constitution" (1971), *Trailmarks of Liberty Series* (Boston, MA.: Houghton Mifflin Company, 1972).

junior and senior high school students.[6] Focusing on how the law works in everyday life, the booklets are entitled "Law and the City," "Crimes and Justice," "Landlord and Tenant," "Law and the Consumer," "Poverty and Welfare," "Youth and the Law." The series teaches that law is an evolving process for balancing conflicting interests and resolving disputes in a democratic society. In addition, L.A.S.F. publishes a quarterly journal for teachers entitled *Law in American Society.*[7]

Other Materials. There are several other curriculum materials that in-service coordinators should consider:

1. The Cornell Law Project has developed a "Basic Legal Concepts" curriculum that includes the *Justice and Order Through Law* series for junior high school and the *American Legal System* for high school students.[8] Each series consists of five student booklets and a teacher's guide. The *American Legal Concepts* curriculum not only provides a comprehensive and interesting treatment of the values, techniques, and limits of the law but also includes cases dealing with the application of the Constitution to the classroom as well as the community.
2. The American Institute for Character Education has developed two sets of law-related curriculum kits for each elementary grade. Entitled *Living With Me–And Others* and *Our Rights and Responsibilities,* each of the kits contain student activity sheets, posters, recordings, evaluation instruments and a valuable teacher's guide.[9]
3. For both teachers and secondary students, the Constitutional Rights Foundation publishes the *Bill of Rights Newsletter.*[10] Each issue of the semi-annual *Newsletter* focuses on a particular theme such as "Sex, Society, and Equality" or "Student Protest" and includes court decisions, cartoons, questionnaires, interviews, and conflicting viewpoints to stimulate class discussion and analysis. In addition, the Foundation recently reviewed *The Bill of Rights, A Source Book,* an

6. Robert H. Ratcliffe, ed. *Justice in Urban America Series* (Boston, MA.: Houghton Mifflin Company, 1974).
7. More information about *Law in American Society, Journal of the National Center for Law-focused Education,* can be obtained by writing to Law in American Society Foundation, 33 North LaSalle Street, Chicago, Illinois 60602.
8. Robert Summers, Bruce Campbell, and John Bozzone, *Justice and Order Through Law*; and Robert Summers, Bruce Campbell, and Gail Hubbard, *The American Legal System* (Lexington, MA.: Ginn and Company, 1974).
9. Character Education Program Staff, *Living with Me–and Others* (1973); and *Our Rights and Responsibilities* (1972) (San Antonio, Texas: American Institute for Character Education).
10. Todd Clark, ed. *Bill of Rights Newsletter* (Los Angeles, CA.: Constitutional Rights Foundation).

excellent background volume for educators who teach about individual rights.[11]

Films and TV. Today there are an extraordinary number of audio-visual materials for teachers to choose from on a wide variety of law-related topics. There are films dramatizing actual court cases, such as Encyclopedia Britannica's the *Living Bill of Rights* series, that presents the background events, the legal arguments and the judicial decisions of six major Supreme Court cases.[12] There are films using hypothetical situations that raise important legal issues but leave the decision and rationale open for student discussion. There are documentaries produced by public television, such as *Justice and the Poor,* that can stimulate student analysis of particular legal problems.[13] And there are a number of full-length motion pictures, such as *Ox-Bow Incident,* that can be adapted for classroom use.[14] In addition, popular television shows about the law might be used to examine stereotypes of lawyers, judges, policemen, and police methods perpetuated by the media. There are also films specially designed for elementary school children, such as *Why We Have Laws: Shiver, Goble and Snore,* an entertaining cartoon that shows why rules and laws are necessary.[15] A comprehensive listing of media in this field has been published by the American Bar Association. Entitled *Media: An Annotated Catalog of Law-Related Audio-Visual Materials,* this free 78-page booklet describes over 400 films, filmstrips, audio cassettes, videotapes, and mixed media kits.[16]

Simulation, Role-Playing, and Gaming. Many people associate law studies programs with one type of simulation—a mock trial in which students enact a courtroom drama and play the parts of lawyers, witnesses, judge and jury. Some criticize this popular activity for its tendency to perpetuate simplistic television stereotypes. Such criticism should remind us that the educational effectiveness of simulations depends on very careful teacher preparation and thorough debriefing

11. William Cohen, Murray Schwartz and DeAnne Sobal, *The Bill of Rights: A Source Book* (Beverly Hills, CA.: Benzinger Publishing Company, 1976).
12. Encyclopedia Britannica Educational Corporation, *The Living Bill of Rights Series* (Chicago, Illinois: Encyclopedia Britannica Educational Corporation).
13. Distributed by Indiana University, Audio-Visual Center, Bloomington, Indiana 47401.
14. Distributed by Film Incorporated, 1144 Wilmette Avenue, Wilmette, Illinois 60091.
15. Distributed by Learning Corporation of America, 711 Fifth Avenue, New York, New York 10030.
16. Susan Davidson, ed., *Media: An Annotated Catalog of Law-related Audio-Visual Materials* (Chicago, Illinois: American Bar Association, Special Committee on Youth Education for Citizenship, 1975). Also, see Gerlach and Lamprecht, *Teaching about the Law,* Chapter 4, "Audio-Visual Presentations."

that compares and contrasts the classroom activity with the real world of law and the judicial process. This is also true of less complex simulations such as the moot court in which students enact an appeals case involving a panel of judges and a set of attorneys. Unlike the dramatic mock trial, the moot court is a more controlled activity involving a written "brief" and oral argument to the judges concerning issues of law (e.g., Was the statute constitutional?) rather than issues of fact (e.g., Did the defendant tell the truth?). Other simulations, role playing techniques, and games place students in hypothetical situations that will enable them to apply their knowledge, develop their imagination, test their decision-making ability, and help them understand the varied attitudes and perspectives of diverse participants in our legal system.

As Todd Clark wrote in the American Bar Association's booklet *Gaming*:

> By taking the roles of other individuals in simulations, students learn how it feels to be caught in a conflict that must somehow be resolved; they can better understand the pressures and learn the skills that are essential to successfully managing conflict in a free society. They can understand that our legal and political system which may seem to be made up of faceless bureaucracies are really run by people.

Gaming: An Annotated Catalogue of Law-Related Games and Simulations describes more than 125 simulation games plus books and pamphlets that can help teachers use simulations more effectively and design their own activities.[17]

IN-SERVICE MODELS AND COMMUNITY RESOURCES

The format of most in-service programs in law-related education follows three familiar patterns. The most effective are the summer institutes, typically full-time programs, three or four weeks in length. Many are free; most offer university credit and include elementary as well as secondary teachers. One popular format devotes morning sessions to presentations by lawyers or criminal justice personnel about substantive topics such as criminal, constitutional or consumer law. In the after-

17. Educators may obtain single complimentary copies of *Gaming: An Annotated Catalogue of Law-related Games and Simulations,* Susan Davidson, ed., from The American Bar Association, Special Committee on Youth Education for Citizenship, 1155 East 60th Street, Chicago, Illinois 60637. Also, see Gerlach and Lamprecht, *Teaching about the Law,* Chapter 9, "Simulation Role-playing and Gaming."

noons, teachers are grouped according to grade level and adapt the "morning knowledge" to instructional use.

The second in-service pattern is a series of minicourses offered by law studies projects during the school year. Typically they involve ten to fourteen weekly sessions for two to three hours in the afternoon or evening centering on the study of one or two particular legal concepts. Like the summer institutes, sessions usually offer substantive law presentations followed by an "education seminar" devoted to translating the legal content into classroom lessons.

The third model developed by the Constitutional Rights Foundation was designed to give teachers more practical experience with the law and its daily operations. In this experiential approach, teachers participate in the operation of the criminal justice system and spend several normal working days at a public defender or district attorney's office, with a court clerk, a probation officer, or in a police squad car. While such activities can have a powerful impact, this model involves extensive coordination and cooperation on the part of public officials, and might best be used as a supplement to summer institutes and courses.

Although most law-related in-service models are not unusual in format, such programs do offer extraordinary opportunities to integrate community resources into the curriculum. In many districts, educators have received help from the local bar association, the police, the F.B.I., the municipal, state, or federal courts, the public defender or district attorney, the corrections department and local law students or professors. Law studies programs, for example, can provide an important, additional perspective by visiting a nearby courtroom and police station and then discussing the visit with a local trial lawyer. Thus, in every community, justice agencies and bar associations can provide both in-service coordinators and classroom teachers with a rich array of resources to supplement a law-studies curriculum.

SOURCES OF HELP

A decade ago, educators who wanted to start a law-studies program were largely on their own. Today there are many sources of assistance. One of the best is a recent book entitled *Teaching About the Law* by Ronald Gerlach and Lynn Lamprecht.[18] Designed for in-service coordi-

18. Ronald Gerlach and Lynne Lamprecht, *Teaching about the Law* (Cincinnati, Ohio: W. H. Anderson, Co., 1975).

nators, this 354-page volume is a comprehensive introduction to the field. It includes chapters on ways to organize a law studies program and prepare the teachers, as well as sections on goals, curriculum materials, community resources, legal references, the case studies approach, and evaluation strategies.

Another excellent source of assistance is the American Bar Association's Special Committee on Youth for Citizenship. Established to stimulate and coordinate projects in law-related education, the A.B.A. committee serves as a national clearinghouse for information in this field and consults with educators, lawyers, and other community leaders in the development of local programs. In addition to *Gaming* and *Media,* the committee publishes a number of other useful booklets, including *Bibliography of Law-Related Curriculum Materials: Annotated* (describing more than 500 books and pamphlets), *Help! What To Do, Where To Go* (discusses a variety of projects and teacher training programs), *The $ $ Game: A Guidebook On The Funding of Law-Related Educational Programs,* and *A Directory of Law-Related Educational Activities.* For anyone starting an in-service program, these free booklets and the committee staff can be an invaluable source of information and advice.

THE RESULTS

Recent books and articles have suggested important differences between the results of the earlier civics and social studies programs and some of the new law-focused curriculum. For example, "traditional" courses, with their emphasis on noncontroversial topics and compliance with rules and authority, resulted in negative feelings regarding political participation and a tendency to allow the government to violate the constitutional rights of individuals.[19] In contrast, it appears that a law-related curriculum, which includes careful and open analysis of controversial legal cases, leads students to develop more positive political attitudes, greater agreement with the Bill of Rights, more tolerance of differences, and more willingness to listen to others.[20] These findings, together with the encouragement of the American Bar Association, have persuaded a growing number of educators to start in-service programs in law-related education as a way of better preparing students for active, responsible citizenship.

19. Gerlach and Lamprecht, *Teaching,* pp. 13–17.
20. Ibid., pp. 17–20.

THE HIDDEN CURRICULUM: TOMORROW'S CHALLENGE

Today, most law-related education projects focus only on curriculum development and in-service education for social studies teachers. However, an effective program must address itself not only to the formal curriculum but also to the "hidden curriculum"—to the environment of the schools and to the behavior of educators who teach by the examples they set as well as by the texts they use. Although there are good reasons for our current emphasis on the formal curriculum, the "modeling" behavior of teachers, administrators, and school boards is at least as influential in demonstrating how our legal system operates. For example, it is probable that a school's use of fair and just disciplinary procedures will do more to shape positive student attitudes and understanding of due process than curriculum materials that accurately describe how due process operates in our courts. Conversely, a school teaches "legal cynicism" if its texts emphasize the value of obeying rules and respecting authority while its teachers or administrators violate the rights of students. This does not mean that in-service programs for social studies teachers are unimportant; rather, it means that in the future we should pay equal attention to educating all of the teachers of the hidden curriculum (from school secretaries and bus drivers to school board members) so that our public schools can become operating models of the constitutional principles we teach in our classrooms.

CONCLUSION

In a 1976 speech before the National Association of Secondary School Principals, the President of the United States echoed the concern of many educators when he said that young people "appear cynical and alienated from our Government and our legal system. Too many Americans see the law as a threat rather than as a protection. Too few have been taught to understand the way laws are created and administered and peacefully changed."[21] The President noted, "we cannot perpetuate our value system merely by telling our children that it is good." Instead, he called for an alternative to the old civics courses that would teach our students to participate effectively in correcting the faults of our legal system as well as in supporting its strengths. It is just this call that law-related education was designed to answer.

21. President Ford's remarks were delivered at the Annual Convention of the National Association of Secondary School Principals, February 16, 1976.

Participation and Personal Growth: Keys to Staff Development

Ambrose J. Furey, Jr.
Forest View High School, Arlington Heights, Illinois

Strange as it may seem, declining school enrollment and the consequent reduction in teaching positions may prove a blessing for in-service education. Since recruitment is no longer a realistic means for revitalizing faculties, the thrust for growth and updating of skills will have to come from programs aimed at currently employed administrators and teachers. Lack of staff turnover will provide, perhaps for the first time, an opportunity for in-service education to become transformed into long-term ongoing staff development.

Whether such staff development is focused on improving instructional or managerial skills or on providing opportunities for personal growth, it must be viewed as an essential part of the educational rather than a remedial frill for the ineffective or the ill-prepared. Providing attractive, significant opportunities for educators to continue their professional growth is the crucial issue in education today.

Too much of "good" teacher behavior is static and maintaining rather than dynamic and growing. (A good teacher is often perceived as one who is rarely ill, has a controlled, quiet classroom, and gets all paper work handed in on time.) Personal and professional growth must be emphasized as open-ended processes rather than goals that are reached when the proper number of degrees or additional approved college credits are amassed. Staff development programs must help establish, within the profession, a model for excellence rather than adequacy by substituting a *becoming a better teacher* model for the *being a good teacher* model now in use.

Planning of staff development programs should include inputs from teachers, administrators, and staff development specialists. Administrators should feel that they can suggest to teachers areas in which growth is desirable; teachers, in turn, ought to be able to feel free to suggest ways in which adminstrators might develop plans for their own educational growth. Shared goal setting and decision-making reinforce the point that both teachers and administrators are educators and colleagues and not part of a worker-boss relationship.

Staff development programs with a participatory base offer teachers a unique source of professional recognition and personal satisfaction. In such programs, teachers can exercise leadership in the profession and share their expertise with colleagues, without having to leave teaching for administrative positions or work in a teacher organization.

Because the need for change in education is crucial, participation in staff development should be part of the terms of employment for all educators, no matter what their role. Each year educators expect, and generally receive, a salary increase based on the questionable assumption that another year on the job has made them better at what they are doing. Mandatory staff development participation would: (1) make it clear to educators that the normal state of the profession is growth; (2) push school districts to reassess, on a regular basis, the needs and issues their staffs must deal with, and make available to them the resources to meet these needs; and (3) make it possible for institutions to invest in programs that would update and improve their staffs in pertinent areas rather than relying on randomly selected conferences and professional meetings to provide necessary growth.

Staff development programs can also be linked to the evaluation and supervision processes. This linkage would give schools considerable power in determining what is asked of teachers in terms of professional growth and change. Disconcerting as this may sound to some teachers and teacher organizations, linking staff development with evaluation and supervision provides some benefits for teachers. Teachers can turn to administrators and school boards and demand the resources for improving their professional competence. By this means, programs for professional growth can be negotiated as essentials and not be relegated to the area of budgetary frills and leftovers.

Educators have come to the conclusion that a uniform presentation of material to a class is not the most effective way to teach children. It seems logical, then, that providing for individual differences among teachers and administrators can only facilitate their in-service learning. The growth needs for individuals who are already *good teachers* are different from those of teachers and administrators who are new to the job or who are simply not as competent as others. Too often concentration on the new or the weak leaves the person who does a good job to find his own growth experiences. Tying staff development into regular professional evaluation is a way to break the *good teacher* model and to give competent people the opportunity they deserve for developing themselves more fully as people and as professionals.

Obviously, the linking of staff development to supervision and evaluation has potential problems. Teachers must be protected from the whims of administrators with regard to how they should change. A well-negotiated contract can provide this protection, yet still indicate that continuous growth in the profession is expected for all staff members. Teachers and teacher organizations, however, must recognize that there are real differences among teachers and that what is an effective, appropriate program for some is not necessarily effective or appropriate for others. It is also conceivable that some teachers may be so incompetent or so unwilling to change that they cannot continue in the profession, even with a specialized and individualized staff development program.

Staff development programs operate in two areas. The first centers on providing new approaches, new skills, and new curriculum materials to the classroom teachers as a means to better classroom instruction, and hopefully, more classroom learning. The second area focuses on providing experiences for personal growth and self-awareness.

There is a supermarket array of options to choose from in the first area (everything from renting a wizard for an institute day to purchasing a new curriculum complete with test booklets, answer keys, and teacher guides) with which to update the education profession, both administratively and pedagogically. The problem is, however, that exposure to new approaches to teaching and supervision are of little use if teaching in the classroom and supervision of the teaching remain exactly as before. No amount of curriculum workshops will bring about improvement unless teachers who will be using the new materials and administrators who will be supervising them are willing to move from "business-as-usual" attitudes and grow into new roles. Unless educators can accept themselves as persons who can initiate and direct change instead of maintenance personnel who respond to community pressure, no amount of educational innovation, no matter how well conceived or cleverly marketed, can make real differences in learning for children.

A staff development program then, should offer opportunities for individual personal growth as well as growth in professional competence. The initial emphasis, however, should lie in the area of personal growth, because the effectiveness of any educational program, whether designed for students or staff, is contingent upon the willingness of an individual to change. For example, think about the years of driver education and drug education in American schools, which have neither lowered insurance rates for drivers under twenty-five nor stemmed the abuse of alcohol and other drugs among youth. What is lacking in such programs is a touching of the learner's values, self-concept and potential for growth that could lead to incorporating the cognitive materials of these courses into a self-directed program of positive, personal behavior change. An effective staff development program will help educators see themselves as changing, growing persons who have the opportunity of shaping the outcome of that growth, and who can recognize their shortcomings as a target for growth rather than a source of defensiveness.

The vehicle used in a staff development program to provide personal growth and heighten self-awareness is immaterial. What *is* important is that educators work together in an atmosphere of mutual concern so that the effects of a comprehensive staff development program can be channeled into behavior that has direct, positive impact on the growth of students in the schools.

Overseas Schools—Diversity in Staff, Students, Setting

Paul T. Luebke

Deputy Director, Office of Overseas Schools, State Department

The teachers of the elementary school assembled for the biweekly in-service workshop. There they were, all eleven of them, graduates of eleven different schools in seven states and four foreign countries, with prior teaching experience ranging from one to eighteen years, including, in one case, an interval of ten years between preservice training and initial teaching experience and current employment. The four foreigners on the staff were graduates of normal schools or other teacher-training institutions in their respective countries, and one held bachelor's and master's degrees from an American university. All the others held bachelor's degrees or higher. (Only five of the seven had been trained in elementary education, one was a secondary English teacher, and one was a chemist with prior college teaching experience.) Four of these teachers held master's degrees in education, one a doctorate (the chemist), and all but the latter held teaching certificates from their respective states.

Where in the world is there an elementary school whose teachers have such varied backgrounds? In many places, as a matter of fact; the school in question is one of a large number of American-sponsored elementary and secondary community schools independently operated in various overseas locations by local associations of parents of students enrolled. These overseas schools have been established for the purpose of providing educational opportunities for dependent children of Americans and other nationals stationed overseas. The schools, located in more than 100 countries around the world, range in size from less than a dozen pupils in what are essentially supervised home study courses, to full-fledged school systems comprising several campuses and enrolling several thousand students. Many of the latter rival good schools in the United States in terms of staff, facilities, and most importantly, quality of educational experiences afforded students.

Some 140 American-sponsored overseas schools that meet certain criteria receive assistance from the Office of Overseas Schools of the United States Department of State;[1] it is this group of schools in particular on which the observations that follow are based, even though what is said would no doubt apply to other overseas schools as well. With combined enrollments of nearly 75,000 students taught by nearly 6,000 teachers, these schools represent a sizeable educational establishment. And large numbers of students and teachers return to schools in the United States each year–perhaps there's one in your school.

Because of their location overseas and the high costs involved in bringing professional staff from the United States, most overseas schools seek to hire local qualified staff if possible. Thus, in the staff referred to here, only three of the eleven elementary staff members were recruited from the United States for the express purpose of teaching in the school. These three were selected on the basis of training and recent experience to serve as a highly-qualified "core" of teachers to guide and assist other members of the staff. The others included the wife of a United States Embassy officer with nearly two decades' experience in public elementary schools in the Washington, D.C., area as well as in three other overseas schools on two other continents. Similarly, the wife of an American businessman, holding a master's degree and certification in special education, had had teaching experience both in the United States and in a variety of overseas schools. Another was the American wife of a local government official who had met her husband when they were both students at the same university. The seventh American, wife of the local CARE representative and a college chemistry instructor before she went overseas, had taught science at both the elementary and secondary levels in overseas schools at other posts to which her husband had been assigned. The teachers who were not Americans included a former director of ele-

1. These schools are described in some detail in Paul T. Luebke, *American Elementary and Secondary Community Schools Abroad,* 2nd ed. (Arlington, VA.: American Association of School Administrators, 1976). This publication as well as additional information regarding the schools may be obtained from the Office of Overseas Schools, Room 234, SA 6, U.S. Department of State, Washington, D.C., 20520. The independent American-sponsored overseas schools are not to be confused with U.S. military dependents' schools operated abroad by the Department of Defense. Information regarding the U.S. military schools may be obtained from the Office of Overseas Dependent Education, Department of Defense, Washington, D.C., 20301.

mentary education of the local Ministry of Education who had been trained in the United States and who taught in a private school for three years before returning to her home country; the wife of a Danish foreign service officer who had had experience in Danish primary schools as well as in several other American overseas schools; the wife of a British Council officer with a number of years' experience in British infant schools as well as in several British overseas schools; and the Indian wife of a United Nations official with training in India and England, and brief teaching experience in her home country some years earlier, before she interrupted her career to raise a family. The elementary school principal was a former Connecticut principal with a doctorate in curriculum and supervision and administrative experience in three overseas schools. The superintendent, a former administrator in California public schools, with a doctorate in administration, was in the third year of his first overseas position. The school's curriculum coordinator, responsible for supervision and in-service programs for teachers of Kindergarten through Grade twelve, had teaching and supervisory experience at the secondary level, plus course work, certification, and college teaching experience in Kindergarten through Grade twelve programs, including intensive workshops (held overseas) in techniques of the individualization of instruction.

With such a heterogeneous "collection" of teachers, chosen more by happenstance than by design, the principal and curriculum coordinator faced a formidable challenge in developing a cohesive teaching team. But they also faced other challenges. The student body, if anything, was more heterogeneous than the staff.

Of the 247 pupils enrolled, just under two-thirds (141 pupils) were Americans. However, these 141 included a number who had lived and attended school in a number of foreign countries where their foreign service and business-connected parents were assigned, as well as a number of "first-termers" whose parents had newly arrived from American small towns and rural communities to take employment in extractive industries and construction projects. Thus, there were considerable differences in background, prior experience, and expectations among the American pupils, a group presumed to be more or less homogeneous. In fact, many of the other dependents of diplomats—Swedes, Germans, Iranians, Canadians, and others, who had lived abroad most of their lives and most frequently had attended American schools at previous posts—probably had greater affinity for the American foreign service dependents than did many of their newly-arrived compatriots. In addition, however, there were several dozen local and third-country children just learning the English language who were also quite unfamiliar with American schools and style of education. Thus, there was a sizeable segment of the school population not attuned to American culture for whom the "strange" ways of their schoolmates posed formidable personal and emotional problems.

A third dimension affecting the school, related to the local students' cultural distance from their schoolmates, was the very fact that the school, an American school, existed in a country far from the United States, both in geographic terms and in cultural terms. Unless the school attempted to exist as a cultural island—as some few schools unfortunately have tried to do—it was faced with the need to familiarize staff, student body, and parent community with both the obvious, and more importantly, the subtle differences between cultures.

Finally, the school, like most overseas schools, was also far removed not only from colleagues and educational resources in the United States, but from other overseas schools as well. When the administrators of the overseas schools in Africa get together for their annual conference, for example, they congregate from throughout an area nearly four times that of the continental United States, and the nearest colleague might well be a $400 plane ride away. Delivery of instructional materials from the United States involved interminable delays; magazines, newspapers, cardboard cartons, public libraries, local supermarkets, the firehouse, and other resources taken for granted at home were simply not available.

The overseas school described here is not "typical," because no two schools are alike. But one or more of the conditions and circumstances noted confront all overseas schools in varying degrees. And conducting effective in-service education programs is difficult enough in a "normal" setting (whatever that might be), without the added problems inherent in the overseas setting. The great diversity in the backgrounds of staff members (both in terms of geography and of time frame), the diversity of students and their backgrounds, and the diversity of school setting add dimensions to the task of staff in-service training that cannot be ignored.

How do the overseas schools cope with these problems? As with schools everywhere, some do poorly, and some do nothing at all, confident that each teacher is best left alone to muddle through. Fortunately, most overseas schools clamor for opportunities for staff in-service training, but some, in their isolation and in their eagerness to latch on to every "visiting fireman" who happens through their city in the belief that anything is better than nothing, have a diet that consists of hit or miss (more often the latter) attempts by uninformed outsiders to say something relevant. (One well-meaning peripatetic art teacher began a description of the use of waste materials with, "Now take a cigar box. . . . You can't get cigar boxes? Well, if you *could* get a cigar box. . . .")

Recognizing the key role of in-service education of teachers, the Office of Overseas Schools has assigned the highest priority to this area, and has long encouraged and supported attempts by individual schools and groups of schools to assess their needs and develop meaningful programs. The impetus for many of the programs is the regional association of overseas schools that exists in each of the overseas regions. These associations sponsor conferences and workshops for administrators, counsellors, teachers, board members, and the like, and several support full-time consultants responsible for curriculum development, coordination of in-service programs, publications, and the like.

Because their overseas location, particularly for smaller and less affluent schools, often precludes the employment of staff with recent "stateside" training and experience, several groups of schools have sought the cooperation of various universities in the development of graduate degree programs. While every effort is made in these programs to be relevant to specific needs of the overseas teachers, the fact remains that they perforce are not infrequently shaped in large degree by academic requirements of the home campus. These formal programs are also supplemented by workshops, short courses, and consultation led by university staff members knowledgeable concerning the overseas school setting. Similar activities are conducted by staff members of school districts paired with selected overseas schools under the School-to-School Program sponsored by the Office of Overseas Schools.

There have also been training programs for teachers involved in special programs such as "Man, A Course of Study" and the various science programs that require special training of teachers before the course and instructional materials may be introduced. There have been special workshops and follow-up activities to retrain teachers and administrators in the concepts and techniques of individualization of instruction. It is these latter kinds of training programs that appear to have met with the greatest success in many overseas schools; they deal with specific problems faced by a unique group of teachers working with a particular student body in a special geographic and cultural setting.

Increasing numbers of overseas schools have instituted in-service training activities that involve staff in considering their own school setting in terms of the host country's cultural values, social structure, verbal and nonverbal language, and the like. They are studying ways of improving classroom effectiveness when cultural values, social background, language, and other elements vary among students or between students and teacher. They are involved in needs assessment and identification of human resources within the local staff, and providing training in interaction analysis and the analysis of instruction in their own classrooms. They are developing learning packets for teachers that are aimed at assisting with teaching and learning problems identified within the local school.

Isolation–with the "neighboring" school often a thousand miles away or more–has been a "blessing in disguise" for some overseas schools in that it has required school boards to employ more highly trained and experienced administrative and supervisory staff than would normally be found in schools of comparable size in the United States. For the same reason, many have higher proportions of other specialized staff members to guide and assist in in-service programs. In 1974–75, for example, nearly three-fourths of the chief administrators in schools with enrollments of 50 to 299 held master's degrees, and another tenth held doctorates. Though the financial outlay is high, so is the payoff in terms of development of staff and ultimate quality of the educational product.

What has been said here is not to imply that all overseas schools are the acme of perfection. Many, for a variety of reasons, provide less than optimum educational opportunity, and even the best are sorely affected by certain adverse factors associated with their overseas location? However, the kinds of staff in-service education programs that circumstances have led a number of forward-looking overseas schools to initiate may well have implications for stateside teacher trainers. With the great mobility of the American population (including teachers) within the country, with the current bringing together in single classrooms of children of divergent socio-economic levels, and the continuing injection of immigrant elements into schools in many areas, is there not a need for increased emphasis on training of staff to recognize and take cognizance of cultural and social dissimilarities among students and staff? Should there not be consideration of possible benefits from increased expenditures necessary to provide local school professional staff capable of developing relevant in-service education programs in each school, in lieu of other more structured programs conducted outside the local school? Is it not time to look at each school in terms of its particular setting, staff, and student body, find out what is unique about them and their interrelationships, and devise individualized staff in-service education programs?

Renewing Educational Leadership: Long on the Issues, Short on the Resolves

Edward J. Meade, Jr.

Program Officer in Charge, Public Education Program, The Ford Foundation

In any discussion of the issues involved in the renewal of leaders in education, the question arises of how leaders come about in the first place. Although there are many schools of thought on this subject, we will be concerned here with just three of those theories, which I call the three C's of leadership development:

Charismatic. Individuals who become leaders do so because of certain characteristics already imbedded within themselves. The only value of training is to reinforce these existing characteristics and make them useful in the hands of those individuals.

Climatal. Situations create leaders. It is the climate of the situation that determines the leader–some situations call for one type of leader, other situations for a different type of leader. Training can involve the creation of various climates or situations in order to see what kind of leaders come from what situations.

Contrived. Leaders can be systematically trained. Utilizing findings of research on leadership development, it is possible to identify and sort out leadership skills and then focus training on the sharpening of these skills so that they become effective tools in the hands of persons being prepared for leadership.

It seems to me that leadership is not exclusively the province of any one of the three C's, but rather comes from a combination of all three. The point is not whether leadership is charismatic, climatal or contrived, but that training should be designed to nurture the leadership charisma inherent in the individual, create the climates for leadership development, and teach identified leadership skills in ways to make the potential leader more effective.

But is there a need for more leadership training in education? Is there really a leadership gap? Many persons believe that education today does not have the kind of leadership it wants or needs. Although many people want to be leaders, for some reason, few seem to be able to be good leaders. Perhaps the training methods we now use are not appropriate to building leaders. It is increasingly evident that problems and issues that must be faced currently by leaders in education probably outweigh the power and authority of these leaders. During the last decade or so there has been a shift from leadership based on position *per se* to one based more on consensus, cooperation, and the like. Are our current training efforts not up to the task of preparing people for this new kind of leadership?

This country currently has more "certified" educational leaders than it perhaps can ever use. We have only to look at studies of educational leadership activities to see this very clearly. For example, Donald Mitchell's study of school principals a few years ago documented that we have trained far more people for roles as principals, assistant principals, and like responsibilities in public schools than we will ever be able to use.[1] In addition, there has been a growth in university training programs for both public and higher education officials such as superintendents, deans, and in some cases, college presidents. Furthermore, thanks to grants from the Office of Education and from private foundations (e.g., Ford, Rockefeller, Kellogg, Carnegie), increasing numbers of persons have been trained in universities or other programs to be leaders in education at all levels. Why are we so concerned about developing leaders if we already have more than we need? Because the issue is quality, not quantity.

A large part of the quality issue has to do with what can be done to help those persons currently in positions of leadership. The need for replacement cannot be ruled out in some cases, particularly when it is necessary to achieve a leadership more closely reflecting the diversity of our society by race, ethnic origin, and sex. It seems unlikely, however, that replacements *per se* will be able to face the kinds of problems American educational leaders are typically facing much better than those currently in the saddle. It also seems reasonable to assume that those currently serving in leadership posts in education (principals,

1. Donald P. Mitchell, "Leadership in Public Education Study: A Look at the Overworked," (Academy for Educational Development, 1972).

superintendents, deans, presidents of higher education institutions, officials in state education agencies, educational leaders in legislative and executive agencies at a state and federal level) will be in these posts for some time to come, and in many cases, ought to stay in these positions. Some may have no other place to go; others may have a tenure of some kind, explicit or implicit. A strong case can be made, therefore, for paying increased attention to renewing our educational leadership.

Most leaders in education are experienced and aware of their need to do better, and realize that they have little training to deal with an array of issues and problems that have emerged or enlarged dramatically in the last five years. Among those major issues and problems are the following.

Civil Rights. While the issue of civil rights has been on the nation's agenda for a longer period than the last five years, in that short span of time it has taken on more complexity, and in some ways considerably more power, as an issue. There is now stronger legal and judicial power regarding racial discrimination and sexual discrimination. We have come to learn about "affirmative action." Employees, particularly public employees, and students in the schools and colleges, see more clearly today what their rights should be. In some cases, civil rights are clashing with civil rights. Think of the dilemma some educational leaders have as they try to follow a program of affirmative action, dealing on one hand with better representation for minorities and, on the other, with women. I'm certain that this kind of conflict can be resolved, but how many educational leaders have been trained to deal with what can be seen as a conflict of two affirmative actions? (If you want to complicate the matter, add the factor of tenure to the affirmative action mix!)

Collective Bargaining. Collective bargaining was once considered to be limited to industrial workers and the like. Later bargaining moved to public employment, and it is increasingly commonplace in both public schools and higher education. Substantially more powerful teacher and faculty organizations are emerging, and even in places without such formal representation, there is substantially more faculty power (teachers, professors, curricular councils, faculty senates and negotiation processes) that all educational leaders need to become intimately familiar with. Yet, how many educational leaders were trained to cope with the nuances of such issues?

Declining Enrollments in our Schools and Colleges. Although there are a few exceptions, the decline is a general national trend. Certainly, one can muster the argument that enrollment could be expanded by finding new constituencies to serve, such as the adult learner or the preschool child. But the resources for such expansion are hardly close at hand, and meanwhile, the consequences of declining enrollment can be felt in terms of retrenchment of organizations, sagging morale, lack of opportunities for promotion and career advancement—all of which make it more difficult for a sustained capacity for hope, change, improvement, and progress. What kind of training helps leadership deal with those matters?

Declining Financial Resources. Obviously this issue is directly tied in with that of declining enrollments. In many cases, schools, colleges and universities in the public sector have budgets based on some kind of enrollment formula. With fewer students, budgets are down. How do we conserve resources as we stretch dollars? How do we compete for fiscal resources that are in small supply with a greater and greater demand from other areas of human activity? Few educators were trained to lead, manage or administer programs, agencies, and institutions with no growth in financial resources to innovate, to add on programs, and to add on people. How can we achieve progress in an age of conservation? Is progress so closely related to financial resources?

Role of Constituent Governors. In earlier time, the lines of governance seemed clear: at the top were the trustees, school boards, college presidents, superintendents of schools and the like. Today, we have the reality of teacher and faculty power and their organizations. In the public sector, we see the state legislator playing more of a governance role than that of a decade ago. The federal government has the largest research funding capacity of any agency in the world, and colleges and universities can't ignore that fact, or its consequences for governance (or control). In addition, parent organizations are growing. In one city, for example, parents have organized into a citizen's union. In still other cities, community boards have been established to serve under a central board of education. Increasing layers of boards, coordinating committees of postgraduate education, and advisory groups abound at all levels of education. Even student government is uppity these days. The crisp straight-line organization charts no longer exist; in some cases, it is nearly impossible to draw an organization chart (if such were ever useful). The point is that governance is more complex and more diverse. What can be done to help leaders better understand governance issues and work with them more effectively?

Conflict of the Values. The recent past gave birth to, or rebirth to, pluralism. Some say that the past few years have brought about the death knell of the melting pot. Try reconciling the value of pluralism with the melting pot. Both have value. One is not really better than the other—or is it? There is a growing conflict of values about education and what it should be and do. What *are* the goals of education? What ought to be the goals of education? Who decides those goals? To what extent is education determined by its establishment (those who serve in it) or determined by its constituents (those whom it serves)? To what extent can those who pay the bills determine those goals? Witness the torture of the recent textbook controversy in Kanowha County, West Virginia. For years there has been a plea for more community participation in the affairs of the schools. Kanowha County citizens showed they wanted to participate, but perhaps not in the way some proponents of participation might hope they would. Witness the controversy over *Man: A Course of Study* supported by the National Science Foundation. This curriculum is unquestionably of high quality in terms of scholarship, and the pedagogy involved makes solid use of findings that social science research is yielding about learning. Some say that children should not have to or cannot deal with such knowledge imparted in this curriculum. Others say they can and should. Again, values and value positions create a conflict. Then, too, there is the interesting conflict tied up with the legal problems of desegregating schools, and of bilingual education. For instance, San Francisco must desegregate its schools and at the same time pay attention to the substantial number of students from a Chinese culture, who are, by law, entitled to get an education in their native language as well as in the language of the nation. How does one desegregate schools and yet continue to create a critical mass of pupils in order to effect a bilingual education program, especially when enrollments are declining and financial resources are harder and harder to get? What can be done to aid the educational leaders who are facing these kinds of issues and other issues of values and goals?

The Worth of Education. Certainly this issue has been debated since the beginning of formal schooling. Still, it is becoming more and more of an issue as more and more people get more and more education. What is the payoff of education for the individual, and for the society? What does it achieve? Mystic notions that more education produces more dollars in the career of an individual is a serious question. How vocational should education be? How enlightening or liberal should it be? How specific, how general?

The questions, issues and problems skimmed through here have been around a long time. The difference, it seems to me, is in their intensity, their complexity, and their interrelationships that add up to a myriad of problems for any educational leader. "Being in charge just ain't easy no more" to put it in colloquial bluntness.

What do we do about it, as persons interested in training and renewing educational leadership? Do our training programs offer systematic approaches to helping current educational leaders deal with these kinds of issues? Hardly ever have our schools and colleges dealt deliberately with training within those institutions and agencies for the leadership required by them. There is no current systematic approach to the job of retooling educational leadership. Nonetheless, the Institute for Educational Leadership (IEL) is making a stab at it. The Educational Staff Seminars sponsored by this Institute at the federal level and those under the Associates Program in the states, at least, are providing opportunities on some kind of neutral turf for current leaders to face the issues outlined here, exchange views, ideas, and expressions about the issues, and learn from the exercise. Most university-based training programs for educational leaders, unfortunately, are long on advice but short on realistic training for leadership. Fads abound in our universities these days, and in other areas of education as well. The latest fad has to do with policy analysis. All well and good—we need to have policy determined on the basis of data and analysis. Still, many leaders are faced with situations and problems that can't wait for all the research data analysis to come in. How then can we help our leaders to develop systems and processes of trust so that decisions can be arrived at and acted on in the absence of hard and conclusive evidence? What can we do to assist leaders to develop appropriate processes within a context of trust and to allow for changing decisions already made when new evidence is found? We need to train our leaders to have compassion, patience, tolerance, courage, stamina and insight as well as provide them with the tools for analysis and the skills of the sciences in the political, economic and social areas.

The conditions outlined here are causing leaders to question themselves. Some leaders are finding that they are just not able to lead. Others are burning out faster than ever. The mobility of our leadership continues (if you can't do it in one place, you try it somewhere else). As an aside, that factor of mobility is disturbing. If one looks at the assessments and evaluations of recent projects and innovations that were considered to be reasonably good or in some cases solid, in recent years, most of them came tumbling down because of the turnover in leadership. Most of them depended on a consistent leadership that sustains over time. Look at the report we issued called *A Foundation*

Goes to School (it analyzed some $30 million of investments in school improvement programs) and learn what the mobility of leadership does to harm such activities.[2] In still other cases, potential leaders are copping out. Why bother getting into the leadership game when you're better off sitting on the sidelines giving advice. John Gardner, in a piece called *The Anti-Leadership Vaccine* sadly points out that many of our educational institutions, particularly those in higher education, were issuing vaccine that made certain that the products of those institutions did not become leaders. This is worth looking up, for some sound advice for leaders and leadership training is offered in it.[3]

Nonetheless, education is better off today than it was ten years ago. Our educational systems are better in a variety of ways, perhaps poorer in others, but better overall. Still, we cannot simply expect that our educational systems and institutions will be even better, more useful, more important or more necessary ten years from now. Past may not be prologue in this case, for in the past we could always reach for more resources. Perhaps life was more simple then, too. Certainly it was less inter-dependent. To some degree, colleges were islands unto themselves; they are less so now. Schools were supported on faith and increasing taxes–hardly the case today! We cannot turn back the clock.

But is the situation hopeless? Again I am reminded of Gardner's *The Anti-Leadership Vaccine* in which he speaks about the confidence of a leader and the leader's responsibility to offer hope.[4] The first task of a leader is to offer hope. Let me underscore that point by trying to conclude on a hopeful plane.

Perhaps those who cut their leadership teeth in the sixties may be better suited to deal with the hard realities of the seventies than many of us realize. After all, they've had moments of triumph; certainly they have witnessed the emergence of these problems, and they are trying to deal with them at this moment. Survival itself demands the acquisition of skills and abilities. What can we do to make certain that they can continue to lead while improving their ability to lead, or, failing that, see the light and allow others to take their place?

The following eight suggestions for trainers or leaders may be worth considering in terms of how they might fit in with efforts to construct renewal efforts.

2. Ford Foundation Comprehensive School Improvement Program (1960–1970), *A Foundation Goes to School* (New York, New York: Ford Foundation, Office of Reports).
3. John Gardner, "The Anti-Leadership Vaccine," (New York, New York: Carnegie Corporation Annual Report, 1965).
4. Ibid.

1. Give leaders opportunities to better understand the issues or conditions elaborated on earlier. (This may not be a simple task.) How do we bring knowledge about these issues to educational leaders? IEL tries through its seminars, through the educational component for its Educational Policy Fellows, through field trips, reports and radio tapes. It immerses people in these issues, not necessarily as they know them in their own organizations, but in problems like theirs somewhere else. In addition, IEL brings before its clients people who display bits and pieces of knowledge about these issues in general—a good first step.
2. Create ways for leaders to take alternative paths. Create optional paths with respect to resolving a particular problem, considering the pros and cons of alternative courses of action. And, consider the possibility that maybe it's good to divert ourselves from one career pattern of leadership in education to another. At least the settings will be different, and new settings often make for new challenges that enable us to muster up more strength. Mobility isn't always a bad thing, at least not when it is planned for and considered in terms of helping, not harming, the institution or the individual.
3. Find ways for leaders to rest a bit and have time for reflection, for considering in depth the solution to a particular problem they have, or must face, as leaders of a particular program or agency. Perhaps sabbatical arrangements for leaders ought to be explored: sabbaticals with focus that afford opportunities in new settings for leaders to draw on resources not available in the home, the institution, or the agency.
4. Create supportive networks for leaders. IEL tries. A former Washington intern, now an Educational Policy Fellow reports that she draws strength from that phone call, that letter, that meeting with persons who have been through that same experience she is going through. Leadership is lonely, and while leadership may always be necessarily competitive, it is also possible to build for more honest, useful cooperation and sharing among present-day leaders.
5. Explore various approaches to helping leaders to understand themselves better.
6. Figure out ways to reward courage. Perhaps courage is its own reward. In the old days when there was a courageous superintendent or college president he or she was promoted to a better job somewhere else with a good deal of public acclaim. This doesn't seem to be happening any more; society doesn't seem to reward courage much these days.
7. Work at creating systems for generating other leaders. It seems to me that the one responsibility of the leader is to make sure that

there are those who could easily take his or her place. Is it not one test of a leader that he or she knows that there are followers who can easily do as well as or better than the leader? A leader who knows that to be a fact is doing the job well! How can we retrain leaders to enable them to produce other leaders?

8. Stop thinking that a final answer will be found to renewing leadership. The job of renewing educational leaders is a job never finished. There are gains and losses, productive and unproductive steps. It is an ongoing process, a process that needs continuous attention.

In-Service Education: Intrinsic versus Extrinsic Motivation

Teresa M. Palmer

Illinois State University

In-service education is a tool to mold better teachers by improving their knowledge, providing ways to help them improve their effectiveness in the classroom and by instilling in them a desire to do a better job of teaching. To accomplish these goals, in-service programs must be designed to satisfy the needs of the participants. The rewards selected to serve as motivational devices are of utmost importance as they can set limits to or encourage the attainment of an optimal level of teaching performance.

Although in-service programs are used for a variety of purposes, most fall into a category that may be called improvement of teaching. This category includes efforts to increase and upgrade content knowledge in the areas of their specialties as well as efforts to provide them with skills to increase their effectiveness in the teaching-learning situation. Another category can be called the communication-indoctrination function. This function includes the use of in-service programs to maintain and improve communication among the professional staff, achieve a sense of unity of purpose within the school system, and enhance the position of the school in the eyes of the community. While the communication-indoctrination function has the promise of being consistent with (and perhaps even essential to) the improvement of teaching, in some instances it has replaced the improvement of teaching as the major purpose of the in-service activity. More effort should be expended in achieving an optional mix of the two categories of purposes, which has the potential for providing increased satisfaction for the proponents of both categories.

Much of the research concerning in-service education has centered around two major areas: the choice of material to be used in the in-service program, and the design of the program itself. The choice of material may be dictated by the perceived purpose of the program, the available resources or the needs of those involved, as perceived by administrators, teachers, community groups or power groups within the professional staff. Such decisions may also be directly influenced by actions of outsiders, as illustrated by the recent federal and state legislation on metrication that has resulted in many in-service programs dealing with this subject. Once the subject of the program is chosen, there remain the problems related to the design of the program itself. Who are to be the participants? Who shall present the program—outside experts, administrators or members of the teaching staff? How shall the material be presented? Decisions must be made concerning the format of the program, the selection of materials and media, the timing and duration of the sessions and the physical setting for the planned activities. Research can give us cues to assist decision-making in these areas to increase the likelihood of the program's success. Of course, success is usually measured in terms of how well the objectives of a given program are achieved, so we're back to the problem of identifying the purposes of the program. It is my belief that the major purpose of any in-service program should be the improvement of the teaching, and that improvement of the communication-indoctrination function will necessarily accompany improvement in teaching in the long run.

The success of any in-service program is dependent upon a great many factors that have already been mentioned: purpose of the program, selection of content, and design of the program itself. These are factors that are to a degree internal to the educational system and controlled by it. There are also factors affecting in-service programs that are largely beyond the control of the system, such as economic environment and community values. Failure to take these factors into consideration can doom an otherwise well designed experience. There is yet another factor that is central to the success or failure of an in-service program, and that is the motivation of the participants. It is not enough to simply determine the degree of motivation (if that is possible); one must examine the nature of the motivation.

Both extrinsic and intrinsic motivation are used to encourage teachers to improve teaching performance. In extrinsic motivation, the impetus may come from rule enforcement (making participation in in-service programs a requirement of the job), or from rewards that are valued by the participants but do not stem from improved performance (such as bonuses, increments, certificates, etc.). Those most susceptible to extrinsic motivation are those who have not adequately satisfied their basic needs or those who do not derive the satisfaction of higher order needs from their teaching. In intrinsic motivation, the impetus for improvement may come from a desire to do a better job of teaching. Intrinsically motivated teachers derive satisfaction directly from the performance of their teaching duties. The rewards here are the rewards perceived by the teacher and are highly dependent upon his or her values and attitudes and environmental pressures. The two types of motivation are not mutually exclusive and it would be wrong to assume that intrinsic motivation indicates a good teacher or that extrinsic motivation necessarily denotes a poor one. Often a difference in the type of motivation apparent at any point is the result of differing external pressures. A teacher might decline an opportunity to voluntarily participate in an in-service program designed to improve his teaching competence for many reasons that have little to do with his desirability as a teacher (such as his perception of the value of the program or the fact that attendance might interfere with other activities such as a part time job that is necessary to meeting financial commitments).

The importance of the differentiation between intrinsic and extrinsic modes of motivation lies mainly in the relationship between mode of motivation and character of commitment to the educational system, which limits the degree of stability that the system can maintain and the attainable limits of teaching effectiveness. When teaching provides intrinsic rewards expressive of the needs of the teachers, they develop a strong commitment to the system and the improvement of the education provided within. When the motivation is chiefly extrinsic in nature there is a much weaker commitment to the system and there is likely to be a fairly high rate of turnover when there are alternative forms of employment that offer rewards that are more highly valued. Since a high degree of stability is essential to the satisfactory performance of an educational system, it would seem logical that school systems should have as one of their primary goals the development and maintenance of a high degree of commitment to the system and its goals on the part of the professional staff. The nature of the commitment will also have an effect upon the sincerity with which a teacher utilizes in-service programs to improve teaching performance.

There are several strategies that may be utilized in attempts to maximize the intrinsic nature of the commitment of members to any system. The most obvious is to use the selection process to hire those teachers (and administrators) who enjoy their work and derive intrinsic rewards from performing their jobs. However, since few schools are doing much hiring under current market conditions this is certainly far from a complete solution. One action that allows intrinsic motivation and high commitment (but does not assure it), is to guarantee adequate compensation to meet the basic needs of the staff. (This can backfire if teachers who would find other types of employment more rewarding stay in education solely because of the money or the security.) Given the constraints of hiring, there are several things that can be done to increase the importance of intrinsic rewards, and in-service programs can and should be instrumental to all of them.

No in-service program for teachers has a chance for success unless it has both the sanction and the support of the administration. In-service programs for administrators could be used to identify priorities and commitments and to educate administrators to the supportive needs of their subordinates. All humans need recognition, need to be appreciated and need to feel that what they are doing is valued by others and it is essential that the administration demonstrate both an awareness of and a sensitivity to these needs of the teachers. If the administrators would set aside a little of their time to communicate with faculty members on an informal basis (without giving the impression of being "big brother") and offer a few words of support and praise when deserved, it would do far more for improving motivation than an annual formal communication. It is the responsibility of the administration to create and maintain a climate that is supportive of efforts to improve teaching. The structure of the reward system is also of prime importance to motivation. While wages, fringe benefits and working conditions do little to increase intrinsic motivation, the absence of adequate rewards in these areas can have a strong negative effect on motivation. Therefore, the administration should work to assure the adequacy of those rewards or their efforts to provide recognition, feelings of accomplishment, and opportunities for advancement and responsibility will be of no avail.

In-service programs can also serve to increase the intrinsic rewards of teaching while increasing the teaching effectiveness of the participants. Everyone values success, particularly his own, and if an in-service program increases the likelihood of success for the classroom teacher it is probable that it will increase the satisfaction he derives from his teaching. Increased teaching effectiveness, as perceived by the participant, encourages an increase in intrinsic motivation by appealing to a previously internalized value–success–rather than trying to change the participant's values. For an in-service program to have this effect it must be carefully designed to meet the needs of the teachers and to provide tools that will assist them directly in their classroom teaching. Programs should be conducted in an atmosphere that is nonthreatening and material must be broken up into segments that are capable of being assimilated. It is much better to have three one-hour sessions than one three-hour session. Teachers must have the opportunity and be encouraged to try out materials from the programs in their classrooms to reinforce the learning. Any facet in the design or implementation of an in-service program that increases the likelihood of the participants' success also contributes to an increase in the sense of commitment and involvement with teaching on the part of the participants.

All of this emphasis on the intrinsic rewards of teaching is not intended to imply that extrinsic rewards and extrinsic motivation are bad or even inappropriate in in-service education programs, only that such extrinsic forms of motivation have been overused while intrinsic rewards have been underused. This may be partially a residual of the market situation for teachers in the early and mid-sixties when available teachers were often lured to those school systems offering the highest salaries and/or the most advantageous fringe benefits. Many school administrators had as one of their major concerns hiring an adequate number of qualified teachers to fill the classrooms each term. Now that the problem of acquiring sufficient numbers of qualified teachers has largely dissipated, schools can and should shift their emphases. Just as individuals have different levels of needs, so do educational systems, and it is only when they have satisfied their essential needs that they can and should move on to the satisfaction of higher order needs. Included in the higher order needs should be a coordinated and ongoing program of staff development whose major objectives include improving communication, striving to achieve unity of purpose among staff members and a high degree of commitment to, and involvement in, the systems goals on the part of the professional staff. These goals are consistent with and even essential to meaningful and lasting improvement in the education provided by the system. Such a program, if it is to be successful, requires a high level of intrinsic motivation.

Do In-Service Programs Teach Anything?

Alan C. Purves
University of Illinois

There are a great number of in-service programs for elementary and secondary school teachers throughout the country—some are good, some are not. A great number of them have as a common thread the fact that they are intended to change the behavior of teachers—to make them nicer or nastier, to make them relate to or control students, to raise or to stultify their consciousness. Some are formed by behaviorism, some by Rogerian psychology; some claim to be "humanistic" (a debased term), some to be "skill developing."

It was not so fifteen years ago. Under the aegis of the United States Office of Education, the College Entrance Examination Board, the National Science Foundation, and others, came a number of courses, workshops, and institutes designed to present teachers with the latest lore about physics, mathematics, linguistics, or social science. The evaluations of these institutes were few, but they warned that too frequently the teachers did not use this new knowledge in their classrooms (maybe they used it indirectly, a question seldom raised). At about the time that this criticism was bruited, the "romantic critics of education"—people such as Holt, Kozol, and Kohl—began to decry the over-academization of American schools. In the political climate of the latter 1960s and early 1970s this news was welcomed and meant for many teacher trainers that they could move to matters other than the latest theory of literary genres or the latest synthesis of biological study. Here was the chance to bring the revolution to the boondocks. Those poor teachers out there needed liberating so that they could liberate the kids. Never mind the fact that the kids were doing all right on that score by themselves, after all they were exposed to the media and could make up their own minds.

Along came the workshops in "opening"–classrooms, schools, teachers, subject matter, and the like. Some of them were fun, some of them were good, some of them even had a theory behind them. In English, for example, there had been developing a theory of "response to literature," which paid attention to the critical variety in a culture as opposed to the somewhat limited schools of criticism in the academy. In pedagogy, there had been developing a theory of pupil-teacher interaction that questioned the dominance of the recitation, and in psychology there was the theory of Piaget about the nature of learning and development. All of these theories could serve the "openers."

As with all "revolutions," of course, a counterrevolution had to emerge, and the reaction to the "romantic revolution" came with the economic recession under the guise of "back to basics." For teachers this meant a resurrection of the three R's, and it meant a concurrent resurrection of the teacher-dominated classroom or the move to highly programmatic individualized instruction. It was the latter that became a prominent part of in-service education, vying for position with "opening."

Such is the present situation roughly sketched. One might go so far as to say that it is a lamentable situation. While teachers are attending workshops and institutes that give them methodology, their students are often learning the same sorts of things that their parents had learned, and very often the state of knowledge has advanced greatly beyond the curriculum. The situation could be likened to the hypothetical one of doctors using leeches despite the centuries of medical discoveries, because their whole training had been in bedside manners, not in *materia medica.*

It has been my lot over the past few years to review many of the protocol and training materials developed for the United States Office of Education. These materials are designed for both preservice and inservice training of teachers. Many of these materials are technically excellent, representing the apex of the manipulation of technology. What is lacking in these materials far too often is attention to what is taught, the content of the curriculum for the teacher and for the student. Teachers have a brief undergraduate training in one or more subject matters; on the basis of this training they prepare lessons, teach them, and evaluate their students. Many of them are nice people, many of them have lovely techniques of working with one child or many children, many of them are hideously uninformed about the material they teach. An in-service education program can give them this information; a good in-service program *must* give them this information. To be sure, there is a need for teachers to look at knowledge not simply as recipients of it but as people who will distill it and impart it. Protocol materials, training materials, and training programs in teaching are important, but unless they have a sound base in the subject matter that the teachers are going to teach they will be useless.

How can the subject matter disciplines best inform the practice of the continuing education of teachers? Just giving them refresher courses in new information and theory is not sufficient. The institutes of the 1960s are not the answer. The disciplines must stand behind materials and programs for training teachers. These are three in kind: the presentation of information and examples for teachers to analyze (often called protocol materials); the presentation of examples of strategies and techniques that may be imitated (training materials); and the organization of the learning situation and its evaluation (a training system).

Protocol materials are intended to be examples of "real" behavior of people in the various roles they play in education (as student, as teacher, as administrator, as parent, as citizen, and so forth) so presented as to allow prospective teachers to see operating in that behavior certain specified concepts. The concepts might be related to pedagogy, to social psychology, to various subject matters, or to other ways of perceiving and thinking about the education complex. Materials related to the various subject matters have for a long time existed; they are in fact the stuff out of which the disciplines have emerged. The concepts of language have emerged from analysis and interpretation of what people have said or written; those of literature have likewise emerged from examination of literary texts; those of physics from examination of certain natural phenomena; and those of history from examination of the actions of individuals and of nations. The need for new protocol materials in the disciplines is limited save in a few areas. There must be some materials that allow prospective teachers to develop the ability to analyze and interpret the behaviors that we have come to call "critical" or "scientific" or "historical" or the like as those behaviors are manifested in children. Prospective teachers see adults (their teachers) behaving like physicists, but they seldom see when little children behave similarly. They need to learn how to see this.

This role of subject matter in the development of protocol materials is important, but less crucial than the role subject matter can play in the development of protocol materials in pedagogy and the social sciences related to pedagogy. In those materials, the behavior manifested is usually that of a teacher teaching students. More often than not, there is a lesson in some content area (reading, say, or mathematics, or social studies). Since these materials present the behavior through film or videotape, there is a high degree of verisimilitude that engages the attention of the viewer, either experienced teacher or teacher trainee. The viewer is asked not to react emotionally or evaluatively but analytically and dispassionately and to focus attention on the form, that is to say the teaching behavior, in the material. By consciously not paying attention to the content of the teaching, the viewer may well tend to assume that the content is acceptable. In many protocol materials such may not obtain. Similarly in those protocol materials that seek to provide data for analysis of behavior in the content areas, the teaching strategy may also be bad and be neglected in the analysis.

This being the case, it is crucial that any protocol material be rigidly scrutinized for conceptual adequacy of the content by a subject matter specialist, and rigidly scrutinized for the conceptual adequacy of the form and technique of the lesson by a specialist in psychology and pedagogy. Not to do so is to run the risk that the materials intended for analysis may inadvertently act as the wrong sort of model for future behavior.

What has been said here applies even more importantly to training materials. Although teaching can be analyzed and defined in a fashion that abstracts teaching from the thing taught, it does not so exist in practice. Even training material that isolates, say, a particular form of teacher-student interaction will show a teacher and student interacting *about* something. The presentation of that something must be intellectually sound according to the best thinking of the discipline that treats it as subject matter. To see a training film in which there was portrayed a beautiful relationship between student and teacher, one that seemed to illustrate the best sort of facilitation of learning, and to see the student learning that no black culture existed before 1954, is to vitiate the whole thrust of the training materials. Such an example is blatant, of course, but subtler errors, misapplications of theory, or discarded notions are even more pernicious than such a blatant falsehood. It is to prevent those subtle errors that provision for a subject matter specialist to help conceive and review the training materials seems hardly a luxury, but a necessity.

It goes without saying that there is an important place for the disciplines in the training system, but to let the matter drop there is to perpetuate a problem that has long plagued the teacher trainer. There is subject matter in the schools and in the arts and sciences colleges of the universities, true, but to infer that the two aspects of subject matter are the same can be risky. Literature in the schools might be said to be the object of critical attention, in the universities the object of historical attention. Or to take grammar as an example, an important function of the schools is to insure that children employ the grammatical richness of the language in communicating in speech or in writing with other people. In the university the emphasis might better be placed on the analysis of grammar and language systems as disciplined forms of inquiry. The function of that analysis might well be to better enable the teacher in the school to understand what the students are doing.

The difference in function and approach to subject matter that separates general from special education may also separate scholarly from pedagogical education. It may be useful for certain kinds of students to be able to perform the functions of the textual editor or the descriptive bibliographer; it would seem more useful for the teacher to be able to perform a content analysis of textbooks in order to discern critical biases.

All of the disciplines are so wide and so complex in structure that it is necessary for the establishers of training systems to determine what aspects of each discipline are most useful to the prospective teacher. In English, for example, it would seem that psycholinguistics and sociolinguistics are more useful than philology. It would further seem that courses dealing in analysis of the concepts and procedures of the disciplines are of greater use to the teacher than courses that simply present the results of those procedures and the scattered details with which those concepts deal. To this end the disciplines must contribute in the planning of the program of the system, but must, in turn, be required to examine their premises, procedures, and conceptual bases, as they are modified in their application to children.

As a result of such examination, programs for in-service training should emerge that have a sense of the conceptual bases of the discipline, of the power and limitation of that discipline as a means of knowing, of the basic procedures of that discipline, and finally of how that discipline might be made available to children of various ages. In literature, for example, we might say that three of the basic concepts of the literary work are voice, metaphor, and form; that as concepts they can tell us a great deal about the aesthetics of a work, but little about the human significance of the work; that critics operate through language to lay forth these three concepts as they operate in specific literary works, and that these concepts may be made apparent to young children through such devices as role playing, word games, and examination of the formal elements of comic strips and children's stories.

It is essential, therefore that scholars in the discipline, particularly those scholars who have a commitment to general education and therefore to teacher training, be a part of the curriculum planning process in a training complex. These scholars must, however, be asked to confront people from the pedagogical fields and from the schools, and particularly people from the community, in order to assure that their conceptions will meet the real needs of the school children and of society. They must be asked to justify the discipline and the selection of concepts in the discipline to the real world. Once they have held themselves accountable in this way, then and only then, should they proceed to planning the training of teachers.

Throughout all of these comments I see two threads, partnership and performance. There must, it seems, be a partnership of the subject matter disciplines and the pedagogical disciplines; neither can effect the training of teachers alone. Whether it be in the planning of models of training, the setting forth of criteria, or the development of materials for analysis or training, the two components must inform each other, must test each other, must harmonize with each other.

To do this, both must look at what they do and what they want the teacher to do. They must examine the performance of professionals and determine the concepts underlying that performance. They must look at the behavior of people in the real world so as to influence the training of teachers for the real world. Performance has a form, how one does things, and a content, what one does. For purpose of analysis, form and content can be separated, but in the performance they cannot. Performance must be analyzed so that the performer can be trained, and the performer must learn about both form and content. Performance in education deals with people teaching or learning something. The disciplines tell us about the something; pedagogy and psychology tell us about teaching and learning; both must help teachers perform at their best.

Changing Patterns of Teacher Education in the United States

J. Myron Atkin
James D. Raths
University of Illinois

SOME POLICY ISSUES

One policy matter that receives little attention on a nationwide basis is the question of recruitment for teacher education programs. When dollar allocations are examined, it is noted that there is an infinitesimal investment in recruitment compared to the investment in the education of teachers. Inasmuch as teacher attitudes are modified with great difficulty, a significant decision is made about the kind of individual who will be teaching in the schools four or five years hence at the moment that individual is admitted to a teacher education program.

Since attitudes and values of teachers play a ciritcal role in the educational system, it is necessary to learn more about the attributes of individuals who choose to teach. Selection criteria of a more systematic sort than are used at present might be employed when admitting each teacher education student.

Alternatively, choices can be made about the particular institutions that are to be authorized to offer teacher education programs. It is known that different kinds of students attend different universities. The characteristics of the student at a particular institution in terms of intellectual attainment, intellectual aptitude, family income, and social class are well understood. Insofar as there is a relationship between these attributes and the qualities desired in a prospective teacher, this policy issue can be approached more analytically.

At the outset, however, it should be recognized that the topic raises political and social questions that are highly controversial, and perhaps for that reason they cannot and will not be broached by teacher certification boards and legislators. Nevertheless the issue is highlighted here because it may well be the one that has the most profound potential for influencing the educational system over the long term.

A second policy issue surrounds the relationship between the award of teaching credentials or a license and the requirements of the teaching position. At the moment in the United States, the prospective teacher is expected to present credentials that may have little relationship to performance on the job. For example, the teacher is expected to have attended college for four years and have completed a large number of courses that are not assumed to bear directly on teaching–though presumably they are valued as a part of general education. It is alleged by some critics of teacher education programs that teacher education should be geared more closely to job requirements. The fact that it is not serves as a device to screen out certain applicants, rather than a device to preserve standards.

Advocates of performance-based teacher education programs point out that PBTE directly addresses this issue. To the degree that employers and teacher educators feel successful in delineating the skills required for successful teaching, there will likely be related pressures to couple licensing directly to the acquisition of those competencies. The educational policy ramifications require careful scrutiny, particularly because a certain model of schooling is implied by such a move; this model should not go unexamined.

The American experience of recent years suggests a policy study associated with the demands for decision-making authority in teacher education by different groups. In the design of teacher education programs and formulation of teacher-education policy, what are appropriate roles for elected school boards, the public at large, the organized profession, the various legislatures, the executive branches of government, the established teacher education institutions, local school districts, and representatives of business and industry? Control of teacher education is in question of course. The competing groups are active. Inevitably decisions will be made as a result of the interplay of political forces. The final decisions, however, might be influenced by analysis of the practical and social implications of the roles suggested by and for the various parties. In fact some experimentation might be inaugurated to study the effects of planned change to test the competing approaches, possibly in combination.

A somewhat related policy question centers on identifying the scientific base for the establishment of teacher education arrangements or practices. It would be useful background for the policy decisions that must be made in teacher education to review in detail those elements associated with the education of teachers that have yielded or are likely to yield to research. If it can be demonstrated, for example, that student achievement is directly associated with definable teacher competencies, then a powerful argument exists for training teachers in the competencies thus identified.

It is characteristic of the current state of decision-making in teacher education that performance-based teacher education programs are being instituted on a large scale without any evidence of the relationship between specific competencies of teachers and children's achievement. The same statement can be made of programs for teachers based on "humanizing" education through "self-development" of teachers, or for programs in open education, or for any other programs. The research is silent on the associations between teacher abilities and children's learning.

It is not the purpose here to question the appropriateness of any element in teacher education programs that is not demonstrably associated with achievement of students. It seems perfectly reasonable that certain attributes of teaching and teacher education programs are desirable in and of themselves, regardless of our present knowledge of their effectiveness in changing behavior. For example it is worthwhile to help the teacher understand the history of teaching children from minority groups, or to help the teacher understand various educational philosophies. It is also desirable that teachers learn to listen carefully to the thoughts expressed by children, and that they become reflective about their own actions. These characteristics are worth emphasizing in a teacher education program whether or not a clear relationship can be established between the attributes and the achievements of children. Nevertheless it would clarify a considerable amount of educational discourse if it were clearly understood which practices were being advocated on the basis of reliable research and which practices were being advocated for other reasons. Of equal importance, it would be useful to identify educational programs that seem most likely to yield to scientific approaches, and that must be approached by understanding value preferences, political constraints, and budgetary limitations.

There is a cluster of policy questions centering around effective strategies for educational change. During the 1960s, educational change was seen largely as a sequential series of steps starting with theory, moving to research, followed by development, then dissemination, diffusion, and finally evaluation. It was assumed, though seldom explicitly, that the teacher or teacher educator was a passive client awaiting the results of developmental activity undertaken by talented groups and based on firm and incontrovertible knowledge.

It became apparent after several years that educational change did not seem to occur the way change was assumed to occur in medicine or agriculture. In the case of medicine, pharmaceutical firms engage in research to develop new treatments for various diseases. When certain medication is found to be effective, pharmaceutical "detail men" carry the word to practicing physicians who try to make a match between symptoms spotted in their diagnosing rooms and the treatment and effects described by the pharmaceutical detail men. When Elliot Richardson was Secretary of the Department of Health, Education and Welfare, he seemed attracted to the analogue of the pharmaceutical detail men and claimed that we needed agents such as these in the field of education to carry the word of effective practices to classroom teachers.

In the field of agriculture, the United States has a well-developed network of extension agents who for decades have been informing farmers about methods of plowing, planting, and cultivation that increase yield. Agricultural practices seem to have been affected profoundly as a result. The agricultural extension agent model, also, has seemed attractive to educational policy makers during the 1960s, and an extensive literature has developed around the theme of educational change agents, their responsibilities and possible impact.

For a variety of reasons, the methods do not seem to work well when applied to the field of education. The teacher does not seem to be interested in "yield" in quite the same way as the farmer. Educational "treatments" do not seem as reliable as therapeutic approaches in medicine. Some observers, in retrospective analysis, point out that incentive systems differ for teachers as compared with farmers or physicians. They point out, also, that teachers, in effect, have considerable latitude since the practice of one is not compared readily to the practice of another.

Whatever the reasons for the failure of recent models of educational change in teacher education or classroom teaching, there is a need to understand more fully how change has taken place and what strategies might be utilized in the future as a basis for policy.

At the moment in the United States there are clear trends, as have been indicated, toward locally-based decision-making authority. This shift to decentralized decisions suits America's present conservative political mood. But, some claim, it is also a more realistic approach to change in education. The task becomes one of fostering and enhancing local innovation rather than implementing what may be an alien instructional plan.

This policy issue entails discovering the optimal relationship between statewide and local decision-making in teacher education through realistic understanding of how it is that teacher education programs can reasonably be expected to change. There are presently a series of practices, effective or not, that have extensive historical roots. They are built into the folkways of teacher education. New approaches that seemed to violate the assumptions of these existing practices can be expected to meet resistance. Analysis may identify those folkways, their strength and shortcomings. Change strategies based on such analysis may prove more effective than strategies that seem to ignore the existing system.

A further cluster of policy issues is associated with uniformity as against flexibility in teacher education. To what degree is it educationally and socially desirable to mandate a single program, however effective it seems, and thereby rule out competing alternatives? Some states are moving toward mandating PBTE programs. How desirable is this practice within a single state, and to what degree should we seek national standardization of teacher education programs? On the one hand, reciprocity across the fifty states in the licensing of teachers argues for a degree of standardization. On the other hand, our lack of knowledge of the effects of various teacher education programs, as well as our apparently conflicting goals for the educational system, seem to argue for governmental policy that preserves diversity.

As has been pointed out in the introductory section, managerial styles that have come into broad usage in the United States seem to suggest a uniformity in planning and management procedures that tend to favor certain kinds of educational programs—those that reflect highly detailed predetermined objectives and carry an evaluation plan for ready assessment. But it is a major question in education whether our educational practices should be limited by the present state of our planning and assessment procedures. If there are significant outcomes of our educational programs that do not seem to be revealed by present planning and assessment methods, perhaps we should rely exclusively on these methods.

Present techniques of management and evaluation tend to emphasize proximate goals. Tangential effects, longterm outcomes, and questions of worth tend not to be examined explicitly. For example a well-engineered instructional sequence can convey to a prospective teacher some specific skills associated with the teaching of reading. It may even be demonstrable at a later date that these skills are effective in teaching reading to children. But what kind of a reader is the teacher, and what kinds of readers does she educate in the schools? Is she broadly read? Is she reflective about the reading she does? Does she help instill a desire to read as well as reading skills? These questions are more difficult to answer than those associated with her possession of specific skills, yet they are important ones. Certain approaches that are effective in building reading skills may be counterproductive if the goal is to enhance the quantity and quality of voluntary reading.

Right now, school superintendents are able to go to the University of Houston or certain other institutions if they want teachers who are certified as having acquired certain specific competencies. They can go to the University of Florida if they want teachers who have been exposed to a "humanistic" program. But in addition to having a basis for judging the quality of these programs and others, superintendents need adequate descriptions of all teacher education efforts if they are to make informed decisions. A policy question focuses on who carries the responsibility for this description inasmuch as program developers cannot be relied upon to provide all the evidence of significance to different audiences.

Clearly, policy issues in teacher education are basic as well as broad. And there is not much background (or skill) in the United States in educational policy analysis. Nevertheless, it seems desirable and in fact inevitable that policy issues will be approached more systematically in the coming years. That being the case, it is hoped that the issues outlined here will be examined carefully by interested parties and that the practices and policy questions highlighted in this document will add to informed discussion and ultimately to improved practice.

RESEARCH AND DEVELOPMENT IN TEACHER EDUCATION: SOME RECOMMENDATIONS[1]

Studies are needed to find methods of judging the correspondence between the needs of teachers and the in-service education they receive. Research findings suggest, for instance, that in passing from teacher

1. The authors acknowledge the major contribution of Professor Lillian Katz to this section of the article.

aspirant to experienced professional, students move through various stages of development. The preservice stage and the early years of teaching are characterized by a desire to do the job well in the eyes of superordinates. There is little room for philosophical analysis or even reflective thinking during this phase. It is suggested by the research findings that once a teacher feels that he is able to meet the demands of the job, he then shows concern about the effects of his work on students. As this stage is passed, the teacher becomes more attentive to the functioning of the school in society.[2]

If these are reliable findings, then it may be a mistake to offer identical programs to in-service and preservice teachers, or even to all in-service teachers. The results of the research suggest that some grouping by stage of professional development would be beneficial. Differentiated teacher education programs should be developed and studied.

Once general dispositions are identified that seem to be desirable in teachers, studies are needed to catalog those behaviors on the teacher educator's part that advance or impede the development of those dispositions. Does grading by the teacher educator help or hinder the development of self-evaluation on the part of the prospective teacher? Does the emphasis on discussion sections that prize the sharing of feelings reduce the chances that teachers will become or remain readers of books and articles dealing with teaching? Do the advocacy positions of professors in colleges of education for or against prevalent ideologies reduce the likelihood that teachers will become critical thinkers when considering issues in education? Empirical studies of these relationships are needed to design appropriate teacher education programs.

At the root of many of the "personal development" approaches to teacher education is the idea that behavior changes in teachers that do not involve a corresponding change in beliefs and attitudes are ephemeral. Longitudinal studies of the belief structures of individuals and how these structures function to affect behavior and perceptions is needed to test this assumption more rigorously. Findings from such research efforts might suggest specific actions that teacher educators might follow both in selecting and training teachers.

As with any institution, the school exerts powerful forces of socialization on any newcomer. If schools are to change and develop to meet the needs of a changing world, so too teachers must change. If the pressures of socialization are inherently conservative, then

2. For a review of this research, see Frances F. Fuller, "Concerns of Teachers: A Developmental Conceptualization," *American Educational Research Journal* vol. 6, no. 2 (March, 1969): 207–226.

researchers must study those forces to understand more completely how they operate to inhibit change. The need for research in this area is especially pronounced since a rapidly increasing number of programs in teacher education are assigning students to schools for a major portion of their training. It may be the case that young students are especially vulnerable to the socializing forces of the public school institutions, to the detriment of innovation and flexibility.

Teacher educators are intent about helping their students acquire a wide range of learnings. Some learnings are routine and mechanical, such as those related to running equipment or to record-keeping responsibilities. Others are subtle such as being sensitive to the preconceptions that students bring to a study of gravitation. Researchers can contribute to teacher education planning by identifying the experiences that are best suited for the acquisition of different types of learnings so that the skills, cognitions, and attitudes acquired in a teacher education program are indeed integrated and functionally related.

More analysis is required of the selection criteria for teacher education programs and their effects. It is our belief that much of the effort that is expended in the in-service training of teachers could be diverted to other areas if there were more astute initial selection of teachers. The measures currently used in selection efforts are mainly convergent ones: How much does an aspirant know, and what problems can he solve? It might be helpful to identify other abilities, for instance receptivity to new ideas, tolerance for ambiguity, ideational fluency, and the ability to anticipate responses of clients (students) in given situations.

Of course, what is deparately needed to advance knowledge in the field of teacher education is the identification of some variable or set of variables that can be accepted as indicators of effective teaching. The problem that has plagued the advancement of knowledge in almost all helping professions–counseling, psychiatry, the ministry, social work, and teaching–is the lack of such criteria. To identify such factors might revolutionize the field of education.

If such features were identified, we could better assess the influences that various elements contribute to the development of a teacher. Clearly students come to teacher education with certain predilections, aptitudes, attitudes, and skills. Almost certainly they acquire additional learnings during the preservice stage of their training. In addition, through experience and in-service programs, teachers acquire other learnings. An interesting research question focuses on the weight each of these sets of factors are likely to contribute to the criterion. Until an ultimate variable is discovered, attempts could be made to assess the weights on the more tentative measures now available to us–ratings of supervisors, ratings of pupils, judgments of parents, self-ratings, and even a measure of pupil growth.

In the United States, a very few institutions have a distinctive quality that is conveyed to most of their graduates. Bank Street College of Education, for instance, apparently instills in its students certain characteristics that are readily discernible. It would be important to identify such institutions to study the strengths and weaknesses such programs possess and to isolate those qualities that contribute to their unique character.

Finally, we need to examine closely the assumption on the part of many teacher educators that learnings stemming from systematic instruction tend to be nonenduring and dysfunctional. Whether we are teaching how to ask higher-level questions or how to compute chi-squares, there is evidence to demonstrate that the learnings that result are short-lived and often misapplied once the student has left the "testing" situation. Are there ways to make changes in the normal procedures used in systematic instruction to diminish this disappointing outcome? Are there ways to capitalize upon the normal bent of human beings to acquire learnings and understandings in a natural and nonsystematic fashion so that they will also acquire the skills needed to become an effective professional?

Forward to Basics

Samuel G. Sava

Vice President, Charles F. Kettering Foundation

Until a while ago, I thought that those of us who entered, or were in, education about 1963 or so participated in one of the most interesting and professionally challenging decades in American educational history. Recently, however, I have begun having second thoughts. It may be that *this* decade will prove to be even more interesting and challenging—but it will, I suspect, be a lot less comfortable and a lot less fun, for both good and bad reasons. For I suspect we have entered upon a period of reaction in American education. Our skill in handling this reaction will help determine how long the period lasts, and whether we will manage to retain the momentum for educational improvement that began in the 1960s.

I have no hard data to back up my assertion that we have entered a period of reaction, just instinct, backed by discussions with colleagues around the country, and a noteworthy indicator here and there. For example, *Newsweek* magazine published a lengthy article titled "Back to Basics in the Schools." The article cited a number of instances in which such innovations as open education, independent study, and so-called "relevant" additions to the curriculum had been rejected by parents in favor of a return to traditional schooling, characterized by letter grades, regular examinations, strict discipline, and a stress on the three R's.

One highly innovative school in Pasadena, California, the article pointed out, has a kindergarten through twelfth grade enrollment of 550 students and a waiting list of 515. But at another Pasadena school, whose stated goals are "Traditional education, order, quiet, and control," the enrollment is 1,700 and the waiting list is over 1,000.

"What is the significance of this astonishing contrast?" the article asks, and then offers an answer: "To many, it suggests that U.S. education's so-called wave of the future has crested. The result is that across the nation, parents, school boards, and often the pupils themselves are demanding that the schools stop experimenting and get back to basics—to reading, writing, arithmetic, and standards of behavior."

Just as one swallow doesn't make a summer, so one article doesn't make a trend, yet my own conversations with parents and colleagues, plus the phenomena cited by *Newsweek,* incline me to believe that the magazine is right—there *is* disillusion with many areas of educational experimentation and innovation. It is likely that all of us here will have to cope with it, if we have not already been forced to do so. What I would like to do, therefore, is summarize my perspective of what has happened these past ten years.

For the last ten years have been a distinctive decade. More happened in American education between 1964 and 1974 than between 1898 and 1908, or between 1931 and 1941.

Those of us who held some position of educational responsibility in 1964, and who paid attention to the social context of our profession, will remember it as a period of high enthusiasm. When President Eisenhower signed the National Defense Education Act in the late 1950s, he stressed that it was an "emergency measure;" the federal government, he suggested, really had no business in education apart from running the military academies, and it would bow out again as soon as NDEA's temporary infusion of funds enabled the nation's schools and colleges to close the training gap implied by the launching of Sputnik.

By 1964, however, NDEA had taken on the characteristics of a continuing Federal allocation. No longer was it an emergency measure; the Federal government was in public as well as private education to stay. Moreover, the original restrictions on NDEA—which limited it to support for scientific and technical aspects of curriculum, instruction, and facilities—had been relaxed to include the humanities, home economics, and a brace of other disciplines unrelated to technology.

This continuance and broadening of NDEA signaled an important shift in our national attitude toward education. NDEA originally stated that education was vital to our national defense, and it viewed "national defense" in terms of hardware. We had to have rockets and missiles and nuclear submarines to match those of our actual or potential enemies; therefore, we had to have engineers and scientists and technicians who could make these armaments, and if state and local school systems, through oversight or inability, could not educate such specialists, the federal government would have to help them do so. *You might recall that it was a demand for a return to basics.*

But by the end of the Kennedy Administration and the beginning of the Johnson Administration, we came to perceive "national defense" in more subtle terms. We saw that the enemies of the United States were not entirely external and military; some of them were internal, and quite civilian. Russia and Cuba and a militant Communism should keep us on our guard, true, but so should such homegrown threats as poverty, the inequitable distribution of income, and the dominance of white Anglo-Saxons in our political, economic, and social institutions. These threats, too, we decided, could cripple our society; these injustices at home also posed a challenge to national defense. The problem was to open up and enlarge opportunity for large segments of the population to whom real opportunity had previously been denied.

The nation delegated a large part of the responsibility for solving that problem to education. Other steps had to be taken: the Constitutional right of all adult Americans to vote had to be enforced–and it was; job barriers built on ethnic restrictions had to fall–and they did. And yet, we realized, no legal steps to make equality of economic or political opportunity real would succeed without equality of *educational* opportunity.

And so, in the mid-1960s we saw a host of laws passed that went far beyond the original intent of NDEA. Those were exciting days to be in education. Virtually every month seemed to bring a new idea, and we got accustomed to a dazzling array of new terms: "Title I" and "sets," "Initial Teaching Alphabet" and "inquiry-directed learning" became part of every elementary school educator's working vocabulary. What had once been a quiet trade, proceeding placidly and predictably from school year to school year, seemed now saturated with innovations–the new math, programmed learning, the talking typewriter, team-teaching, nongraded classes, classrooms-without-walls, cross-age teaching, multimedia packages, even computer-based instruction. More and more newspapers, which once had regarded education coverage as ritual reporting of the school bond election, now found it necessary to assign a reporter to the schoolbeat. The cover of *Time* magazine, for the first time in memory, carried the portrait of the U.S. Commissioner of Education.

Yet after a few years of enthusiasm, something happened. Our colleagues in higher education, after rhapsodizing about their acquisition of new dormitories and electron microscopes and language-and-area centers, suddenly found themselves confronted with a student generation that refused to be impressed by all these academic trappings. While university administrators fretted about a new creation called the "multiversity"–at times, its major problem seemed to be student parking–the students themselves marched to protest what they viewed as the "lack of relevance" in the curriculum. President Johnson, once confident that we could afford guns and butter both, now thrashed around in a quagmire composed of Vietnam and civil disorders, Weathermen and Black Panthers, and a growing restiveness caused by a fear that we had tried to go too far, too fast. The recognition dawned on us that the resources of the United States, while perhaps still greater than those of any other nation, were nonetheless limited. A certain mood of self-doubt and disillusion crept over the land.

This was particularly true in education. The Coleman Report, the Moynihan Report, and the Jencks Report all suggested that our strenuous efforts to improve the nation's health through education had failed; improvements in schools, it was alleged, simply didn't make much difference. And educators were further pummeled in such books as *Death at an Early Age* and *36 Children* that suggested that some schools and their teachers might be doing harm.

In sum, it's a trying ten years we've come through since the high enthusiasm of 1964 and educators can be forgiven if, now and then, they survey what they tried to build in that time and find nothing but the wreckage of wasted efforts.

The truth, perhaps, lies somewhere between the extremes of fulsome praise and savage criticism. My view is that the nation's enthusiasm for education during the last ten years produced some solid gains–less than we had hoped, to be sure, but progress nonetheless. And the greatest impediment to further progress is that we may lose our sense of enthusiasm and purpose.

American education, perhaps, is both better and worse than we commonly assume. The results of the International Association For the Evaluation of Educational Achievement's survey, for example, demonstrate that while the average scores of American students are not particularly impressive, our top 10 percent compare quite favorably with the elite of other nations. Presently, 75 percent of our eighteen-year olds graduate from high school. This is the highest percentage in the world. Our great achievement, in short, is that we have sought to educate a larger portion of our population than any other nation, and in large measure succeeded. These figures, of course, provide quantitative measures–they suggest how accessible education is, not how good it is. The search for quality, it goes without saying, must continue. We still do not know how to pinpoint the "hidden curriculum" that characterizes the home life of some of our children, nor how to incorporate it in the overt curriculum of schools where youngsters fail in disproportionate numbers. We still do not know how much of our high school curricula makes sense for youngsters who will spend most of their lives in the 21st century. We still do not know how to measure quality in teaching.

There are, consequently, some strong arguments for the continuing professional education of teachers. From 1966 through 1972, /I/D/E/A sponsored a comprehensive study of change. The results suggest that the dynamics of the school—the patterns of professional rewards, staff jealousies, and human morale that operate within a school and give it a distinctive personality—have a profound effect upon teaching and learning. Our ten years of experience with IGE, moreover, have made it clear that teachers are anything but alike. Some are excellent lecturists, some are not. Some are stimulated by outstanding students and respond well to them, while others have a special gift for diagnosing the learning difficulties of children with less than average ability. Nonetheless, our experience would seem to suggest that it is in the school unit, where the staff and administration have a unified set of goals, that efficient improvement can most easily occur. Sustained efforts to promote professional development are therefore indispensable.

We must also avoid confusing the form of an educational innovation with its purpose; in focusing with such intensity upon the accomplishment of an objective we should not overlook its fundamental intent. It is in this regard that the continuing education of teachers and administrators can offer additional advantages. It is not innovation, per se, that is our aim; rather it is the improvement of the educational process. Among other things, then, professional development experiences should help school personnel make intelligent judgments as to when change is, and is not, desirable.

These, I cannot help but believe, are important points to remember as we begin the difficult decade ahead.

In-Service Staff Development and the Right to Education

Hannah N. Geffert
Robert J. Harper II
Daniel M. Schember
Lawyer's Committee for Civil Rights under Law

All is not calm in the world of in-service teacher education. Those seeking to conduct "business as usual" in this field are facing increasing challenges from others who insist that the business should not be theirs to conduct. While the former attempt to concentrate on the substantive questions of in-service, the latter are pushing the questions of authority and decision-making procedure in in-service to the fore, saying the substantive questions should be addressed after the power to implement the proposed answers is properly reallocated.

The national symposium that generated this volume manifested the growing uneasiness. "The critical issues . . . ," asserted the program announcement, "have to do with the new kinds of teaching requirements that are associated with community-based learning, moral and civic education, the impact of children's television on early childhood education, the individualization of learning, and the humanistic aspects of schooling"—all substantive issues.

"In-service," came the response, "is a teacher power issue."[1]

This is a dispute over action priorities. The teacher power perspective does not deem the requirements associated with the humanistic aspects of schooling irrelevant. Rather, this perspective simply demands that the question of who governs be properly answered first, or at least concurrently with substantive issues.

1. Statement of William L. Smith, Director of Teacher Corps, United States Office of Education, at the National Symposium: Critical Issues in Teacher In-Service Education, Chicago, Illinois, October 3, 1975. Mr. Smith's remarks also include the significance of right to education developments for in-service training policies.

The dispute is serious. The American Federation of Teachers may be prepared to boycott efforts to address the substantive questions until the question of power is more favorably resolved.[2]

Nonetheless, it is important not to judge, in a vacuum, the significance of this dispute, or the significance of any of the "critical" issues mentioned above. There are many other complicating factors. The purpose of this article is to address one of them—a major legal development, a part of the frequently unstated context in which the teacher power dispute and the substantive issues will necessarily be resolved, if at all. This development is the growing body of law concerning the right of each student to an education suiting his or her needs.

The right to a suitable education was won initially in landmark federal litigation by handicapped students,[3] non-English-speaking students,[4] and disciplinary pushouts.[5] Subsequent cases have significantly expanded the scope of this legal concept.[6]

Implicit in the right to a suitable education is the right to instruction by suitably trained teachers. Hence, this right has direct implications for in-service training.

In fact, a mandatory in-service training program is one of the major responses that right to education litigation has evoked. The reaction to the pressure of bilingual education litigation illustrates this point and exemplifies the type of response that right to education litigation in other areas is likely to generate.

The California legislature has made in-service training a mandatory component of district bilingual education programs.[7] Similarly, train-

2. So that the reader may independently assess the likelihood of this development we would like to say that this statement is based solely on the following occurrence: At a planning conference for a national meeting on in-service professional development, Eugenia Kemble, Special Assistant to the President, American Federation of Teachers, announced the withdrawal of the AFT from participation in the conference for specific reasons including, first, that the federal effort behind the conference does not support freeing up the teaching profession to develop its own ideas; and second, that no one in the AFT runs a professional development center. Minutes of the Planning Conference for SPRING INSTITUTE, Washington, D.C., November 18–19, 1975, p. 3.
3. Pennsylvania Association for Retarded Children v. Pennsylvania, 334 F. Supp. 1257 (E.D. Pa. 1971) (consent decree), 343 F. Supp. 279 (E.D. Pa. 1972) (consent decree). See also Kirp, *The Schools as Sorters: The Constitutional and Policy Implications of Student Classification,* 121 U. Pa. L. Rev. 705 (1973).
4. Lau v. Nichols, 414 U.S. 563 (1974).
5. Mills v. District of Columbia, 348 F. Supp. 866 D.D.C. (1972).
6. Peter W. Doe v. San Francisco City and County, Cal. Filed November 20, 1972. See also Abel, *Can a Student Sue the Schools for Educational Malpractice?,* 44 Harv. Ed. Rev. 416 (1974).
7. Hannah Geffert, Robert J. Harper, and Daniel M. Schember, *The Current Status of U.S. Bilingual Education Legislation,* (Center for Applied Linguistics, May 1975), p. 46.

ing institutes are mandatory in Texas.[8] In Michigan the state board of education must "develop and administer a program of in-service training for bilingual instruction programs."[9] Federal standards covering all states include the requirements that in-service training be "directly related to improving student performance," and must include an "evaluation design . . . and performance criteria for individuals receiving the training." Districts opting to use in-service training "must continue" the training "until staff performance criteria has [sic] been met."[10]

The important features of these legal requirements are the facts that the programs are mandatory; they are oriented to student needs; and they must have specific objectives and accountability measures.

It is important to stress that although these in-service standards are for bilingual education programs, the impact of these precedents will, for several reasons, vastly exceed their current application. First, the in-service requirements concern minority cultures as well as languages. In California, for example, training programs must be "designed to rapidly produce teachers . . . who are sensitive to cultural differences and knowledgeable about the origins of such differences. . . ."[11] Provisions such as this set strong precedents for mandatory training concerning all cultures represented in desegregated school systems without restrictions concerning language proficiency or orientation.

Second, educational isolation of cultural minorities–either through segregation or discriminatory tracking–is illegal.[12] Some bilingual education programs are expressly transitional, requiring the rapid movement of students into the mainstream of the curriculum.[13] Thus, all teachers are potential instructors of students from cultural backgrounds different from their own, and the logic of current developments compels the inclusion of all school staff in appropriate in-service training.

Third, the same compelling case for system-wide in-service training applies to ending the educational isolation of disciplinary pushouts and

8. Geffert, et al., *Current Status,* p. 113.

9. Ibid., p. 83.

10. *Task Force Findings Specifying Remedies Available for Eliminating Past Educational Practices Ruled Unlawful Under Lau v. Nichols,* (Washington, D.C., Office for Civil Rights, Department of Health, Education and Welfare, Summer, 1975).

11. Geffert, et al., *Current Status,* n. 7, p. 50.

12. Brown v. Board of Education, 347 U.S. 438 (1954); Hobson v. Hanson, 269 F. Supp. 401 (D.D.C. 1967), aff'd sub. nom. Smuck v. Hobson, 408 F. 2d 175 (D.C. Cir. 1969).

13. Illinois and Massachusetts are prominent examples. See Geffert, et al., *Current Status,* n. 7.

exceptional students–an emerging legal requirement.[14] Mandatory mainstreaming of such students demands that all teachers be effectively trained to meet unique student needs in an integrated setting.

Fourth, the pattern of bilingual in-service requirements is already being replicated in response to right to education litigation having a much broader scope. In *Robinson v. Cahill*[15] the Supreme Court of New Jersey invalidated virtually the entire state education system and ordered the legislature to enact new legislation to fulfill its state constitutional mandate to provide each student a "thorough and efficient" education.[16] The legislative response to the court order requires the formulation of specific educational goals to be attained by students and grants the state commissioner of education the power to order "necessary budgetary changes" and "in-service training programs for teachers and other school personnel" as part of "corrective action" to make sure the goals are accomplished.[17]

Two other aspects of *Robinson v. Cahill* are important to note. First, the case clearly indicates, as do many other cases, that fulfilling the right of each student to a suitable education is the responsibility of the state. Second, *Robinson v. Cahill* is a school finance equalization case signifying the imperative of linking statewide equity in resource allocation with state-enforced efforts to ensure that each district's students meet established educational goals. The incorporation of a state-enforced in-service training requirement in this context implies the allocation of scarce in-service resources according to state priorities for "corrective action."

In summarizing the important elements of these developments and assessing their significance for the teacher power dispute and the debate over substantive in-service issues, it is important to reiterate that education is the responsibility of the state. If the current pattern of in-service developments continues, mandatory in-service training programs will be implemented in response to the expanding scope of right to education litigation. The programs will either be directly, or ulti-

14. Burt, *Beyond the Right to Treatment: Strategies for Judicial Action to Aid the Retarded.* President's Committee on Mental Retardation and the Project on Classification of Exceptional Children, (Nashville, Tenn.: Vanderbilt University, June, 1973).
15. 62 N.J. 473 (1973).
16. Twelve states presently have "thorough and efficient" or similar language in their constitutions: Colorado, Idaho, Indiana, Maryland, Minnesota, Montana, New Jersey, Ohio, Pennsylvania, South Dakota, West Virginia, Wyoming. *State Constitutional Provisions and Selected Legal Materials Relating to Public School Finance* (Washington, D.C., Department of Health, Education, and Welfare, 1973).
17. New Jersey Senate Bill 1516, 1975.

mately controlled by the state. They will be oriented to meeting established, system-wide priorities. These priorities will emphasize (1) the special educational needs of exceptional children and disciplinary pushouts; (2) understanding and responding to cultural differences; and (3) implementing corrective actions necessary to impart basic communication and mathematical skills to students whom the schools are currently failing to serve. Resources will be devoted to these priorities according to the more equitable distribution schemes won in school finance litigation. State control and established priorities will demand, and at the same time facilitate, the incorporation of performance evaluations and other accountability-oriented measures to insure that in-service training is relevant and effective. While these developments will be the enacted policies of the states, they will occur in the context of court-ordered imperatives, implementing a concept central to contemporary American life—the right to a suitable education.[18]

The teacher power dispute and the debate over the substantive issues deemed "critical" by the symposium program stand to be totally subsumed by the paradigm of legal principles emerging from right to education litigation. An open-ended demand for teacher power in in-service—no mandatory requirements, no accountability, individual teacher control of the topics, purposes, and settings of in-service—is incompatible with this paradigm, as it has evolved to date. It is conceivable, moreover, that all of the "critical" issues for the symposium will be relegated by this paradigm to the category of less than compelling priorities. At the very least, this paradigm will demand that the relevance of these issues to the more basic needs of educationally-deprived students be clearly demonstrated.

All of these issues, however, must be studied from a variety of perspectives. While legal principles stemming from right to education litigation will be dominant factors influencing the teacher power dispute and the debate over substantive in-service priorities, these controversies are also subject to other complicating, and perhaps counterbalancing, factors. State statutes mandating in-service training stand on no firmer footing than state statutes mandating collective bargaining. To the extent that aspects of in-service training are, and continue to be, mandatory subjects of collective negotiation, teachers

18. This is not to say that courts are the only sources of pressure for policies implementing the right of each student to a suitable education. Many forces influence the enactment of legislation and the adoption of policies. New Jersey, however, is an example of a state enacting in-service legislation in direct response to a court order. Robinson v. Cahill *supra,* n. 15; Senate Bill 1516, n. 17.

will be able to substantially influence in-service developments.[19] Moreover, arbitrary impositions of irrelevant in-service training are of questionable legal validity, especially if teacher performance evaluations from such training are used to make critical employment decisions.[20] Study of these and many other issues will be required to avoid the errors of analyzing in-service policies in a vacuum. Nonetheless, the right of each student to a suitable education remains a prominent and compelling priority.

19. Negotiations under Iowa's law include in-service training by express provision. See Megel, *Guide for Legislative Action and State Collective Bargaining Laws* (American Federation of Teachers). In-service may also be a bargainable "working condition."

20. See Rebell, *Teacher Credentialling Reform in New York State: A Critique and a Suggestion for New Directions* (Omaha, Nebraska: University of Nebraska Study Commission on Undergraduate Education and the Education of Teachers).

In-Service Education in Schools of the Poor

William L. Smith

Director, Teacher Corps, U.S. Office of Education

Twice in the last two decades, national and international events have forced public school administrators to make dramatic revisions in educational policy. In both instances, the Federal Government served as the catalytic agent through which the school adjusted to changing world events. With the advent of Sputnik, and the need to reinvigorate the curriculum, sizeable modifications were prompted. Major alterations were again initiated, a few decades later, when newborn social consciousness mandated a more liberal public school.

Programs developed through federal funding cannot in themselves affect pupil achievement. Money for research and development is important but constructive change is not the automatic consequence of dollar expenditures; the decisive factors, instead, have to do with fundamental reform in school structure and organization. These reforms in turn, cannot be accomplished without professional retraining directed at the beliefs, commitments and skills of the practitioners who are directly responsible for the accomplishment of educational objectives.

If one conceives of a continuum with (a) federal program intervention at one end, and (b) significant change in the organization of schooling at the other end, it is difficult to establish a direct cause and effect relationship between a and b. A large number of variables affect what is started at one polarity of the continuum and what eventuates at the other. While all of these variables are not completely understood, there seems to be little question but that three particular factors are of considerable importance: (1) the actions taken by the building principal; (2) the corresponding response of the school faculty; and (3) the ways in which the consequence of these are perceived by both the student and the community.

Humans, after all, are remarkably adept at avoiding unwanted constraints, at interpreting program provisions in accordance with their biases and predispositions, and at bending both the spirit and intent of policies in order to patronize their own beliefs. Moreover, since instructional innovations sponsored by the Federal Government cannot be tightly bound up in mandates, but rather must have sufficient flexibility to fit local circumstance, the latitude for acting upon personal prejudice is great.

PRINCIPAL BEHAVIOR

Leadership, or the absence of leadership, works in strange ways. Principals, as experiments have repeatedly demonstrated, have considerable impact on the operation of schools, both through calculated actions and through deliberate failure to act. Much depends upon teachers' perceptions of a principal's educational philosophy and on the extent to which they trust executive judgment, feel supported, and are thus inclined to aid and abet the cause. Leadership behavior is often less significant than the motives followers ascribe to the behavior—well-intentioned administrators, seeking to accomplish worthwhile goals, may be forgiven and aided when they blunder. On the other hand, when their actions and aspirations are viewed by the faculty with either suspicion or disdain, loyalty, trust and commitment are substantially reduced. It is largely for these reasons that the brightest and best educated of principals are not always the most successful: faculty response to administrative maneuver has the capacity both to blunt genius and enhance ordinary leadership ability.

STAFF BEHAVIOR

Teaching faculties not only respond to leaders, they also act out their own predilections. It has often been observed that teachers habitually filter suggested innovations in instructional method and content, as well as other suggested changes, through their own value-system. While administrative pressure may have some impact upon these value-systems, it is probably naive to assume that they can be completely remade through even imaginative and powerful manipulation. It follows, therefore, that changes in curriculum and instruction cannot be achieved on any permanent basis if the virtues of these changes are not understood and endorsed by practitioners. The implications for staff development, hence, are obvious.

Teachers are no less intelligent than administrators and, in many instances, equally well-trained. It is not uncommon, consequently, for disparities to exist between a particular teacher's view of the educational world and the view of a particular principal. Moreover, since it is the teacher, in the last analysis, who determines what goes on in the classroom, teacher autonomy often overrides administrator preference as well as the recommendations incorporate in a given innovation. Practitioners can, of course, be "ordered" to comply with stipulated procedure but most dissidents find it relatively easy to meet such requirements without abandoning their own prerogatives. These circumstances notwithstanding, it would be misleading to say that professional agreement between teacher and principal conviction is impossible, or to deny that large numbers of teachers willingly implement suggested changes when their merits are obvious.

As an occupational group, teachers are victimized by conflicting allegiances. Like other professionals, they hold personal beliefs regarding what constitutes good practice, effective teaching, and useful learning They are also beholden, however, to a dual set of clients (students and parents), to prescribed school policies, to the expectations of their peers, and, at times, to pressures created by their professional organizations In view of these often contradictory demands, it is not surprising that they frequently feel trapped in a doublebind wherein any teaching decision will alienate some segment of their constituencies.

COMMUNITY EXPECTATION

The heterogeneity of community expectation creates further complications. Particularly in poverty areas, it is not uncommon to find widespread "dissatisfaction with the school," and on deeper probing to discover that different community factions have diametrically opposed expectations. Young parents, for example, may object to a continual reduction of the school budget whereas older citizens—confronted with increasingly burdensome tax bills—press for further cutbacks. Community groups also vary in their perceptions of what schools "do to the children" and the appropriateness of leadership policy. The professional short life of superintendents, caused by the high rate of Board hiring and firing, provides an obvious illustration.

The poor cannot help but feel that their plight is largely the result of oppressive public policy and they are therefore anxious to ensure that the schools do not deprive their children of an education that will enable them to cope, more effectively, with the social system. It is imperative, consequently, to work toward a mutual feeling of trust among teachers, administrators and parents. This, however, is easier said than done. For such trust involves, first, a belief among all concerned in the ability to influence decisions; second, a degree of consensus as to what schools are for; third, a confidence in the integrity and judgment of the other partners; and, fourth, a basic faith in the democratic process.

The concept of "parity" can be viewed as a potential vehicle for achieving these requirements. In this context, *parity is defined as the deliberate, collaborative sharing of decision-making among those who render and receive services.* Its effect is to increase power equalization and reciprocal involvement. The underlying assumption is that parents—given greater opportunity to influence the course of their children's education—will (a) become more effective collaborators; (b) help reinforce designated learning objectives in the home; (c) cooperate more intelligently with school personnel; and (d) develop greater confidence in the schools' procedures. A second assumption, moreover, is that principals and teachers will function more effectively if both play a hand in policy determination. Once parity has been accomplished, and a more equitable power distribution exists between professional and client, resistance to reform and change may not only diminish but, of even greater importance, program adaptations can be directed toward goals that parents and teachers alike regard as significant.

True parity will necessitate a greater degree of communion between school and community, as well as stronger alliances among the subgroups within each. In the school hierarchy, for example, it will require a greater division of power among teachers, building administrators and central office. In the community, on the other hand, decision-making influence must be distributed more broadly among the different sectors, and efforts must be made to increase congruence in expectation. Importantly, whatever provisions for parity are put into play, a balance must be maintained between public and private good. Schools are intended to serve the societal welfare as well as the special interests of students and parents. Thus, to tilt too far in serving vested interests would be to ignore the basic mission of public education.

Beyond realignments in the politics of education, moreover, fundamental revisions will be necessary in basic educational philosophy. Rather than conceiving of schools as social agencies designed to impose selected doctrines on a captive clientele, they must be regarded as agencies intended to serve or facilitate, at least in part, the educational preferences of those who, by law, are compelled to attend. Similarly, the curriculum will need to be viewed as a tool for accomplishing personal as well as societal objectives. And, perhaps of greatest moment, professional educators must envision themselves, not as the final arbitrators of what goes on in school, but rather as public agents expected to facilitate the realization of parental aspirations. It is this last, self-evidently, that poses a definitive target for in-service education.

Unfortunately, little exists in the way of operational theory for promoting parity. A large number of clues, however, probably can be derived from conventional constructs on organizational systems, community organization and managerial process. Each of these, to a greater or lesser degree, touches upon some aspect of the five principal tasks:

1. restructuring decision-making procedures for determining educational policy;
2. achieving a rational distribution of power in curriculum planning among parents, teachers and administrators;
3. developing greater consensus regarding educational purpose among different community groups;
4. reorienting teachers, through programs of professional development, to function in a parity-based system;
5. enabling administrators, through programs of staff development, to assume leadership responsibility for accomplishing the above.

It is the last two of these tasks that are particularly relevant to this volume. The administrator's role is critical because principals alone can create a work environment that lends itself to decision-making parity. The professional preparation of most administrators is not geared toward shared authority in decision-making, the fine-lines distinguishing leadership from management are blurred, and, as a result, some retraining will be mandatory. Similarly, the preservice education of teachers has tended to focus on autonomous action, within established protocol, and a shift toward greater collaboration with parents and community groups, as well as a more forthright accommodation of student and parental interests in the instructional program, also will necessitate professional reorientation.

Contemporary theory on teacher in-service education, it might be noted, is well ahead of practice. Whereas most schools, for example, still rely upon general institutes, afterschool meetings, and nondescript summer workshops, recent research evidence suggests that retraining is most efficacious when it occurs in the actual work setting. The thrust of most staff development programs, furthermore, is toward traditional conceptualizations rather than toward adjustments to a rapidly changing society. And, while some improvment has taken place, the content of professional improvement programs still tends to be based upon administrative fiat rather than upon the perceived needs of the practitioners involved.

The morale of teachers, at present, is at low ebb. Dispirited by sustained criticism, teachers in poverty areas feel torn between parental critics who do not comprehend the essence of good education, and administrators who are insensitive to the impediments and constraints inherent in the teaching environment. Not uncommonly, therefore, many teachers avoid participation in decision-making, preferring to allow administrators to establish policy and assume responsibility. Realistically, however, teachers have the ultimate power to influence student achievement and they therefore can legitimately be expected to hold responsibility. So, much of the in-service education activity aimed at decision-making parity will need to deal with the teacher's presumed sense of powerlessness. That is, teachers must be induced to accept a larger role in the decision-making process; they must be given greater freedom in achieving their educational objectives; and, correspondingly, they must be held accountable for the net results.

When all is said and done, the communities do not want to run the schools. What most parents seek is an educational program that seems sensible and effective. Especially in the inner city, many parents have come to believe that the only way to insure good schooling is to carefully monitor the activities of teachers and administrators. Given an open and flexible system of communication–wherein parents are informed about ongoing instructional activities, the reasons underlying their selection, and the benefits to their children–most parents would not only be receptive but supportive and protective as well. Such goodwill would, in time, have a salutary effect upon the teachers–appreciated and reinforced by their administrators and constituencies, they would be inclined toward greater dedication and commitment. The existing state of affairs, in contrast, tends to beget attacks and counterattacks, defensiveness, suspicion, distrust, and an educational system weakened by a general malaise.

A good deal of difficulty stems from the pronounced lack of sophistication, particularly among young teachers, regarding the cultural milieu of the inner city. The indictments that have been levied against teacher training institutions aside, teaching in the ghetto is far more difficult than teaching in the affluent suburbs. Resultingly, teachers with seniority gravitate to greener pastures, leaving the vicissitudes and turbulence of the poverty belt to those just beginning their careers. Assigned to predominately black, or Spanish-speaking, or Appalachian white schools, apprehensive over what seems like a hostile parent cohort, and aggravated by students with less than normal motivation, young teachers quickly embrace the idea of "getting out as soon as possible." The fact remains, nonetheless, that some teachers render distinguished service and derive considerable gratification from working in inner city schools. The satisfaction attached to making a significant contribution seems to overshadow the extra effort. Effective in-service, one would think, might serve to infect neophyte teachers with similar attitudes.

It has also become fashionable, recently, for teachers to regard "professionalism" as dispensation to disregard parent and community expectations. No profession, however, can survive such a posture–in law, medicine, social service, the ministry, and everywhere else, the professional must satisfy the client. It can be no different in teaching. Good in-service education, consequently, must also be concerned with the teacher's obligation to the consumer. Few parents are likely to impose demands that are totally inappropriate, ill-suited, or irrational. Most, in fact, will happily endorse whatever can be demonstrated to be good for their children. Parity in decision-making will remain ineffectual as long as teachers and parents misunderstand one another, question each other's motives, and work at cross-purposes.

Finally, something should be said about the necessary readjustments in the internal relationships among teachers, principals, supervisors, district administrators, and central office specialists. If parity is to flourish, the ancient pecking-order must be abandoned so that "subordinates and superordinates" respond to one another as colleagues rather than as superiors and inferiors.

All of this suggests that quality in-service education must pay considerable attention to how teachers feel about themselves, the materials they use, their children, and their communities. Inspired teaching can only come from those who are inspired: yet, perversely, the children most in need of inspired teaching are also most likely to be taught by teachers who have been driven knee-deep in alienation. People, teacher training institutions and school organizations have an obligation to do something in a systematic way about this deplorable state of affairs, now.

Do Staff Development Practices Make a Difference?

Charles A. Speiker

Association for Supervision and Curriculum Development

Research findings, current trends, legislative policies and opinions from various experts have been reviewed in an attempt to bring light to the question "Do staff development practices make a difference?" Collections of information from varied sources were obtained including interview statements from association leaders representing educators, dentists, lawyers, and engineers.

An informed answer to the question was "yes, but. . . ." *Yes,* staff development practices made a difference, *but* not always in the manner or mode desired. Frequently, the real difference was probably a depletion of scarce resources. However, if practices were carried out under certain conditions, then, hoped-for results would be obtained.

One of the more current and comprehensive reviews of research on in-service education was done by Lawrence. In that report it was clear that staff development programs under certain conditions were effective. He found patterns of effectiveness from an analysis of ninety-seven studies. Findings from that collection include:

1. School-based in-service programs concerned with complex teacher behaviors tend to have greater success in accomplishing their objectives than do college-based programs dealing with complex behaviors.
2. Teacher attitudes are more likely to be influenced in school-based than in college-based in-service programs.
3. School-based programs, in which teachers participate as helpers to each other and planners of in-service activities, tend to have greater success in accomplishing their objectives than do programs that are

conducted by college or other outside personnel without the assistance of teachers.

4. School-based in-service programs that emphasize self-instruction by teachers have a strong record of effectiveness.
5. In-service education programs that have differentiated training experiences for different teachers (that is, 'individualized') are more likely to accomplish their objectives than are programs that have common activities for all participants.
6. In-service education programs that place the teacher in (an) active role (constructing and generating materials, ideas and behavior) are more likely to accomplish their objectives.
7. In-service education programs that emphasize demonstrations, supervise trials and feedback are more likely to accomplish their goals than are programs in which the teachers are expected to store up ideas and behavior prescriptions for a future time.
8. In-service education programs in which teachers share and provide mutual assistance to each other are more likely to accomplish their objectives than are programs in which each teacher does separate work.
9. Teachers are more likely to benefit from in-service education activities that are linked to a general effort of the school than they are from "single-shot" programs that are not part of a general staff development plan.
10. Teachers are more likely to benefit from in-service programs in which they can choose goals and activities for themselves, as contrasted with programs in which the goals and activities are preplanned.[1]

Lawrence presented a note of optimism toward certain *current* (1970s) practices; Haas looked at practices that accompanied the 1950s and 1960s curriculum development projects, and judged them as ineffective.[2] The hoped-for union of subject matter competency and appropriate uses of new curriculum did not occur.

Ingersoll surveyed 745 elementary and secondary school teachers in 26 school districts.[3] A Teacher Needs Assessment Survey was de-

1. G. Lawrence et al., *Patterns of Effective In-Service Education: A State of the Art Summary of Research on Materials and Procedures for Changing Teacher Behaviors in In-Service Education* (State of Florida: Department of Education, December, 1974), pp. 8–15.
2. John D. Haas, *Diffusion of Curriculum Products Through In-Service Education* (Denver, Colo.: ERIC–ED 098 120, November 1974).
3. Gary M. Ingersoll, *Teacher Training Needs, Conditions and Materials: A Preliminary Survey of In-service Education* Report #8 (Denver, Colo.: ERIC–ED 108 407, February 1975). Gary M. Ingersoll, *Assessing In-service Training Needs Through Teacher Responses.* Paper presented at the Annual Meeting of the American Educational Research Association, Washington, D.C., April 1975. (Denver, Colo.: ERIC–ED 104 820).

signed during this study and an analysis of the data from the instrument was similar to the summary data by Lawrence. Ingersoll found that areas of concern were usually selected by persons other than the in-service participants, follow-up and evaluation were inadequate, and statements giving directions were not clearly stated. It was recommended that more attention in the development of in-service programs and materials be given to individual teacher needs, skill development (not only motivational materials), and to the uniqueness of in-service and preservice materials.

Other researchers also found that in-service strategies were making a difference. Johnson on a release time program, Peters on strategies in rural schools, Brous with teacher attitudes toward career education, Simmons in an elementary school science program, and Yarger with teacher centers, found reason to judge staff development programs as making a difference in teacher behavior and cognition under certain conditions.[4]

Questions relating pupil performance to staff development created a heated debate. In Georgia an attempt was made to refine methodology relating teacher behavior to measures of pupil growth.[5] This long-term project was intended to reduce the inconsistencies that plagued other similar projects.

When various associations were contacted, a less than optimistic picture—in an organized sense—emerged.[6] Many of the comments by spokespersons for those associations gave the impression that what was happening was just happening. "Our programs are fragmented," "we cannot keep track of the activities," "we're going through congresses because we cannot upgrade our membership any other way," "it's a mixed bag," and "nothing is done to measure the effectiveness of practices" were a few of the comments received in response to the question "Do your professional renewal efforts make a difference?" Persons at the National Education Association (N.E.A.) were contacted and the responses were different. Extensive needs assessments throughout districts across the country have been initiated. According to Lois Krarsik, "It makes a difference." Evidence suggested that

4. Herbert Nelson Simmons, *Research on S.C.I.S.* (Denver, Colo.: ERIC-ED 114 251). In 1973 Simmons sampled 224 teachers studying the Science Curriculum Improvement Study program for elementary schools. He found "strong indicators" that the experimental group resulted in a more student centered teacher.

5. Robert S. Soar, *Validation of Competencies.* Paper presented at the annual meeting of the American Educational Research Association, Washington, D.C., March 1975.

6. Associations for Dentists, Engineers, and Law Officers were initially contacted to determine whether there were practices that teacher educators could look at or adopt.

staff development practices definitely made a difference with respect to teacher attitude and performance. Three items of importance based on their surveys that were being processed toward policy statements were:

—who should pay for staff development programs,
—when should certain staff development occur,
—who should determine staff development programs.

The N.E.A. has advocated that employing districts should pay for staff development activities planned with teacher involvement that occur as part of the contract week. The research and advocates for sound staff development practices concur that teachers ought to be involved in determining the program activities.

Yet, programs planned from an informed position seemed to be in the minority. Almost every area of education was calling for a fresh look or a rejuvenation of program practices, whether for administrators,[7] for health care personnel,[8] higher education teachers,[9] or educators in general interested in staff development.[10]

In *Improving In-Service Education: Proposals and Procedures for Change,* Louis Rubin has drawn fifty-five operational implications from eleven chapters written by educational leaders on the topic of in-service.[11] The exhortations from Rubin and the other writers reaffirm many of the findings from the research, including:

1. Teachers must be given time and other resources with which to assess their professional needs and to carry on improvement activities.
2. The continuing education of the teacher should bear directly upon the problem he or she encounters in his or her work . . . give teacher greater contact with his or her social environment.
3. Teacher in-service education should emphasize instructional alternatives rather than single methods.

7. *Administrative Staff Development,* The Best of ERIC Series, No. 8, April 1975. (Denver, Colo.: ERIC ED 102 643). Called for a complete "rejuvenation of administrator training."
8. Helen M. Tobin, *The Process of Staff Development: Components for Change* (Denver, Colo.: ERIC ED 096 534, April 1974). She noted that staff development becomes more significant as major changes are occurring in the field of health care.
9. Robert M. Caldwell, *Critical Issues in Faculty Development* (Denver, Colo.: ERIC ED 105 523, March 1975). This publication describes efforts directed toward higher education faculties.
10. Thomas J. Sergiovanni, *Professional Supervision for Professional Teachers,* ASCD (Washington, D.C., 1975).
11. Louis Rubin, ed., *Improving In-Service Education: Proposals and Procedures for Change* (Boston: Allyn and Bacon, Inc., 1971).

4. Most in-service education activities should be carried on within the setting in which the learners normally work together.
5. A systematic program must be developed . . . programs demand long range planning.
6. Whenever possible teachers should be asked to compare their goals with their actual results.

The six statements above relate specifically to teachers. But, the in-service program neither begins nor ends there alone. A number of players need to be involved in the development of appropriate policies that encourage reform; supervisors and administrators need to evolve as part of this total renewal process; and at all times our focus should ultimately return to how these activities may help children learn, and by learning, become free to learn.

The findings of social psychology suggest that people with similar interests can, through interaction, contribute to one another's welfare. Programs of professional growth should take advantage of teachers' potential for teaching one another.

Ben Harris said:

> In-service education is at a crude level in most American schools. Therefore, most programs are quite ineffective. This is not surprising when you consider:
>
> –little or no money is available,
> –little or no staff is available for planning,
> –policies and guidelines in districts are weak or nonexistent.
>
> State departments such as Florida and Georgia are doing a fine job. When monies from federal sources, staff, and planning are properly utilized, results occur. Results in teacher classroom behavior and cognition occur. The research is most reassuring in teacher performance. Student learning is another question.[12]

According to Rubin, "It has been astonishingly easy for clumsy and inept programs to survive. We have now reached the point, however, where our ancient infirmities may do us in, for it has now become clear, first, that better–perhaps different–schooling is an indispensable element in sustaining the society, and, second, that better schooling will necessitate continuous readjustment in the time to come."[13]

We are in the decade of the 1970s now and practices have not changed at a meaningful level. Forces that have long-standing tradition

12. This was part of a telephone conversation on June 16, 1976. Dr. Harris reviewed this quote and gave permission for its use.

13. Louis Rubin, "The Case for Staff Development" in *Professional Supervision for Professional Teachers,* Thomas J. Sergiovanni, ed., ASCD (Washington, D.C., 1975), p. 35.

in American education still need to be reckoned with in an age of unequaled technological advancement. In a state-of-the-art article, Edelfelt and Lawrence pointed to twelve "concepts" that have been historically important in shaping in-service education. "Some of the concepts were operating at the beginning of American education or before; others have emerged more recently. They are:

1. The primary role of the school is the giving and receiving of information.
2. Learning is the receiving of information to be stored and used later.
3. Curriculum and teaching are relatively fixed elements in the school.
4. The main business of teacher education is the quest for mastery of some relatively stable subject matters and methods of teaching.
5. In-service education is training that is designed, planned, and conducted for the teacher by persons in authority.
6. The central purpose of in-service education is the remediation of teachers' deficiencies in subject matter.
7. Leadership is "direction from above," and motivation is "direction from outside."
8. Supervision is diagnosis, prescription, modeling, inspection, and rating.
9. Teacher education in teacher preparation institutions and teacher education in schools are separate and discontinuous processes.
10. Intellectual leadership in goal setting and planning for in-service education appropriately comes from outside the school.
11. The teacher is a solo practitioner rather than a group member involved in cooperative planning of common goals and related actions.
12. Prescriptive legislation is an appropriate vehicle for improving the quality of teaching standards.[14]

It seems that leaders should now begin to seriously rethink current practices, in light of old exhortations that call for an increase in systematic (not standardized) theory.

How one goes about the process of staff development is to do it. This simple answer ought to make one comfortable after a few distinctions are made. There is a difference between change and progress. There is a difference between authoritarian and authoritative. All of this is meant to say that techniques that work are available.

14. Roy A. Edelfelt, and Gordon Lawrence, "In-Service Education: The State of the Art" in *Rethinking In-Service Education,* Roy A. Edelfelt and Margo Johnson, eds., N.E.A., Washington, D.C., 1975), p. 9.

A myriad of needs assessment instruments and specific models have been developed for the person who wants to go about the development of an effective staff development program. The National Public Relations Association has succinctly presented several techniques, models and examples of these techniques in a recent publication.[15] It contains goals from Tucson, Birmingham and Los Angeles, an assessment survey from New Oxford, Pennsylvania as well as specific plans and activities from other cities throughout the United States. Another publication with the theme, "Models of Staff Development," contains models and plans of actual programs from eleven different cities and regions in the country.[16] Another publication, *Staff Development: Sources and Resources,* contains hundreds of annotations on the full range of the topic.[17]

Individual state efforts have been previously mentioned such as Florida and Georgia. Other states are also taking a closer look at the topic. An excellent article has been written in a Wisconsin document.[18] This article with its historical perspective, mentions experience from states such as Arkansas, Vermont, Texas, New Hampshire, Tennessee, and Minnesota.

Legislative action is also a means whereby progress in staff development programs is affected. A report from the Lawyers' Committee for Civil Rights Under Law has collected and indexed all state legal standards affecting education. *State Legislation Affecting In-Service Staff Development in Public Education* represents the most recent attempt to orderly present data that "constitutes the basic legal structure for the development and implementation of in-service staff development programs."[19]

In summary, it is clear that certain staff development practices make a difference; leaders believe that the current state of staff development practices leaves much room for informed improvement; and, there exists a great supply of resources for those persons who are earnest about improving staff development practices.

15. *In-service Education: Current Trends in School Policies and Programs.* N.S.P.R.A. (Arlington, VA., 1975).
16. Jack R. Frymier, ed., "Models of Staff Development," *Theory Into Practice* vol. XI, no. 4, (October, 1972).
17. Ione L. Perry, and Leslee J. Bishop, *Staff Development: Sources and Resources.* (Athens, GA.: University of Georgia, College of Education, 1974).
18. Allen T. Slagle, "In-Service Education" in *A Candid Discussion of the Issues in Education,* James M. Lipham, ed., (Madison, Wisconsin: Department of Public Instruction, 1975).
19. Hannah Geffert, et al. *State Legislations Affecting In-service Staff Development in Public Education,* Model Legislation Project, Lawyers' Committee for Civil Rights Under Law (Washington, D.C., 1976).

However, improvement will not come about in a sustained form until:

At the university level:

1. A greater awareness of the uniqueness of preservice and in-service activities is achieved.
2. Greater attention is given to the education of supervisors and administrators from an informed and organized base.
3. Greater awareness of administrative constraints placed on teacher preparation programs is achieved.

At the district or building level:

4. Policies and personnel guiding and coordinating staff development practices are upgraded (or developed in the case of absent policies).
5. Programs are planned and executed with strong teacher involvement, not merely teacher approval and passive participation.
6. Programs are *planned* that avoid "one shot affairs" or faddism, and systematically incorporate the elements of: the teacher's conception of purpose, sensitivity to students, grasp of subject matter, and a basic repertory of teaching skills.[20]

At the personal, individual educator level:

7. Each educator takes a personal responsibility for his or her improvement, acquiring a learner attitude—"becoming teachable."
8. Each educator becomes aware of false notions of security, power, prestige and change, understands that change and progress are different, but that certain changes can be progress—and progress is essential to growth and survival. (Speiker, 1975)

20. Rubin, *Improving In-Service Education,* 1975. p. 48.

Practical Observations from the Field

John C. Thurber
Palm Beach County Schools

It should be noted at the outset that my observations on in-service education stem from practical experience. Insofar as my professional assignment includes direct administrative responsibility for the professional development of a large number of teachers, working in a large array of different schools, my observations are based upon the teachings of the practical world. In-service, in my judgment, now faces two sets of problems—one has to do with an extension of theoretical thought, and the other with a refinement of operational procedures. While teachers routinely ask for usable solutions to everyday problems, and while in-service should make these available, it must, in the last analysis, be more than simple retraining and gadgetry. We must aim, ultimately, at the self-enlightenment and self-actualization of the teacher. Two circumstances prompt this point of view: first, the problems teachers encounter are directly related to their teaching goals, and to the ways in which they seek to accomplish them; and second, ready-made solutions to problems are not always as effective as those teachers create in response to the requirements of their personal situations.

Adaptability and flexibility are critical to teaching success. In these uncertain times, when enrollments, budgets and curricular objectives are all subject to abrupt modification, the ability to continually readjust is vital. It is this capacity to alter technique, as situations change that, more than anything else, enables teachers and administrators to cope, and to maintain their resilience.

Looking backward, it would seem that three judgmental errors are primarily responsible for past failures. One, the substance of in-service programs has not always reflected the true concerns of teachers; two, the retraining activities have been excessively short-term, lacking adequate follow-up and reinforcement; and three, the evaluations of the activites have relied predominantly upon opinion, with little attention to tangible evidence of teacher growth, pupil achievement, and undesirable side effects.

Through trial and error, we have gradually concluded that central office personnel must serve a dual role—that of idea-infuser and that of facilitator. Teacher involvement in determining the thrust of in-service activities is now mandatory. Irrespective of whether teachers make their recommendations on the basis of random judgment or deliberate analysis, the recommendations must be accorded a full measure of respect. Teacher-determined programs, however, gain considerably when they also have the endorsement of building administrators. The generation of support for an in-service program, and the coordination of its implementation, therefore become major central office responsibilities. The fulfillment of this obligation, however, does not prohibit central office personnel from also suggesting potential in-service objectives. We have found, for example, that teachers and administrators respond favorably to a process of a program-selection wherein a variety of possible activities are assembled by central office personnel, particular options selected by designated teacher committees, and principal approval solicited. The element of choice, in short, is essential.

Professional development is often viewed by citizens, boards of education and even administrators, as an unnecessary luxury. In times of economic hardship, moreover, funds for in-service education generally are cut sooner rather than later. It is important, therefore, to not only make use of collaborative decision-making but to also maintain a constant communication program that draws attention to the value of professional enhancement. Participation in decision-making should be shared by teachers, building-level administrators, central office personnel, board of education members, university personnel, parents and other interested citizens. It is true that the self-interests of some of these factions occasionally conflict. By and large, however, a cooperative spirit is possible, particularly if the importance of the undertakings are understood. Collaboration, furthermore, is likely to heighten if good communication successfully conveys tangible evidence of the programs' worth.

Again on the basis of trial and error, we now emphasize school-based programs that are planned jointly by teachers and administrators. We also stress the desirability of "individualization" provisions. In cases, these provisions amount to no more than insuring a range of alternatives, and in other cases a deliberate attempt is made to identify developmental activities particularly appropriate to a given teacher.

There is of late an unfortunate tendency to expect instant results from staff development activities. This is understandable when conditions make it necessary to decide upon the best ways to use limited resources. It is important to remind both participants and critics, however, that although we are unable to leap tall buildings, we can climb them on ladders, step by step. Quantum leaps in professional development are rare. In most instances, change is evolutionary and relatively slow. Some in-service objectives are reachable in comparatively short periods of time, but others can only be achieved through gradual change over substantial periods of time. Those involved in in-service activities sometimes need to be warned that expectations of instant success, and early evaluation, are irrational when long-term objectives are involved.

We sometimes forget that there is a direct connection between the in-service education of teachers and that of administrators. Not only must administrators themselves engage in routine professional growth, but their ability to work collaboratively toward teacher improvement depends upon their sophistication, educational awareness, and leadership skills. We have, for these reasons, made it a practice to precede the organization of teacher institutes and workshops with preliminary administrator orientation sessions. Our objectives in these orientation sessions are two-fold: first, to increase the personnel management skills of department heads, supervisors and principals; and second, to enlarge their understanding of current educational trends. These steps greatly facilitate teacher in-service activities.

We have also felt it desirable, in recent times, to substantially increase our public relations endeavors. Educational innovations, whether radical or conservative in nature, are often upsetting to parents. We deem it wise, as a result, to advise and inform the public in all possible ways. Changes in program offerings, alterations in grading procedures, and revisions in the procedures for student counseling, for example, can be communicated and justified for the larger community without too much difficulty. It is important to recognize the value of these operations, and to take the necessary time for their organization and implementation.

Our projections for the future suggest that continual change is likely. We therefore feel that teacher and administrator flexibility, including receptivity to constant readjustment, are vital. All of our staff development activities, therefore, are directed not just at a specific program objective, but also at the more general effort to accomplish three secondary purposes: to encourage flexibility and adaptivity in work style; to stimulate a desire for self-directed personal renewal; and to induce a willingness to experiment with alternatives. These objectives, it must be admitted, are not easy to achieve. People resist change if only because the familiar is easier to deal with than the unknown. Nevertheless, as long as we remain convinced that professional life will continuously alter, we think it necessary to stress professional resilience.

A word should be said finally, about the equilibrium that must exist among district objectives, school objectives and teacher objectives. We have learned over the years that conflicts sometimes develop among the three. Our effort is to keep district mandates at an absolute minimum, so as to provide the individual school with a maximum of latitudes. The building administrators are then advised to restrict their imperatives so as to give every teacher as much autonomy as possible. This approach, we think, provides for the necessary degree of internal consistency and, at the same time, for a variety of teacher options. Although all teachers are not particularly interested in a multitude of options, those that are can function more imaginatively and creatively.

In conclusion, I cannot help but believe that professional growth is the critical factor in achieving better schools. Such growth, to the maximum extent possible, should be self-directed. While we invest considerable money and energy in organizing a great variety of professional learning experiences, we subscribe to the belief that the purpose of variety is to increase personal relevance. Our goal is to achieve a highly motivated teacher willing to do everything possible to improve the learning of children. We want, in a phrase, a thoughtful and independent educator rather than an obedient conformist.

In-Service Education: Some Ruminations from the Firing Line

Ian Westbury
University of Illinois

Current discussions of in-service education seem to assume that the practicing teacher is a new discovery for the college of education. By implication it is being said that individually and collectively the in-service teacher poses new problems for those of us in the colleges that, if embraced, will give our work a new purpose and allow us to address (more directly than we have in the past) the needs of the schools. Three themes seem to stand out: (1) traditional activities of the colleges of education have been irrelevant to the needs of the schools; (2) if colleges of education address the in-service needs of teachers they will become relevant in a way that they have not been to this point and will be able to work with teachers for the improvement of education; and (3) if we accept this mandate, there is a new population for the colleges of education that might, somehow or other, ameliorate our current enrollment problems.

The charge of irrelevance brought against us in colleges of education is, of course, an old one that is probably well taken, and the implication that our problems of enrollment might well be solved if we go down the road of in-service is an exciting one. However, before our eyes gleam too brightly with the prospect, perhaps some caveats are in order. Because the analysis being offered of where we are is an accurate one or the difficulties that face us in addressing the in-service needs of teachers have been adequately explored, I fear that we might end up missing the real point that should be addressed. My goal in these observations is to suggest a different target for our concerns and propose an agenda for action. I am assuming that I am addressing the interests of faculty as they ponder in-service, although, as a university administrator, I want to also raise some issues of my colleagues in schools and State departments of education.

My point of view reflects my role as both a university administrator and as a faculty member.

I believe that the mission of the university is research and teaching, and that any acceptance on the part of the faculty of colleges of education of an in-service mission must be compatible with the primary mission of the institutions in which we work. As a realist I would point out that even if we do not accept the norms of scholarship, our colleagues across campus do, and that tenure decisions, promotion decisions and prestige in the university depend fundamentally on the acknowledgment by our peers on the campus that we are true members of the intellectual community. If we are to accept a greater responsibility for in-service activity, that activity *must* assume a form that is compatible with the conceptions our institutions hold for us. It is not clear to me that in-servicing is, in fact, readily compatible with these norms. Nor is it obvious that the forms of our institutional lives are in fact readily compatible with the needs of the field. The effective delivery of extension services requires an ability to respond quickly to the needs of the programming marketplace (the schools) and perhaps requires evaluation of our activity in very simple market oriented ways. Are we prepared to accept the consequences of responding to these needs for our institutional ways of life? Is academic freedom consistent with the demands of the market? Is tenure and the way of life tenure connotes consistent with the needs of the schools to have reprogramming now? Would we be prepared to terminate one of our colleagues because his skills were not consistent with what the schools need now to make room for another faculty member whose skills were?

I believe that the answer to these questions is no, but let me put these concerns in more concrete terms, concerns that bear on two in-service demands that the state of Illinois at least is making on my institution at this time. The State is asking for active in-service programming in the area of metrification. My department has one faculty member at present in the area of mathematics education and three faculty members in the area of science, and I would assume that were we to follow the State's lead, these are the faculty we would call on. But these faculty are at present deeply involved in a number of projects that have little to do with metrification; one is working on the development of curricular materials in statistics and probability, another is working on environmental education, two others are working on program development in preservice education. Should I ask these faculty to stop this activity and instead think about servicing the needs for a workshop activity on metrification? How can an administrator make such a decision given a commitment both to academic freedom and a prudent concern for the kinds of thinking that the university at large rewards at tenure, promotion, and merit raise time? But, if the probability is high, I suspect, that we will do little or nothing to address a need that the state has high on its list of priority items.

Similarly, the State is asking all of its universities to develop programming that addresses mainstreaming, not as a question but as a state policy. My department has no faculty members who have the slightest competence (given the traditions of the schools) in this area. Should we clear a position to make an appointment to satisfy the state demand for services in this area? Even if this involves termination of a tenured faculty member? And should we pressure faculty to act in this area even if they have profound reservations about the wisdom and sense of the State's decision? Is the demand that the state pushes so insistently because of its policy commitments more important than my college's feeling and my faculty's feeling that our priority is to develop our capability in a quite different area–instructional applications of computers?

I have outlined these concerns in black and white terms (they are not black and white of course) to highlight what seems to me to be an almost fundamental incompatibility between the missions and practices of the university as I see them and the proper needs of the schools for programming that addresses *their* needs. And I invoke our concern for the role of computers in the instructional programming of the schools to highlight the concern that I believe will be manifest in the state within the next ten years. My argument, of course, would be that IAC will become a state priority soon, and that when this happens we will have built the capability that the state will need to move more coherently than it can at the moment given its current priorities. It seems to me that the long run is our *proper* concern and that our priorities are right given our mission; but the implication of my position is that in-service focusing on state priorities as they seem now will not be served by this posture.

This seems to me to be the fundamental problem all discussions of in-service must face. What is it? What is its agenda? How is in-service delivered? I believe that there are answers to these questions that are compatible with the norms of the university, but the thrust of my argument goes in a different direction from the conceptions expressed in these pages.

Before beginning the development of my own position, however, let me return to assumptions. In-service is not a new notion for the College of Education; it has been one of our central activities for at least the past twenty years or so. The problem is less one of discovering a new sphere for our work than of reconceiving our traditional mission. I am referring, of course, to our graduate programming in which, for many years we have offered courses for in-service teachers who wish to advance on their salary scales as they secure their masters. And, in this mission, we have had the full support of schools and states, inasmuch as both have made a massive investment of dollars in the incentive systems they have developed to encourage teachers to attend universities to secure course credits. The problem is not that the College of Education has not been undertaking in-service instruction but, instead, with the form of the in-service we have been conducting.

There is, of course, an obvious problem with the in-service activity we have been undertaking. I know of no school administrator who believes that the tax monies he or she invests in encouraging his or her teachers to secure their masters, or their masters plus thirty or sixty are being well spent; and when the costs of incentives are calculated at the state level and seen as a major component of the costs of salaries, the lack of conviction in the efficacy of either the programs or the expenditures becomes a major source of concern. The question is, why did this particular form of heavily subsidized in-service activity begin in the first place? Why did we ever get into this trap we now seem to be in? Faculty members can probably ask this question as easily as can their colleagues in state offices, inasmuch as few of the faculty I know have much belief in either the forms or the efficacy of the graduate instruction that is one of their primary functions. I would suggest that if we are to examine in-service constructively, it is the masters that we have to examine. And, if we are going to assess what we have done and perhaps ponder some new and different undertaking, it is the masters that we have to reform. If we fail in this task of examination, I fear that our colleagues in the schools will accuse us of wanting only reform that does not affect our existing vested interests. We want them to take our new in-service programs as well as our existing programs; the problem is, that if the case for in-service is endorsed, the case for requiring the masters and the like as a regular part of the career line of the teacher is less strong. Let me devote the remaining pages of these reflections to this theme.

Some years ago, I was associated in a peripheral way with the development in a Canadian province of mass American-style masters programming. The province decided to create a research, development and training institution for its schools, and as a central part of the millions of dollars it decided to spend, it expected to see its teachers taking the masters degree we were authorized to offer on a part-time basis. The background for this development was unclear at the time, but the story seems to go like this. Until that time the province's teachers received only either two years of normal school training plus a degree or four years of college plus one year of teacher education. Few teachers had any systematic exposure to education after basic training, although many took subject masters and course work. This pattern of teacher education seemed at the time to be one of the major sources of problems that the province's ministry of education was experiencing. Examinations were being converted to a multiple choice format because of the press of the number of examiners, but the teachers were saying that nothing could be tested by a multiple choice form. The ministry of education was urging locally-based curriculum development, but teachers were asking how and why. Somehow our masters was supposed to solve this problem.

The missing link in this argument can be filled in fairly readily if we assume that to be responsive to the moves the provincial department of education was, initiating teachers needed more *information* than their prior teacher education had given them about what might be possible. In the absence of any information about Bloom's taxonomy and validity studies and the like, it is difficult, for example, to be enthusiastic about multiple choice testing formats of any kind. In the absence of any information about new curriculum developments the question "why change?" is reasonable. In the absence of any systematically gained information about new developments in governance and the like, the concerns of the department for those issues might well appear mysterious. It was the role of our institution, I would suggest, to disseminate such information, to encourage teachers to discuss the issues of the day, and in so doing, to develop their openness to new ideas. If we were able to reach two teachers in every school with our messages of modern ways and modern technologies of testing, curriculum, mental health, and the like, part of the province's problem would be solved. This goal justified our curricula, and our forms of instruction and the payoff to the province from the diffusion of the kind of information we were retailing justified the province's investment both in our salaries *and* in the incentives it offered teachers by way of salary scales to take our degrees. The investment was, I believe, justified and cost-effective given the needs of this school system at this time. To double from three to six percent the number of teachers knowing about the new curricula of the "sixties" and having modern conceptions of the "goals" of education was an important good.

But what happens when the number of teachers who have been exposed to this kind of information is of the order of fifteen or twenty percent? I would suggest that the marginal yield on an investment in information dissemination structures declines drastically and that these structures begin to serve the system less and less. This is, I fear, where we are now in most states in the United States, and this is the reason that we hear more and more criticism of the ineffectiveness, in systemic or personal terms, of the time and money both systems and teachers spend in coursework of the traditional kind. We hear the charge that a masters does not improve the competence of the teacher in the classroom in any way at all; but if my analysis is correct this was not the goal of these programs. We hear administrators saying that courses and programs do not bear on local needs, but again I will suggest that this kind of locally targeted training was not and is not the goal of these programs. We hear districts saying that the money they spend on incentives to justify teacher investments of their time in coursework does not have any real return to the district; my analysis would suggest that this is probably true at this point in time, but might not have been so true fifteen or twenty years ago.

In other words, all of us, faculty, teachers, administrators, school boards, are victims in a sense of training and career structures that have outlived their usefulness and justification. Yet, they are structures with such power and personal utility that it is difficult to imagine us being without them. I want to suggest that, given this world, the payoff to the system, and to teachers, of investment in rethinking what we do within these structures is enormous. If we were able to turn these structures towards skill training or competency-enhancement the cost benefits would be well nigh incalculable—and much greater than almost any other existing investment in educational improvement. Title I, Title III, Right to Read, and curriculum development projects can all be seen as mechanisms designed to effect the quality of schooling we offer students. Given the existing fixed costs associated with masters and the like and given even a small but growing increment in the competence of teachers that resulted from such programming, investment in the redesign of the masters would have significant multiplier effects and might well represent the most cost-effective intervention into the governing of schools that any governmental unit could undertake at this time.

Imagine, for example, a model of in-service education embedded in the masters that took unit and course development as its focus with the goal, say, of the improvement of the reading abilities of students. Imagine the effects, for example, of a year of more or less concentrated attention to this problem by a cohort of elementary teachers, not merely reading specialists. Imagine, for example, an administrative program that took as its focus the analysis of the achievement problems of a district, or the race relations problems, or "local problem-solving capabilities." Imagine, for example, a program that focused on the development of units exploring local resources or applications of science. Imagine, for example, a year's concentrated focus on the problem of mainstreaming. In each of these cases it would seem that not only much of the true residual of the present kinds of programs could be achieved but in addition, much more could be gained because of concentration and the implied demand that students should spend the entire year working their problem area through, not a third of a semester or a quarter. Such programming would require that both teachers (faculty) and students (in-service teachers) truly come to grips with their problems and authentically address the true needs of schools in a way that is rarely possible within the real constraints of existing models.

Many other benefits might also be derived from the exploration of such a model. To control and monitor the search for real solutions to real problems should truly engage faculty in the tasks associated with the traditional missions of universities while at the same time permitting these goals to find a focus in local, real problem-solving. New paradigms of inquiry and new conceptions of what schools might achieve must be a part of the search for real solutions to real problems that this task entails. New collaborations between faculty members of different backgrounds would be required. Teachers must benefit, it would seem, from a real engagement in the development of the knowledges and skills that such tasks would require. And school systems would benefit if their teachers gained more than they currently do from the programs that they end up paying for.

The kind of program I have attempted to outline here is different from anything currently undertaken. The task of developing the prototypes of such programs would not be easy, since none of us know yet whether we can, in fact, address the real needs of the schools in any sustained way. Furthermore, the structures that would be required by such programming would be different from those we now have; in my own institution, for example, it would seem that the bulk of a student's time would be spent with those faculty members who are, or could be, most centrally concerned with programs other than traditional research and theory. Although such programming would be more expensive than existing patterns, that is probably an affordable luxury if our administrations were convinced that we were either seriously searching for something new or were doing something our colleagues in the schools and the state departments regarded as cost-effective.

Perhaps this model seems the self-evident thing to do; but, if it is, why don't we do it? We don't partly because we have not been recruited and socialized to do it; partly because we were not able to escape from the pull of old forms when we were coping (unreflectively) with more students than we knew what to do with; and partly (now) because we are fearful about our enrollments. Given this fear, it is perhaps more rational to work to build our enrollments in existing programs by easing the access barriers to those programs than it is to build new forms. It is this feeling that we can build new clientele that leads us to interest ourselves in in-service to work busily to devise new ways of justifying our activity in other than conventional terms, and to be so protective of the course and distribution requirements of the present programs that give us our existing student bodies.

Given our fears and anxieties at this time, I am not optimistic about our ability in the university to explore new models. But, I am convinced that we could and would willingly respond constructively to the demands of our new world if we were required to, and I would see the most powerful set of such requirements coming from increasingly hard-pressed states, governments that need to justify their expenditures in terms of meaningful cost-effectiveness assessments. In this context it would seem reasonable to expect the states to ask us to engage in a dialogue with them about what we are doing; I only hope that as we entered such an inevitable dialogue our colleagues from the states would ask the right questions, push us in the right direction and recognize us for what we are, autonomous scholars who have the right and the duty to go our own way. Perhaps it is *hubris* that leads me to suggest this, but I would guess that we, more than they know what the problem is and what might best be done, and that they would best serve their own interests, and those of the schools, by insisting only that we focus on the problem and work with them in the collaborative search for solutions. Our goal and their goal is the same—the improvement of the educational experiences the schools offer our children. As one state superintendent has implied, we have the luxury that he does not have of looking into the middle and far distance in a search for ways and means by which we can truly actualize this goal. If we are asked to fulfill our true role in the intellectual and educational community, our record suggests that we will deliver, albeit haltingly; if we are asked to do what we cannot do, satisfy the needs of the moment, we will fall flat on our faces.

Career Long Staff Development: An Educational Necessity

Sheila Wilson

Township High School District 214, Mount Prospect, Illinois

Changes in our society have come about very rapidly in the past few decades, and all indications are that the rate of change will become even more dramatic in the future. As the rate of change accelerates, it will become increasingly important for educators to update themselves and become familiar with the newer techniques and areas of emphasis in education. This need will be further emphasized by the fact that school staffs are becoming more stable and will continue to do so in light of declining enrollments in many school systems. With fewer new staff members entering the profession, we can no longer rely on them as our natural source of vitality and fresh ideas. Efforts to maintain vitality and to insure that new ideas are constantly being considered will have to be more deliberate than they have often been in the past.

School staff members, who are continuously learning, provide excellent models for students and may be better able to relate to the learning needs of students than those staff members who think they have learned all they need to know. A staff development program that encourages and enhances career long learning is, for many reasons, in the best interest of students as well as staff members.

It is the purpose of this article to explore some of the characteristics necessary to comprehensive staff development programs that will successfully meet current and changing needs. Any professional growth activities that have the potential to increase a person's effectiveness in his role within a school system will be considered staff development activities for purposes of the article. The ideas presented are probably most appropriate to public school systems with multiple schools but could easily be adapted to single or private school situations.

DEVELOPING A PHILOSOPHY

A staff development program should have a clearly identifiable philosophy, one that has been agreed upon by representative groups within the system and one that can be clearly communicated to all involved. Ideally, the philosophy should be general, not restrictive, and yet it should be specific enough to give some general direction to the program without ruling out purposeful diversity. The degree to which the philosophy is compatible with the system's philosophy of educating students may also be a critical factor in its acceptance. If a school system expresses a belief in individualization, self-direction, and choice for students, and does not recognize the same value in these concepts for adults, it may be difficult, at best, to obtain staff commitment to the implementation of these concepts.

Compatibility doesn't necessarily imply sameness, but at minimum a staff development program should be built upon the same basic assumptions about the individuality of learners. Expanding from there, it can continue to develop around assumptions that take into account the adult nature of the learner and permit him to use his adult competencies to further his own development. Examples of positive assumptions that might give direction to the philosophy and activities of a staff development program are as follows:

> The school system will be most successful if it provides the type of environment that facilitates continuous learning on the part of staff as well as students.
>
> Given a choice in staff development activities, a staff member will choose something that has meaning and value for him or her.
>
> Learning occurs most readily through methods that are suited to the individual.
>
> There are very few goals that are best achieved by requiring everyone to engage in the same activity at the same time.
>
> Much of school success is best achieved through people working together rather than in isolation.
>
> A person's attitude toward staff development activities will be more favorable if he or she has had a voice in the planning and selection of those activities.

The provision of staff development opportunities is a natural part of a school system's function.

Many have talents to contribute to the achievement of staff development goals.

STRUCTURING THE GENERAL PROGRAM

Each year in most school systems staff members receive increases in salary because it is assumed that their added years of experience cause them to be more effective with students and consequently of greater value to the system. Therefore, it seems that a system has the right to expect each staff member to grow professionally each year. Growth, however, may not come about solely through experience. The quality of the program that is provided to encourage reflection on experience, in such a way as to facilitate growth, will have a great deal to do with the degree to which that growth occurs.

A list of general criteria for a school system's program is provided to suggest areas that should be considered by those who have responsibility for staff development. The degree to which a system would choose to emphasize, delete or add individual criteria depends upon the local situation and priorities that have been agreed upon by those involved.

Through appropriate coordination, a system's staff development program should meet each of the following criteria to the extent that it is desirable.

The program should provide the opportunity for building activities to differ according to individual building needs as long as these activities are compatible with the system philosophy. Since individual school buildings serve varying communities and have undoubtedly developed their own personalities and goals, it follows that they will have some needs that will require individually designed programs.

The program should provide for communication among buildings concerning their staff development needs, programs, and ideas. In this way, it might be possible to utilize the diverse strengths of building staffs and programs, to foster learning and sharing ideas rather than competition and defensiveness.

The program should provide the opportunity for buildings to cooperate in areas in which their needs are common or where additional people are needed in order to establish a program that would be worthwhile.

The program should provide the means for establishing system wide programs that would meet general system needs and/or supplement building programs.

Some purposes may be better through the participation of people from a variety of settings.

The program should make use of system and community resource people who have strengths appropriate to various staff development activities. Many staff and community talents are unknown to the majority of people in a school system. Most programs could be greatly enhanced by the recognition and use of many of these talents. In addition, the recognition might serve to enhance the self-images of those involved.

The program should make use of resource people who may be available through local universities or other institutions. Many institutions are willing to share resources through some sort of cooperative arrangement. Often school systems can supplement their own resources by entering into one of these cooperative endeavors.

The program should provide the means for bringing in consultants and resource people in areas of need that could not be covered by system, community, or other available resource people. Most school systems have specialized needs that cannot be met adequately without outside assistance. This type of assistance may also be needed from time to time to stimulate people, bring new ideas into the system, or offer an objective view of what is occurring within the system.

The program should provide the means for releasing staff members for participation in staff development activities when released time is desirable and/or when other arrangements are not feasible.

The program should provide a means for assessing staff development needs. Programs based on whim or the fad of the hour rarely have long lasting results. Efforts should be made to diagnose needs, establish goals, and design ongoing programs to meet those goals.

The program should provide the opportunity for all staff to assist in defining needs and to have a say in determining what their building, system, and individual staff development goals should be. If this is not done, valuable input could be overlooked and the likelihood of program success reduced.

The program should provide a continuum of growth from preservice through in-service. If at all possible, a school system should serve as a setting for the preservice experiences of teacher candidates and should use participation in such a program as a form of in-service staff development. Each end of the continuum has something to contribute to the development of the other.

The program should provide staff development opportunities for all staff members, not just the instructional staff. All system employees contribute in some way to the development of the system, and all should have opportunities to increase their effectiveness in doing so.

The program should provide services and materials that are supportive to staff development activities (professional books, articles, tapes, student opinion questionnaires, evaluation tools, information about local workshops, conferences, etc.). Many services can serve to facilitate teacher self-evaluation and other forms of professional growth.

The program should offer a variety of alternatives for purposes of staff development (seminars, workshops, visitations, travel, independent projects, courses, etc.) We have long recognized the need to individualize instruction for students. Staff members, too, have individual learning styles and preferences. More may be accomplished by catering to these individual styles and preferences.

The program should provide adequate rewards and recognition for professional growth.

The program should provide meeting locations that facilitate professional interaction and growth. Is there any place in the school that is conducive to professional activity, to staff members spending time on developmental or analysis efforts that are of importance to them? If high priority is given to staff development, a place such as this might be considered.

The program should draw upon existing learning theory and principles of psychology rather than solely upon past experience. All too often we fail to use the knowledge we have about learning. Programs of staff development should be of the highest quality possible and should serve as models for program development and evaluation.

The program should be responsive to individual requests for assistance with professional growth goals. The availability of a person or people who can advise others on alternatives available to them in reaching their professional goals is an important aspect in the program.

The program should be evaluated systematically as a basis for decision-making and program improvement.

The program should be supported by top level administrators, philosophically, financially and through their participation. While some types of staff development activities can be conducted quite inexpensively, without adequate funding and coordination, both the scope and quality of the program could be jeopardized.

One of the most difficult tasks associated with the planning of staff development programs is the balance of time available to various types of groups that have needs for professional growth. System, building, and subject area groups, as well as individuals, all have staff development needs related to their varying purposes and goals and may all voice demands for the time available. Whenever possible, activities should be designed to meet mutually beneficial, individual and organizational goals, but this isn't always possible. Care must be taken to insure a balance of time that will honor the needs of all groups and individuals to the greatest extent possible.

Another question that must be answered is who shall have the responsibility for initiating and planning various kinds of activities. Logically, it seems that those who have voiced the need for growth would be in the best position to participate in the planning. In addition, others who would be affected by the activities should be involved along with those who have responsibility for expertise in the area of staff development. Examples of purposes for which various people might initiate programs are as follows:

Central administrative personnel might initiate programs for purposes such as: (1) assisting staff in complying with state guidelines for curriculum, certification, and program planning; (2) increasing the effectiveness of district organization and administration; (3) drawing attention to important new instructional developments; (4) assisting staff in the achievement of system goals; and (5) developing programs related to system priorities for improvement.

Building administrative personnnel could initiate programs when there is a need to: (1) assist staff in the achievement of building goals; (2) work on the improvement of building programs; (3) increase the effectiveness of building organization and administration; (4) orient new staff members to building programs and operation; and (5) increase staff awareness in relation to new educational developments.

Subject area personnel would seem to be the potential initiators when they want to: (1) assist staff in implementing new subject area curriculum; (2) increase awareness of new teaching methods related to the specific field; (3) assist staff in achieving subject area goals; and (4) assist staff in increasing effectiveness in any of a number of things related to their specialty.

Individuals could be interested in initiating programs that would enable them to: (1) pursue learning in relation to their individual needs; (2) fill gaps in their individual experiences; (3) gain new teaching techniques; (4) do research in an area related to individual's area of responsibility; and (5) engage in dialogue with others concerning common interests and concerns.

Once programs have been initiated, the responsibility for implementing and evaluating could rest with many. Obviously, those with responsibility for staff development could do much to facilitate the programs that have been initiated by various groups. Assisting with program design and evaluation, suggesting appropriate human and material resources, and providing support services might be among the responsibilities of staff development personnel. Emphasis should be placed on reaching agreement concerning the various responsibilities for the program and on insuring that those responsible are also reasonably capable.

RECOGNIZING THE VALUE OF STAFF DEVELOPMENT

As mentioned earlier, it is imperative that the value of staff development be recognized through the availability of adequate financial resources. Without the financial commitment neither the variety of activities nor the quality of the programs offered will be sufficient to meet more than the simplest needs of the system. While staff members may be willing to assume some of the financial responsibility for their own development, they will be more likely to do so when they receive some degree of support and encouragement from the system. The more value they perceive that the system places on continuous growth, the more likely they are to feel motivated to pursue that growth.

Obviously, financial commitment alone will not insure a quality program. The personnel commitment must be adequate to provide continuous coordination, evaluation, and development of the program. Without skillful coordination, it is unlikely that the system potential for staff development will ever be fully explored.

Administrators and others who are influential within a school system can do much to create an atmosphere wherein staff development is encouraged and valued. Whether they realize it or not their behavior has a substantial impact on those with whom they work. For example, by acknowledging their own needs for growth and seeing to it that those needs are met in a constructive and professional manner, they may be modeling an attitude toward staff development. Giving frequent attention to staff development in important system councils and other meetings may reinforce its importance as a system function. The discussion of staff development expectations during interviews might encourage the hiring of those with positive attitudes toward their own responsibility for continuous growth. Looking beyond grades and courses to other experiences potential staff members have had can give recognition to meaningful forms of staff development.

Supervisors who recognize new skills staff members have gained, and who provide opportunities for them to use those skills are probably rewarding and encouraging growth. Showing interest in a staff member's plans for a professional visit to another school rather than complaining about having to contact a substitute would be supportive of the cause rather than squelching future visitation plans. Those who willingly support reasonable new ideas rather than routinely opting for the way things have *always* been done undoubtedly encourage purposeful creativity in staff development.

Staff evaluations that give recognition to real growth, not just to things like completing paperwork on time and conforming to school policy, foster further growth. Providing people with written forms of recognition for the successful completion of professional growth activities emphasizes the value of the activities and the possible relevance to their professional files or resumes. Active participation in professional conferences and preservice teacher education may suggest a commitment to the improvement of the profession. These and many other day to day interactions like the examples given provide or deny attitudinal support for staff development.

CONCLUSION

From the arguments set forth in this paper a number of conclusions can be reached. In order to meet the demands of changing times as well as to continuously upgrade the quality of educational opportunities, it is critical that a school system provide a variety of opportunities for career long growth. Staff development has the potential to have substantial impact, not only on those it serves directly, but also on those for whom it serves as a model of active learning. As such, it should be as well thought out, as comprehensive, and as highly valued as any other instructional program in the school system. Finally, influential staff members continuously act in subtle and indirect ways that either promote, overlook, or hinder the development of an attitude of career long development. Through thoughtful consideration and planning, we can cultivate those attitudes and behaviors that demonstrate commitment to career long growth.

Teacher: Automaton or Craftsperson?

Arthur E. Wise

Education Policy Research Institute

Advocates of educational change who once asserted that only a "new breed" of teachers could achieve their purpose are now calling for in-service education of the existing teacher force. To issue such a call is to expect or desire changes in the teacher's behavior or thought. To achieve its purpose, the program must be potent; it must convert teachers to the cause (whatever the cause is) and having converted them, train them to the preferred purpose. While developers of new instructional materials, school administrators, purveyors of in-service teacher education, teachers' organizations and teachers themselves generally favor in-service teacher education, the goals each group seeks may vary. The purpose of this article is to examine the policymaker's advocacy of in-service education to promote accountability in education.

Although teachers and advocates of accountability occasionally use the same vocabulary–leading us to think that they are in the same world–they are not in the same world. Teachers have fundamentally different conceptions than do advocates of accountability of the role of teachers and of how the process of education operates. To think that an in-service teacher education program that focuses on the technology of accountability will link these two worlds is folly. Those who support accountability have low expectations of the role of the teacher; their concept of accountability rests upon a theory of education that has never been validated. That theory runs counter to the ethos of teachers who tend to hold an atheoretical view of education. Because accountability begins with such a disparate concept of teaching, there are serious limitations to in-service teacher education as a mechanism for its implementation. Moreover, most teachers would question the sanity of teacher educators' schemes designed to reduce teachers to automatons.

My secondary purpose is to suggest that some sophistication be brought to the process of educational reform. There are frequent demands for reform in education and as long as there is perceived to be an excess supply of teachers, one route to such reform will be in-service reeducation of the existing force. As long as there is lingering doubt about the efficacy of education, legislative efforts to make education accountable will continue. As long as the larger economic situation remains grave, concern about the "productivity" of teachers will remain. As long as teachers organize, school boards and legislators will redouble efforts to increase productivity. One hopes that a sounder model of accountability and productivity than has thus far been devised will be developed.

Many legislative efforts to reform education assume a "hyperrational" view of the process of education. The rationale of the accountability movement (and its derivative movements) involves a specific view of the role of the teacher. Accountability is based on an assumption that a set of goals for education can be agreed on through the policy making process. Another assumption is that these goals can be translated into educational objectives. The educational system (including teachers) is then to produce students who can meet these objectives. Tests will be devised and administered to ascertain whether the objectives have been achieved. Finally, a management system will integrate and monitor the accountability process. This "hyperrational" view of education presumes the existence of a science of education.

In the simple accountability model, the teacher is allowed discretion (in principle, at least) to determine how the educational objectives are to be achieved. In the derivative models, built from and upon the simple model, the discretion of the teacher to determine how the objectives are to be attained is systematically eliminated. When implemented, all the derivative models generate a view of the teacher as an automaton. And since most teachers are not yet automatons, it remains for in-service teacher education (training?) to make them so!

Let us assume a hypothetical school district in a hypothetical state. (Actually, if all the accountability laws on the books in California were implemented, it could be substituted for the "hypothetical state.") This forward-looking school district in the forward-looking state is, by state law and its own school board ruling, moving toward full accountability. This school district is now (1) operating under competency-based education (CBE); (2) hiring teachers who are graduates of competency-based teacher education (CBTE) programs and who have been certified "competent" by competency-based teacher certification (CBTC) procedures; (3) using only instructional materials that have been learner-verified (LV); and (4) managing its affairs with a planning, programming and budgeting (PPBS) system. Obviously, an in-service teacher education program is required for all teachers who are not graduates of CBTE programs or who have not been certified by CBTC procedures. Additionally, all teachers will need to be introduced to CBE, LV, and PPBS. Let us consider the cumulative impact upon the role of the teacher of CBE, CBTE, CBTC, LV, and PPBS. (Note also that I have said that the hypothetical school district is *moving toward* full accountability for it is omitting program evaluation, management-by-objectives, cost-benefit analysis, etc.).

Competency-based education is perhaps no more than the simple accountability model revised. The competencies that a student is to demonstrate are prespecified so that the teacher knows exactly what he or she is to accomplish. Since the school system knows what it expects of its students, it hires teachers who demonstrate in advance that they can teach in the manner necessary to ensure that the students master the desired competencies. Hence the school system hires only graduates of CBTE programs and/or persons certified as competent by CBTC procedures. It is assumed that research will have identified those competencies of teachers that enable them to develop the desired competencies in students. (This can only be *assumed,* however, since research has not thus far identified such competencies in teachers.) All teachers entering the system will demonstrate the appropriate competencies and all teachers presently in the system will receive in-service education. In this way the range of teacher behavior will be narrowed to the point at which the *method* of achieving student objectives will be prescribed. Both what and how the teacher is to teach, then, has been determined through the application of general accountability theory and its derivatives, CBE, CBTE, and CBTC.

However, in the event that CBE, CBTE, and CBTC do not operate effectively, alternative derivatives of general accountability theory will provide fail-safe guarantees. "Learner verification" is a less well-known derivative of accountability theory and deals with assessing the effectiveness of instructional materials. When this legislation is operative, a publisher will have to provide evidence that his materials have been tested with children and revised on the basis of this experience. (This is based on the underlying assumptions that there is a best way to use the materials, and that the publisher must make that best way known through in-service education.) Florida legislation, for example, requires that "such text revision . . . be interpreted as including specific revision of the materials themselves, revision of the teachers' materials and *revision of the teachers' skill through retraining.*"[1] If the teacher's behavior (1) has not been sufficiently defined by the expected goals and expected objectives; or (2) has not been properly trained by CBTE; or (3) has not been properly selected by CBTC, then the residual discretion in his or her behavior will be limited by learner verification of the materials of instruction.

Should learner verification not complete the task, then a managerial derivative of accountability theory will. A planning, programming and budgeting system is a means by which the administrative apparatus of the school system sets and tracks the accountability process. Given a set of goals, the administrative apparatus plans for their implementation, programs the system (including its teachers) to achieve the goals, and budgets accordingly. The teachers in this hypothetical school district have once again been programmed.

The goal of accountability appears to be total control by policymakers of the instructional process. Policymakers assume a "hyperrational" view of the process of education and see education as a closed, deterministic system. The relationships of the elements of the system are assumed to be known so that the manipulation of one element will have predictable consequences on the other elements. Accountability presumes a science of education.

Accountability contains a theory of education that is foreign to that which the average teacher holds. Unless these two conceptions of education confront one another, accountability is destined to have a negligible impact. So far the advocates of accountability have failed to recognize this discrepancy, except in the most superficial terms.

In *School-Teacher: A Sociological Study,* Dan C. Lortie paints a picture of the teacher that is radically different from that assumed by advocates of accountability.[2] In his picture, teachers far more resemble craftspersons than automatons. If advocates of accountability wish to have more success in the future than they have had in the past, then they must examine the teacher's conception of role and of education. The teacher's orientation to role and task has evolved as the result

1. Ch. 74-337, [1974] Fla. Stat. 1065. (Emphasis added)
2. Dan C. Lortie, *School Teacher: A Sociological Study* (Chicago: University of Chicago Press, 1975).

of the structure of schooling and the demands of the task. As such, and by definition, this orientation has certain functional consequences. Unless this orientation is changed, it is not likely that change in education will occur.

Those who advocate accountability assume that the process of education rests on an underlying order. According to Lortie, teachers may not share this assumption:

> A scientific approach, however, normally begins with the assumption that there is an underlying order in the phenomena under study. It is not clear that all or most teachers make that assumption about their world. Some see teaching outcomes as capricious and describe short-term results in almost mysterious terms. If that viewpoint is widespread, it is not surprising that teachers do not invest in searching for general principles to inform their work. If they suspect that classroom events are beyond comprehension, inquiry is futile.[3]

Accountability not only assumes predictability, but also simplifies the complexity of reality and creates a model of the educational process that may seem simplistic to the teacher:

> Those trained in behavioral science are used to accepting short-run measurements as evidence of effectiveness; it would be easy to assume that these teachers do not want to confront the possibility of low impact on students. But one wonders: styles of thought which pervade science may not work for those who take personal responsibility for the development of children. Science moves ahead through deliberate and sophisticated simplifications of reality, but there is little to suggest that this is the approach of classroom teachers.[4]

While science can legitimately abstract and simplify reality, a teacher cannot; he or she is responsible for the whole child.

Lortie argues that a powerful force in the orientation of teachers is their observation over the years of their own teachers. Conceptions of teaching are formed before exposure to teacher training. Accountability schemes adopt a view of education drawn from the behavioral sciences:

> Teacher training is increasingly influenced by ideas drawn from behavioral science. Those trained in behavioral disciplines are inclined to conceptualize teaching in instructional terms—to talk of "treatments" and "options" and to assess outcomes in terms of measurable and discrete objectives. One wonders how effectively such professors communicate with the many students who, it

3. Lortie, *School Teacher,* p. 212.
4. Ibid., pp. 146–147.

> appears, see teaching as the "living out" of prior conceptions of good teaching. Students who conceive of teaching (consciously or not) as expressing qualities associated with revered models will be less attuned to the pragmatic and rationalistic conceptions of teaching found in behavioral science. The two groups–students and professors–may talk past one another.[5]

Teacher training and teacher retraining must come to terms with teachers' prior conceptions of teaching.

Accountability schemes make important assumptions about how the school hierarchy operates. For example, accountability schemes assume that the goals of education are set politically, transmitted through the school district and school hierarchies, and then come to rest with the teacher for implementation. To what degree does this assumption accord with reality? To what extent do the formal goals of the school system guide the actions of teachers? According to Lortie:

> If teacher pride were ordered in strict adherence to organizational, formal goals, we would expect to find heavy emphasis on results attained with entire classes; school systems present themselves as concerned with the learning of all students. It is provocative, therefore, that fewer than one-third (29 percent) of the Five Towns teachers mentioned generalized outcomes with entire classes, and that most of these did so in an offhand manner. Such responses seemed to occur with teachers working in particular subjects and grades–the more tangible and visible the learning they were seeking to promote, the likelier they were to emphasize general gains with students. Examples are initial reading, physical education skills, typing, and skill subjects in home economics. A few elementary teachers linked pride to favorable outcomes on achievement tests, but they seemed hesitant to do so.[6]

Perhaps surprisingly, teachers do not naturally emphasize objective group results. Yet, accountability schemes assume that the underlying objective of the teacher is to maximize aggregate achievement test scores. Advocates of accountability will argue that accountability schemes are designed to focus the teacher's attention on output measures. And indeed, teaching for the test has occurred. However, whether the teacher has fundamentally altered his orientation is quite another matter.

A priori, it would seem that teachers would use group tests as a way of assessing their performance. For a variety of reasons, they appear not to be disposed to fasten upon achievement test scores as a personal gauge of teaching success. Until it can be understood why

5. Lortie, *School Teacher,* p. 66–67.
6. Ibid., p. 127.

teachers do not now use tests as a gauge of successful teaching, accountability systems that assume that teachers are trying to maximize test scores are not likely to succeed. Goals will only affect students as they are mediated by teachers. Teachers translate general goals into specific objectives:

> Educational goals are often stated in global, even utopian terms . . . [W] e observed that teachers "reduce" such goals into specific objectives they use in their daily work. This reduction apparently involves two conservative tendencies: relying on personal convictions and obtaining high satisfaction from outcomes that are less than universalistic. When teachers cannot use stated goals to guide their actions, organizational objectives give way to personal values; the personal values of teachers, as we saw . . . are heavily influenced by past experience.[7]

The process described by Lortie takes place naturally, i.e., in the absence of special efforts to control the behavior of the teacher. Unless the underlying reward system is altered, the process of goal redefinition will likely continue.

Lortie's characterization of the ethos of teaching does suggest some dimensions of teaching that must be taken into account if an accountability system is to be installed successfully. The persistent failure of accountability schemes demonstrates the need for this. An in-service program that prepares teachers to understand PPBS or to write behavioral objectives will have little effect upon school practice. In-service education for teachers designed to instruct them in the use of these new techniques is generally mechanistic. The mechanics of the new system are taught, but nothing is done to modify the incentive system within which the teacher operates. Teachers do not "naturally" adopt the goals that policymakers set. Unless explicit steps are taken to modify the goals that teachers employ in the classroom, accountability is destined to fail. Whether a more sophisticated in-service teacher education program (or some other means) to bring about responsibility is desired depends upon whether one believes that education will improve more and more rapidly if teachers are treated as automatons or craftspersons.

7. Lortie, *School Teacher,* p. 208.

Section IV

Operational Concepts

Some Postulations and Principles on the Continuing Professional Education of Teachers

Louis Rubin

University of Illinois

POSTULATIONS

1. Retraining should increase the competence of the teacher. It should enable the teacher to use specific tactics to accomplish a specific purpose. To be competent, the teacher must have a repertoire of efficient techniques, a sound knowledge of the intellectual ideas to be taught, an ability to respond spontaneously to teaching opportunities that emerge from the activities of the classroom, an accurate perception of the educational process, and a capacity to interact sensitively and compassionately with the learner.

2. Teacher retraining should be dealt with in small, discreet units. Each unit should be based on an analysis of a teaching task. The unit should prepare the teacher to perform the task and also provide criteria for determining the teacher's degree of success.

3. Training activities should be in sequence so that teachers can progress through a cycle of retraining units that will gradually increase in complexity.

4. The training unit should be sufficiently flexible to allow teachers to begin at their own level of ability and to progress at their own rate.

5. The units should make use of alternate training methods in order to accommodate the individuality of the teachers.

6. Teacher retraining should become a permanent part of the educational system so that professional growth is sequential and continuous.

7. Retraining should take place during the teacher's work day.

8. The teacher's ability to perform a teaching task should be assessed cumulatively. The initial assessment indicates the kind of retraining required; the final assessment verifies performance competence. When possible, these assessments should not only estimate improvements in performance, but should also diagnose teaching behavior that can limit the teacher's effectiveness.

9. The efficiency of a training program should be judged by a comparison of the teacher's ability at the beginning and at the end of the program.

10. The assessment of a teacher's ability should be based, as much as possible, on measured student achievement.

11. The training unit should enable the teacher to acquire the knowledge, skills, and attitudes that are prerequisite to achieving desired competence.

12. Training units should give priority to general teaching tasks that have wide applicability.

13. Wherever possible, retraining should make use of actual teaching situations involving students.

14. The retraining program should be adjusted to the requirements of each school to fit the instructional setting that exists, the nature of the school's students, the materials and resources available, and the school's instructional objectives.

15. Retraining should not interfere with individuality in teaching tyle so long as performance effectiveness is not impaired.

16. Teacher retraining should be joined with performance incentives that motivate the teacher to use acquired skills.

17 To the largest possible extent, selected classroom teachers should be used as instructors in the retraining program.

18. Teachers who supervise retraining programs should also undergo a special training program.

19. Teacher retraining should be accompanied by a correspondıng effort to increase specialization and decrease the range of the teacher's functions.

20. The training units should give teachers alternate procedures for achıevıng a desired end, as well as the ability to decide which alternative is particularly appropriate in a specific instance.

21. Teachers should have feedback on their cumulative growth du ing the training program.

22. Teachers should have an opportunity to practice new skills in the course of their regular teaching.

23. Retraining should advance educational innovation wherever possible.

24 Time for teacher retrainıng can be gained through new patterns of staff deployment: team teaching, flexible scheduling, the use of para-professionals and other teacher aides, and student-tutors

5. Teacher retraining programs should be compulsory. A teacher should be able to conclude a training unit when a specified performance ability is achieved. Therefore in some cases, competent teachers may not need to engage in a particular training unit

26. The time devoted to a training unit should be commensurate with its complexity and the strengths of the individual teacher. Different retraining objectives require different amounts of training time.

27. Teacher retraining is enhanced when the total school staff is involved in the retraining program.

28. A training program that demonstrates tangible benefits will be more successful than one that does not.

29. Teachers involved in retraining programs should have continuous access to an available facilitator—a trained technical resource.

30. The principal of a school should not, for many reasons, serve as the supervisor of a retraining program.

31. Skills acquired in a retraining program in most instances will go unused if they are not valued by the administration of the school.

32. The purposes of a retraining program should be based on classroom tasks that the teacher wishes to accomplish.

33. The teacher should be motivated in some way to participate in the retraining program.

34. The retraining should increase the teacher's sense of job satisfaction and nurture the unusual abilities that exist among teachers.

PRINCIPLES

35. In the near future we will see the introduction of new technological devices, the extension of the classroom to the resources of the community-at-large, and the emergence of new instructional materials and methods. Each of these will demand special teaching skills. We must capitalize on the time remaining, identify these skills as soon as possible, and institute programs of professional growth that will guarantee skill mastery.

36. The improvement of teaching performance should be handled with reasonable precision. Principals, supervisors, and others who work with teachers in the area of skill development should acquire systematic procedures through which the diagnosis of teaching strengths and weaknesses can be accomplished.

37. Teachers should participate in the governance of their own professional growth. Those who serve as instructors must also acquire the skills of collaborative interaction that permit them to work effectively with teachers.

38. The improvement of teaching skills should become a routine aspect of professional life. Teachers should be given time and other resources with which to assess their professional needs and to carry on improvement activities.

39. Effective teaching is characterized by the ability to make rational choices through which the means are adapted to the ends. Programs of continuing teacher education should increase rather than decrease the teacher's instructional options.

40. Teachers should have knowledge of the consequences of their work in order to grow. Programs of professional growth should provide teachers with the time and tools necessary to conceptualize their experiences, and to reach insights that alter their perception of their role.

41. Professional growth should relate to life in the classroom. The continuing education of teachers should have a direct influence on the problems they encounter in their work.

42. As the reform of educational practices continues, heuristic learning, individualization of instruction, and teacher specialization will likely increase. We must develop efficient programs that will enable teachers to deal with these and other modifications that lie ahead.

43. The ability to function effectively and to accomplish a specified objective is itself a powerful source of motivation. Teacher incentive for

professional growth should be based on the satisfaction that is derived from authentic competence.

44. Continual change will occur in the educational system in the future. The provisions we make for the professional enhancement of teachers should reflect three dominant aims: flexibility in teaching style, capacity for self-renewal, and desire to perform skillfully.

45. The findings of social psychology suggest that people with similar interests can, through collaborative interaction, contribute to one another's welfare. Programs of professional growth should take advantage of teachers' potential for teaching one another.

46. Effective teachers have a variety of methods that can be used to achieve a goal. Teacher in-service education should emphasize instructional alternatives rather than mandatory methods.

47. Classrooms frequently lack relevance to life itself. Acquiring teaching methods that result in a stronger connection between the subject matter of the classroom and life outside should be a major goal of in-service programs.

48. The continuing education of teachers should provide opportunities for acquiring a deeper understanding of the changing society. The training program should promote activities that will give teachers greater contact with their social environments.

49. Some of the knowledge that teachers require is most easily obtained by interacting with others in a group situation. Groups of teachers, engaged in a collaborative analysis of their functions, represent an effective instrument of professional growth.

50. Professional growth should be managed with precision. It is essential to specify—to the extent that circumstances permit—performance criteria for many of the tasks teachers perform, and to also specify the specific objectives of particular staff development activities.

51. Individuals have unique talents. In order to capitalize on these differences we must develop procedures through which variation in teacher activity can be easily accommodated.

52. Teachers are responsive to different kinds of training stimuli. We should develop diverse methodologies through which subject matter knowledge, personological skills, pedagogical techniques and professional values are enhanced.

53. Many processes of professional growth have received little attention. It is essential that we enlarge our conception of the ways in which professional growth can occur.

54. Improvements in teaching and systematic research on professional growth can be mutually facilitative. Much remains to be done with respect to exploiting the potential inherent in the research storehouse.

55. Some knowledge and skill should be acquired before the teacher enters service; some can be acquired only after the teacher is in service. In the development of teachers, we must determine where, when, and how particular skills and understandings are best nurtured.

56. Curriculum development and professional growth share a common ground. Much could be gained if greater efforts were made to interrelate the two.

57. Teacher performance represents the only rational base for determining professional growth needs.

58. Little professional growth will occur without the provision of adequate time. Teachers' work schedules should be reorganized so that there is routine opportunity for improvement.

59. Teacher's talents should be used in whatever way they can best serve the learning of the young. We would be well advised to adapt instruction and schooling to the nature of the teacher rather than to require conformity.

60. Because many teachers have had unsatisfactory experiences with in-service activities, it is essential that teachers be involved in the identification and articulation of their own training needs. When teachers participate in the determination, initiation and organization of their own growth, the incentive to improve is greatly strengthened.

61. Ideally, most in-service education activities should be carried on in the setting in which the learner normally functions. Teachers can—while engaged in teaching—learn to identify and analyze pedagogical problems and search for solutions.

62. The human resources for in-service training reside in a variety of places. Technical assistance can be provided by individuals within the local system, by specialists, and by experts available elsewhere. A systematic program should be developed in which inside and outside resources can be conjoined.

63. If efforts to improve the performance of teachers are to succeed, provision must be made for continuity of action and support. Professional growth depends on long-range planning, systematic coordination, appropriate sequencing of improvement activities, and continuous evaluation.

64. Teacher training programs are an indispensable element in perpetuating innovation and reform.

65. Group efforts at problem solving encourage the sharing of acquired skills and of workable methods for dealing with common problems. Thus teachers themselves can contribute to the body of knowledge on professional growth.

66. The modification of behavior is facilitated by a direct confrontation with the outcomes of the behavior. Teachers should have an opportunity to analyze and evaluate the results of their teaching.

67. In order to judge their results, teachers must have some recourse to objective data. Much is gained when teachers can analyze their own

work through systematic feedback from learners, audio and video tape recordings, and peer observations.

68. In general, teaching involves patterns of actions rather than isolated tactics. Hence, teachers must not only master a technique but must also learn the conditions under which it can be most intelligently used.

69. The discrepancy between teacher perception and student perception of a lesson is a useful basis for identifying teaching strengths and weaknesses. Teachers should be encouraged to compare their goals with their results.

70. Clinical supervision provides a vehicle for principals and teachers, or teams of teachers, to collaboratively consider instructional practices.

71. The schools belong to the people; students, parents, teachers, and administrators should interact more closely in the setting of instructional policy.

72. It would be shortsighted to base the continuing education of teachers on an outdated school. Professional growth activities should anticipate the necessary reforms.

73. Teacher retraining should be more pragmatic and potent. Truly superior teachers should be involved to a far greater extent in facilitating the growth activities of their colleagues.

74. The humanistic aspects of education will become increasingly important in the future. The in-service education of teachers should anticipate this circumstance and give increasing attention to the emotional development of teachers.

75. The improvement of teaching should go hand-in-hand with the establishment of high standards of performance expectation.

76. The development of a teacher begins in the training institution

and concludes in the school. Supervisors who work with prospective teachers in preservice training institutions should perhaps continue their training relationship after the teacher enters service, or, those who supervise teacher in-service should perhaps establish a training relationship in the preservice period.

77. The management of programs of professional growth is a highly specialized aspect of personnel administration. We would do well to create and legitimize a new kind of management role—that of a training specialist concerned exclusively with the improvement of teaching.

78. It is unlikely that any teacher will ever reach his or her ultimate performance potential. Therefore, continuing education, on a systematic basis, should become a routine aspect of professional life.

79. True teaching competence embodies a number of specific capacities. Professional growth activities should go beyond the mere mastery of teaching technique and deal with attitudes, beliefs, and values.

80. Professional standards normally stem from a body of reliable knowledge. Wherever possible the perennial training of the teacher in service should relate to such standards.

81. Time is an essential factor in the formula for acquiring new understanding and skills. Schools should have a sizeable teaching staff so as to enable individuals to devote a portion of their time to professional growth.

82. As a group, practicing teachers constitute a rich source of new ideas and practices. Teachers should be encouraged to engage in the systematic field testing of potential new techniques.

83. Many teaching competencies can be acquired only after the teacher has become familiar with the particular school and the children with whom he or she works. Consequently, the mastery of some essential skills must be achieved through repeated practice and regular evaluation *in situ.*

84. An interest in teaching artistry does not occur as a matter of course. Even when it does exist, it is easily dissipated by excessive organizational constraints or weak morale. The evidence seems to suggest that greater emphasis should be placed on both intrinsic and extrinsic incentives to high achievement.

85. The teacher's performance is often undermined by fundamental disagreement with the instructional goals he or she is asked to accomplish. Far more attention should be given to the attitudes, values, and beliefs that influence teacher behavior.

86. The responsibility for revitalizing the professional growth of teachers lies with educational leadership. The principal, the supervisor, and the superintendent must all regard the establishment of procedures for the improvement of teaching as a primary obligation.

87. The observation of skilled teaching is a significant stimulation to professional growth. The regular observation of master teachers should become a routine aspect of professional life.

Section V

The Tasks Ahead

A Field-based Research Agenda

Louis Rubin
University of Illinois

Staff development must deal with a vast spectrum of professional activity. Successful teaching depends on a large body of miscellaneous knowledge, an extensive repertory of skills, and an appropriate constellation of attitudes, beliefs, and values. The extraordinary complexity of pedagogy mandates that its mastery be developed cumulatively, over time.

Precision in professional development can be accomplished in two primary ways: (1) we can help teachers acquire generic, universally applicable competencies such as individualizing learning, motivating children, and pacing lessons; or (2) we can focus on the special teaching skills associated with a particular instructional program. For example, the current effort to improve citizenship education requires teaching practitioners who have a strong belief in the preservation of student's autonomy; are sensitive to the social problems youth considers relevant; are skilled in the techniques of individuation; have a high tolerance for ambiguity; are adept at making spontaneous teaching decisions without rigid reliance on a stipulated course of study; and are sophisticated in matters involving ethical behavior.

For example, teachers lacking these attributes are not likely to perform well when using Kohlberg's method of analyzing moral dilemmas. If this occurs, the potential of the method itself is diminished, the teacher is beset with feelings of frustration and inadequacy, the children suffer from clumsy direction, and the quality of the learning environment is dissipated. It is perhaps permissible to observe one more time that the failure to anticipate the teaching requirements of new instructional innovations has seriously impeded educational progress for the past twenty-five years. We have concentrated on the production of effective new pedagogical tools with little regard for the corresponding need to educate practitioners in their intelligent use. The result has been a double loss: a good invention has been poorly deployed and—in the face of disappointing results—interest in its potential has disintegrated. The seeming inability of the ivory tower to serve the arena may be more attributable to inept implementation than to a lapse in creativity. All of which suggests that while future research on teacher in-service education can profitably continue its concern with general competencies, it must also make a deliberate and systematic effort to cope with specific problems associated with specific educational changes. (Rubin, 1978)

The time lapse between the development of a new educational idea and the beginning of a corresponding staff development program is far greater than one might expect. When a new program becomes available it must prove itself in the eyes of the early adopters, undergo a period of cumulative popularization, and if all goes well, it eventually achieves something approaching wide-spread utilization. Only at this point does the program attract some sort of in-service attention. The odds are, therefore, that it will be used irrationally or ineffectively for a considerable period of time. It is hardly surprising, then, that team teaching still falters on occasion because teachers have not had an opportunity to develop a sensible division of labor; that in many schools the individualization of instruction is no more than a slogan; and that considerable havoc is sometimes committed in the name of humanistic education.

These hazards are not necessary. There is no reason why essential technical skills cannot be identified as program developments proceed, or why retraining mechanisms cannot be planned and tested during the final phases of program refinement. Ideally, staff development would take place *before* an innovation is introduced. Fenton's efforts to achieve such an end, a rare exception to custom, are described in an earlier section.

Plainly, the need for a reciprocal process between educational change and teacher reorientation is great. However, because of the scarcity of relevant research, we know very little about the ways in which this process might work. One is hard put to know in reviewing the major educational innovations derived from the research of the past two decades, whether an innovation survived or failed because of its own inherent strengths or weaknesses, or because of the way in which it was put to use. Even worse, if one probes the total research on teacher in-service education, its primitive nature and myopic vision give rise to a sense of dismay. Viewed as a whole, in fact, the literature consists of one part data and four parts opinion.

Perhaps the most widely discussed document in this meager literature is the James Report, published in England in 1972.[1] Although the text is more a compendium of deliberations than a research summary, its central arguments are clear. In Lord James' words:

> The first, and in many ways, I think, the most important conclusion that was reached, was that an entirely new scope and emphasis must be given to in-service training. We felt this so strongly that we did, as it were, write our report backwards, and actually end it with the education and training of the serving teachers. This was not simply a gimick; it was a measure of the importance which we attached to this aspect of the problem. To ascribe such a priority to this element involved to some extent an act of faith, for surprisingly little hard information exists as to what effect various kinds of post-experience training actually have on teaching and the teacher; how long do those effects last; the most appropriate kind of education to accomplish ends which might be quite different for different individuals; and the effect on the schools themselves in-service education of the staff has.[2]

In essence, the report suggests that in-service education is crucial because knowledge, society, and teachers are all subject to continuous change. There is, moreover, a powerful argument for the current tendency to conceive of preservice and in-service education as parts of a sustained continuum. To quote Lord James again, "It would be a remarkable piece of self-deception if we believed that the preparation of a student for any of the great variety of tasks that we include under the word 'teacher' could be completed in two or three or four years."[3] In addition the recommendations heavily underscore the importance of a professional "coach" for beginning teachers:

> We also make another proposal which we believe will have an important effect on the development of the inexperienced teacher. That proposal is that in every school a suitably experienced member of the staff be designated as a professional tutor. Being normally given a lighter teacher timetable, his task would be to exercise general guidance over the work of the probationary teacher, and in addition he should familiarize himself with the field of in-service training so that he could advise all his colleagues on suitable courses to attend.[4]

1. Lord James of Rusholme, "The Education and Training of Teachers" in *Innovation Now, International Perspectives on Innovation in Teacher Education,* ed. Frank H. Classen and John L. Collier (Washington, D.C.: International Council on Education for Teaching, 1972).
2. Ibid.
3. Ibid.
4. Jung, Charles, "Instructional Systems for Professional Development," *Theory into Practice,* XI (December 1972): 5.

Not only is the research base—on professional consultation—poor, but there is a conspicuous lack of attention to the critical questions of content, method and rationale. Continuing professional education is obviously essential in the adaptation of new curricula, in improving the organizational cohesiveness of a school, in the introduction of new technological apparatus, and in providing teachers with an orientation to prevailing social problems. Beyond these somewhat global aims lies the more intricate objective of technical adeptness. The typical teacher requires literally hundreds of distinct competencies. In the absence of usable research evidence, it is difficult to know which are most important, which are most responsive to retraining, and which primary skills are essential in the acquisition of more sophisticated techniques. Underlying all of these, is the fundamental issue of training methodology. Philip Jackson, a perceptive student of life in the classroom, distinguishes between the "defect" and the "growth" approaches to staff development:

> The first of the two perspectives from which the business of in-service training might be viewed is found in the notions of repair and remediation. For this reason I have chosen to call it the "defect" point of view. It begins with the assumption that something is wrong with the way practicing teachers now operate and the purpose of in-service training is to set them straight—to repair their defects, so to speak.
>
> Thus, for reasons that are not immediately obvious, persons who espouse the defect view of in-service education, typically, though not always, are behaviorally oriented and tend to emphasize the more molecular aspects of the teacher's work. Their goal seems to be that of equipping teachers with specific skills—teaching them how-to-do-it.
>
> Yet as we all know, experience, though it may be the best teacher, is often insufficient to stimulate continued growth. To achieve that end we must not just *have* experience; we must *benefit* from it. This means that we must reflect what happens to us, ponder it, and make sense of it—a process that in turn requires a certain distancing from the immediate press of reality. As everyone who has been in charge of a classroom knows, it is very difficult to teach and to think about teaching at the same time. What is needed, therefore, is both the time and the tools for the teacher to conceptualize his experience, to imbue it with personal meaning in a way that alters his way of looking at his world and acting on it.[5]

5. Jackson, Philip, "Old Dogs and New Tricks, Observations on the Continuing Education of Teachers," in *Improving In-Service Education,* ed., Louis Rubin (Boston MA.: Allyn and Bacon, 1971).

In effect Jackson's dichotomy outlines the prevailing controversy surrounding Performance Based Teacher Education. PBTE simultaneously subscribes to Skinnerian theory and to cybernetic systems. Its conceptual underpinning is described here:

> A competency-based (or performance-based) teacher education program is a program in which the competencies to be acquired by the student and the criteria to be applied in assessing the competencies of the student are made explicit and the student is held accountable for these criteria. . . .
>
> Three types of criteria are used: (1) knowledge criteria, which are used to assess the cognitive understandings. . . . ; (2) performance criteria, which are used to assess the teaching behaviors. . . . ; (3) product criteria, which are used to assess the student's ability to teach by examining the achievement of pupils. . . .[6]

Another distinguished analyst, Harry Broudy (In-Service Teacher Education), weighs PBTE's assets and debits somewhat differently. He observes that there are three distinct teaching functions: the didactic, the heuristic, and the philetic. He says:

> Didactics refers to the impartation of knowledge by the teacher to the pupil; heuristics refers to the effort to help the pupil discover for himself either the contents of a body of knowledge or the methods of arriving at such knowledge and assessing it; philetics is merely a Greekish name for love or securing rapport with pupils or, as the current jargon has it, 'relating to pupils.'

Broudy makes it clear that PBTE, if pursued with diligence and integrity, will turn out better didactical technicians than the present conventional programs. But he makes it equally clear that where heuristics and philetics are concerned, the situation is quite different. When the teacher wishes to help a student clarify his values, modify his attitudes, or deepen his insights—when teaching artistry is a matter of making what is relevant seem irrelevant—a knowledge of technique alone is not enough.

Broudy tells us, "The performance of a specified task in a predetermined form is the criterion of success in teaching, programs of teacher preparation could not only be unnecessarily abstract and theoretical, but perhaps otiose altogether." But if success in teaching is defined in a larger vision, a vision requiring the teacher to take the child's mind beyond the obvious, and summon imagination and curiosity to new flights, then we must have a teacher who blends technical skill with a

6. Jackson, Philip, "Old Dogs and New Tricks."

rich and intuitive understanding of theory. What we need, says Broudy, is a training program "in which laboratory work, clinical teaching—after the model of medicine—and internship are used to illuminate, exemplify, and utilize theory."

While it is clear that preparatory education and continuing education are confronted with many of the same obligations, it is not certain that the proper solution to the problems of one is also the proper solution to the problems of the other. There are, after all, patent differences between preservice and in-service learners. To wit, the experienced practitioner may need to unlearn old habits as the first step in acquiring new ones. Experienced teachers are likely to measure recommended new pedagogical techniques against the lessons of their experience, whereas preservice teachers, who lack such experience, are more likely to accept such prescriptions as articles of faith. In-service teachers can benefit from staff development activities specifically geared toward their workday problems; teachers in preparation, however, can only be given a general orientation that will hopefully have some pertinence to the job they eventually take.

Another major controversy (one confounded by inadequate research) is the presumed contradiction between the development of the teacher as a person and as a skilled technician. Smith (In-Service Education in Schools of the Poor) takes this position:

> The first purpose of teacher education is to protect the clients of the school against incompetence, not to develop the teacher as a person. That is the primary task of general education. Naturally, choices among courses should be allowed when they are in line with the teacher's career goals, but these must always be made within a program designed to discipline the teacher in the knowledge and techniques essential to his competency.

Other, more humanistically inclined commentators, believe that the crucial ingredients in the formula for good teaching demand a psychologically intact teacher, knowledgeable about the world in general and about the child's subculture in specific. Once again, however, the substantive data is inconclusive—little has been done in the way of clarifying high-priority objectives; apart from a few notable exceptions, the retraining methods in use are untested and imprecise; there is not much in the way of a solid bond between means and ends; the pertinent findings from basic research in psychology and sociology have only tangentially been brought to bear on applied problems; and instruments for both interim or terminal evaluation are in extraordinarily short supply.

Four conclusions, therefore, seem justified:

1. There are few definitive research studies on the problems of continuing professional education.
2. We have not identified, in any validated form, the crucial competencies experienced teachers find indispensable.
3. A limited number of retraining mechanisms are moderately successful in changing simple teaching behaviors.
4. We have yet to achieve any real success in the systematic improvement of complex teaching behaviors.

The net result of all of this is that the well-intentioned school district, interested in upgrading the performance of its teachers, has no recourse other than to rely on ancient and infirm mechanisms such as lecture and exhortation, or on the most appealing cures that emerge in the educational marketplace. Yet, these circumstances notwithstanding, staff development no longer encounters innovative resistance. Its need has become apparent and hundreds of school districts annually spend thousands of dollars on procedures that have only limited potency. In short, the moment for reform has arrived.

THE NEED FOR A THEORY OF TEACHER PROFESSIONAL GROWTH

The great value of theory is that it tells us how to achieve the goals we seek. It is for this reason that philosophers have so often observed that "nothing is as practical as good theory."

Theories evolve out of a consideration of problems and issues. They can neither materialize in a vacuum nor in the abstract because they must relate, in one way or another, to a set of events or occurrences.

To build a theory it is necessary to examine assumptions, to define expectations, and to form conceptions about the meaning of observed phenomena.

It follows, therefore, that in order to understand observed phenomena we must ask questions about the events involved; to form conceptions, we must ponder the answers and speculate about their potential meaning.

Consider, for example, the twenty-two questions that follow:

1. Can the system of staff deployment in schools be reorganized so as to provide regular school time for teacher professional growth?
2. If such a reorganization occurred, what operational problems would result?

3. Does the simultaneous involvement of a school's total teaching staff in a program of professional growth offer any special advantages?
4. Does such total involvement produce excessive management problems for principals?
5. Does the cumulative practice of a teaching skill automatically produce a greater degree of competency?
6. Are teachers successful agents for facilitating the professional growth of their colleagues?
7. Does the use of a teacher-coach create special problems for the school administration?
8. Do teachers respond favorably to a teacher-facilitator?
9. What kinds of coaching activities are of greatest value in promoting professional growth?
10. What personal characteristics are most likely to contribute to a facilitator's success?
11. What training is most valuable for teacher-trainers?
12. Can teaching methods be communicated to teachers through the use of carefully arranged printed materials?
13. Can all teachers use some teaching methods with equal success?
14. Do all teachers learn a given method in the same way?
15. Do some teaching situations require *ad hoc* teaching?
16. What factors cause teachers to resist professional retraining?
17. Is intrinsic motivation sufficient impetus for professional growth?
18. Is it more practical to train teachers in technical skills without reference to their underlying theoretical principles, or is it more practical to demonstrate the theoretical basis of a method?
19. Should teaching techniques, subject-matter knowledge, and professional values be dealt with in conjunction or disjunction?
20. Do urban and suburban school environments present different training impediments?
21. Do elementary, junior high, and senior high school teachers require entirely different training materials?
22. Is there a relationship between length of experience and particular retraining procedures?

These questions, of course, are only illustrative; undoubtedly, better ones exist. But even a partial search for their answers would yield some raw data with which to work. With this data we could begin to reexamine our convictions regarding staff development—what it is, how it functions, and what it should accomplish–and we could attempt the formulation of a rudimentary taxonomy of teachers' professional growth. We could at least partially identify some of the basic principles and elements of a prospective science.

Other questions–the nature of which are not now known–must also be asked. Without their answers we have an incomplete theory. In time, as these other more subtle and penetrating questions are asked and answered, the bones of the theory will take on more and more flesh until, eventually, we will acquire an organized collection of ideas that will define the means by which to reach the ends.

The need for such a theory is very great. Without it, we are reduced to random, undirected behavior, dependent on the hope that, through repeated trial and error, we may somehow stumble on a usable pattern. Even if we were lucky and some sort of pattern emerged, it would in all likelihood be the offspring of convention rather than of creative imagination. The virtue of a calculated search for new theory lies in the fact that the search forces us to look at old problems in new ways, to unfetter ourselves from habit, and to go beyond the prosaic.

The fact is that our present understanding of staff development and teacher professional growth is very slim indeed. We are uncertain about the objectives toward which we should strive, and even more unsure of the tactics to use. Few problems in education, it might be argued, are more in need of a concerted effort at theory building.

THE NEED FOR OPERATIONAL SYSTEMS

Given a tentative theory, we can set about the task of experimenting with a variety of alternative systems. The design of a system stems essentially from five sequential actions: (1) determining the desired end results; (2) determining the pursuits most likely to achieve these results; (3) initiating the pursuits; (4) determining whether the anticipated results have in fact been achieved; and (5) remodeling as required.

The building of a system also demands careful attention to a number of other variables. Using a tentative theory as a point of departure, the available mechanisms must be sorted, organized and categorized into a set of operational procedures. Allowance must be made for environmental constraints, differences in school setting, and flexible implementation. It is also of importance to note that in the betterment of continuing teacher professional education, the fabrication of an operational system need not be delayed until more basic research has been recorded. The available evidence can be reexamined, reclassified and reorganized into a variety of experimental forms. It is for this reason that, in reference to the system, the verb "fabricate" rather than "create" or "invent," has been used.

More research is critical in the following areas: devising superior procedures for fitting professional development activities into the work schedule; providing effective training facilitators; identifying powerful training tactics; selecting objectives; and limiting program costs. Our knowledge base in these matters is indeed shallow and superficial. We are, however, somewhat better off with respect to a syntax of teaching methods that can be used in attacking those aspects of professional growth involving pedagogical technique.

An enormous amount of research on teacher education has already been accumulated. While the quality of this research is uneven, much of the data is ignored in practice, mainly because the implications have not been fashioned into a manageable scheme that accommodates the demands of reality. In the fabrication of experimental systems bits of basic and applied research may occasionally be necessary but a good deal of the didactic component can be constructed from the available data on teaching methodology.

Whatever the structure of a professional growth system, it should enable faculties and individuals to deal with their own designated goals. Moreover, it must be based on a specific set of procedures through which these goals can be attained. We are in dire need of investigations that will help us to learn what retraining devices work, for what objectives, and under what conditions. If we are to overcome our present infirmities we must seek a tested set of operations that, under given circumstances, will deliver desired results. The search for these workable systems, it should be noted, does not preclude open-ended, informal, or even unstructured approaches to professional enhancement; even goal-free endeavor, however, must take place within some sort of framework.

The most appropriate and efficient means for discovering these frameworks, and their attendant operations, is to: (1) analyze past successes and failures; (2) cull, from the research and development record, the best of the practices now in use; and (3) conjoin the yield from both of these activities into methodical experiments. To accomplish these tasks with reasonable effectiveness, both the analysis of past endeavors and the assessment of successful practices must proceed according to some sort of matrix. In other words, we must know beforehand what problems are to be solved, what prospective solutions can be tried, and what criteria govern their feasibility within the existing constraints. In the absence of such a matrix, the gradual evolution of functional systems that provide a range of alternatives would be impossible.

To illustrate how such a matrix can be used, a series of problems, prospective solutions, and feasibility criteria are set forth here:

Problem 1: *Since educational improvements will continue during the foreseeable future, retraining must become a routine aspect of the teacher's professional life.*

Solution: Reorganize staffing patterns so that retraining activity is a built-in facet of the job assignment, permitting new teaching skills to be acquired and refined as the teacher is at work.

Feasibility Criterion: ***Can time for retraining be provided within the normal workday without undue disadvantage? Will teacher organizations accept the necessary reorganization?***

Problem 2: *Satisfactory training programs must integrate three basic elements: knowledge of subject, knowledge of educational processes, and technical skills. In existing in-service programs, these are treated, if at all, in disjunction from one another.*

Solution: Design training units that (a) integrate the three elements; (b) are directed at specified performance capability; (c) are arranged in logical sequence; and (d) provide outcomes that are a perceptible improvement over present procedures.

Feasibility Criterion: ***Can such training units be designed? Are there teaching skills generally useful to all teachers? Can these be developed in conjunction with the teacher's routine work assignments? Will school personnel regard the required time investment as useful?***

Problem 3: *Present training programs often ignore vast differences in teachers' work situations. Profes-*

sional growth activities must fit the conditions that prevail in the particular school.

Solution: One, study the teaching-learning environment in which the teacher must function. Two, identify the teaching objectives and methods particularly appropriate to the students. Three, design continuing professional education programs tailored to the situational context. Four, utilize these programs with the total school staff.

Feasibility Criterion: ***Can the four steps of the solution be accomplished with reasonable ease? Will the resulting reorientation experiences be of tangible worth to the teachers?***

Problem 4: *Experience suggests that it is advisable to provide a guide or coach in the form of a "training agent," who is regularly accessible to teachers. Earlier investigations have shown that, because of role conflict, neither the school principal nor the external supervisor can adequately serve in this capacity.*

Solution: Utilize a selected teacher as the "agent" who (a) has the esteem of other teachers; (b) demonstrates leadership ability; (c) has undergone a preparatory training program; (d) is given time to facilitate the professional growth of others.

Feasibility Criterion: ***Can teachers be trained to serve as facilitating agents? Can leadership time be provided without excessive budgeting difficulties? Can both principals and teachers work cooperatively with such teacher-facilitators?***

Problem 5: *Even when quality training protocols have been adapted to the special requirements of a school, teachers in the school will progress at different rates and master the training objectives in different ways. The training, therefore, must accommodate teacher individuality.*

Solution: Organize the training materials for self-directed use. Provide alternative explanations, practicums, and activities that achieve the same objective in different ways, thus affording teachers

	personal options. Enable the in-school training agent to encourage and promote individual adaptation of the protocols.
Feasibility Criterion:	***Can training materials that allow for individualization retain their effectiveness? Will teachers exercise personal autonomy? Can the in-school facilitator cope with individualized professional growth?***
Problem 6:	*The successful individualization of teacher growth will permit two major modifications. One, the combination of special aptitude matched with special training will make it possible to use teachers for purposes for which they are particularly suited and bypass those for which they are not; and, two, the nurture of special capacities will allow exploratory efforts to improve the "fit" between the natural styles of teachers and learners.*
Solution:	Coordinate professional growth with specialized teaching assignments, and experimentally "couple" teachers and students with similar predispositions.
Feasibility Criterion:	***Will teachers react favorably to specialized assignments? Can their particular strengths be determined accurately? Is selective teacher-student matching possible? Are the logistical problems manageable?***
Problem 7:	*Teacher organizations, school administrators and individual practitioners all wish to determine professional growth objectives and control the corresponding programs.*
Solution:	Constitute, school by school, professional education commissions, including representatives of all interested parties, that approve proposed in-service programs.
Feasibility Criterion:	***Can the various factions work cooperatively and achieve consensus?***

From the foregoing, the logic of the proposed experimentation perhaps becomes clear. By analyzing past and present in-service education problems according to an agenda of conceptual questions, we can gain a better understanding of the phenomena involved, as well as a deeper insight into their function and meaning. These, in turn, will make it possible for us to reconstruct the necessary character of continuing professional education, and to take preliminary steps toward the building of a suitable theory. Then, if we use the theory to tentatively identify potential developmental activities and test these according to a matrix of problems, solutions, and solution-feasibility, we can ascertain successful in-service training procedures that constitute first-generation operational systems. What will then remain, obviously, will be the need to verify—through secondary replication—the validity of the theory and the potency of the system.

What all of this comes to, in sum, is an effort to determine whether the difficulties of in-service education are attributable to faulty problem conception, and a parallel effort to achieve improvements through field-based experimentation. Sometimes, when dilemmas are removed from their customary context and recast in new formulations, unsuspected answers materialize. And sometimes, when we acknowledge the limits of rationality and try the promising ideas in the actual scene, powerful visions that are elusive in the usual process of translating scientific data into everyday policy, occur.

Index